Hiram Warner
To
Mrs H. Jackson
April 16th 1857

A

PASTOR'S SKETCHES:

OR,

Conversations with Anxious Inquirers,

RESPECTING

THE WAY OF SALVATION.

ὁ λύχνος αὐτῆς τὸ Ἀρνίον.

BY

ICHABOD S. SPENCER, D.D.

PASTOR OF THE SECOND PRESBYTERIAN CHURCH BROOKLYN, N. Y.

Second Series.

SIXTH THOUSAND.

NEW YORK:
M. W. DODD, PUBLISHER,
Corner of City Hall Square and Spruce St.

1855.

STEREOTYPED BY
THOMAS B. SMITH,
216 William St., N. Y.

PRINTED BY
E. O. JENKINS
114 Nassau St.

Contents.

Preface.

THE following Sketches have no necessary connection with those formerly published, and contained in another volume. Each volume is complete by itself, though the two are fit companions for each other.

The favorable reception which the former volume met with from the public,—the numerous testimonials of its usefulness to private individuals, which have been received from many different parts of the country,—and more especially the similar testimonials received from many of his ministerial brethren, have induced the author to believe it to be his *duty*, to issue this additional volume. The former one has a thousand-fold more than realized every expectation that was ever entertained by the author respecting it; and although this volume may be less interesting in tender and affecting incidents, it is believed there are some reasons to hope, it will not prove less useful.

The author has aimed to present here such sketches as are *unlike* those of the former publication; so as to avoid, as much as possible, the needless repetition of the same ideas and arguments, and to make the volume a fit companion for the one which preceded it.

In these volumes, the author is not to be understood as professing to exhibit all the phases of Christian experience. To the varieties of such experience there is no assignable or *conceivable* end. Experiences are varied and modified by a thousand circumstances, which no pen can describe,—by age, by condition, by illness, by peculiarities of mind and disposition, by the kind of preaching which has been heard, by associations, by habits of life, and perhaps, by the sovereign and infinite wisdom of the Divine Spirit, in His enlightening and saving influences Sometimes one doctrine, or class of truths, and sometimes another, will take the lead in the reflections of an anxious mind; and so varied will these reflections become, that (it is believed), no wise man will ever attempt to describe religious experiences, which shall embrace all possible varieties. The circle of religious experience is immense, if not infinite. But this fact need discourage no inquirer, need embarass no minister of the Gospel. The truth of God, after all, is simple: there never *was* a soul to which it is not applicable, and it is the sole instrument of the Spirit in the sanctification of the soul; and therefore there will be *points* of very distinct resemblance in all the *saving* experiences of men. And if what the author has written upon this subject tends to show, that the same truths are applicable to all souls; his work may not be valueless in illustrating the simplicity of the Christian religion, in conducting bewildered minds to the path of truth and salvation, and in showing, that the power and excellence of the Gospel lie in the great doctrines of grace,

—doctrines applicable to all souls who would find the way to Christ and eternal life.

The purpose of this book is not sectarian. It is confidently believed, that nothing which is here written can give any offence to evangelical Christians of any denomination. Not willingly would the author wound the feelings of any human being; and he has aimed here, to deal only with the religion of the heart, and the truths which promote it.

It is not probable, that all readers of this book will entirely approve the *mode* of the author's conversations with the inquiring. He has only to say, that his reliance has been placed upon the *truth alone*, as the instrument of the Holy Spirit in leading sinners to heaven; and consequently his aim, in these conversations, was simply to cause the truth to be understood, felt, and received, as the sole and sure guide. The *matter* of his teaching can be better judged of, by this book, than the *manner* of his teaching. The propriety of manner has respect to the person, his age, state of mind, and other things; and to give such a minute description of all these personalities as to justify the manner in which he spoke, the author knew full well would make the book too large, and diminish the power of its truth. But he has always been unwilling to utter a single sentence, which could wound the feelings of an anxious inquirer after truth, aiming to find his way up to the Cross, and perplexed and harassed with the doubts, and difficulties, and darknesses of his own troubled mind. And he may be permitted to say, that some of the expressions contained in this book, (and the former one also,) which, to a mere reader, will probably sound abrupt, and perhaps *severe*, are expressions which assumed their peculiar style, from the supposed propriety of it in the case. It was felt to be an important thing to *condense* the truth, to make it plain, and pointed, and incapable of being misunderstood; but he hopes and trusts there are no expressions here which will be found offensive to refined taste. Christianity, certainly, is kindness, and good manners, and good taste; and the author is confident, that he never uttered an unkind expression upon the ear of any inquirer, and never unnecessarily wounded the feelings of any one, who ever did him the favor to come to him. About the *mode* of conversation, men will entertain opinions somewhat unlike: the author can only say, he aimed to impress the truth upon the mind in the most effectual manner; and he feels fully satisfied with the kind regards towards himself, which are entertained by those who have been led to Christ under his ministrations. They both prize and love him far more than he deserves.

Some of the conversations recorded here, (as well as those contained in the former volume,) have a character which they could not have possessed, had it not been for an advantage, which the author always strove to improve. Whenever it was practicable, he studied the subjects beforehand. Having met an individual once, and expecting to meet him again, he carefully considered his case, aimed to anticipate his difficulties, studied the whole subject intensely, and, in many cases, wrote sermons upon it, the substance of which afterwards came out, to a greater or less extent, in the conversation. Thus, the conversations aided the sermons, and the sermons aided the conversations. If he might be permitted to do so, the author would commend this mode of ministerial action to younger ministers of the gospel.

What is here presented to the public, has been submitted to the inspection of some of the author's ministerial brethren, in whose judgment and taste he has great confidence; and, without their approval, these pages would never have been printed.

If this humble volume, by the blessing of God, shall be the means of aiding sinners in the way of salvation, and of any little assistance to the younger ministers of the Gospel, in directing the anxious, and guiding the perplexed, and comforting the broken in heart, the author's hopes will be realized.

Brooklyn, N. Y.,
March, 1853.

The Universalist's Daughter.

THERE was something, as I thought, not a little peculiar in the religious aspect of a young married woman in my congregation, whom I sometimes visited, and strove to influence on the subject of religion. She was not a pious woman, but greatly respected religion, and was a constant attendant at church. It was her seriousness which first made me particularly acquainted with her; though before that time, I had sometimes urged her to attend to the concerns of a future life. At her solicitation, as I understood, her husband, with herself, had left my congregation about six months before, and they had attended another church, until they were induced to come back to our church, one evening, by the expectation of hearing a clergyman from a distance. As she found I was to preach (for the stranger clergyman was not there), she whispered to her husband, proposing to leave the place and go home; but he refused to go, for he said it did "not look well." They constantly attended our church after that evening; and when they became seriously disposed to seek the

Lord, I became more intimately acquainted with them. She had become deeply serious, but appeared strange to me. I could not discover precisely what it was that was peculiar about her, but there was *something*. She was uniformly solemn, appeared to me to be frank and candid, was an intelligent woman, had become prayerful, and at times deeply anxious about her future welfare. And yet, as weeks passed on, she appeared to make no progress, but remained in much the same state of mind, unsettled and without peace.

She had no resting-spot. Whenever her thoughts were directed to the subject of religion, a pensiveness would spread over her soul, like the shadow of a cloud over the summer landscape. I pitied her. She was an interesting woman. Her naturally fine mind had not been neglected. She had received the accomplishments of a careful education. She was young, she was beautiful, she was tasteful; and the ease of her manners threw an additional gracefulness over her tall and graceful person. But a cloud was on her brow. It was out of its place—it had no right there. Such a brow ought to be bathed in the sun-light. A heart like hers ought not to be the victim of some secret and mysterious sorrow, and such a soul as hers ought to find in the kindness of Christ the balm for its sorrows.

She had been married about a year, and her husband, like herself, had become interested in the subject of religion. But they were very unlike in their religious successes. He seemed to get onwards; she remained stationary and sad. They were about the same age (twenty-seven, perhaps), and in other respects much resembled each other; but they were unlike in religion.

She was born and had been educated in a distant part of the country, and among people of somewhat different manners; and I thought that she might perhaps have some feelings of melancholy and loneliness, as she had come to reside among strangers. But I found she had no feelings of that kind. On the contrary, she was delighted with her new home; was easy and familiar, and friendly in her social intercourse with her new acquaintances. Several times I called upon her, and aimed to discover what made her so downcast in mind, and especially what hindered her from attaining peace with God, through faith in our Lord Jesus Christ. But I could gain no light on the subject. After all my conversation with her, the peculiarity which hung around her was as mysterious to me as ever.

At one time I suspected that her seriousness might arise more from mere fear than from any just sense of her sin; and therefore I aimed, by explanation of the law of God, and by application of it to her own heart, to render her conviction more deep and clear. But, to my surprise, I found that her sense of sin and unworthiness, and of the wickedness of her heart, appeared to be more than usually deep and solemn.

At another time I feared that she might have a very imperfect idea of the freeness of divine grace; and therefore I aimed to show her how 'the *kindness and love of God our Saviour*' offers to every sinner pardon and eternal life as a free gift, by us unmerited and unbought. And again to my surprise, I found that her ideas on this point also appeared as clear and as strong as any that I could express.

So it was with her, as it seemed to me, on every part of evangelical truth. I could discover in her mind no error or deficiency: and could not even conjecture what kept her from flying to Christ in faith. Evidently the Holy Spirit was with her, but she yet lingered; and her state appeared to me the more wonderful, because her husband had become, as we believed, a follower of Christ, and was cheerful and happy in hope.

As I was conversing with her one day about her state of mind, she somewhat surprised me by suddenly asking,—

"Will you lend me the Presbyterian Confession of Faith?"

"Certainly, Madam," said I, "if you want it; but I advise you to let it alone."

"I want to know," said she, "what the Presbyterians believe."

"They believe just what you do, I suppose," said I; "they believe the Bible,—they believe just what you hear me preach every Sabbath."

"Other denominations," said she, "who disagree with you, profess to believe the Bible too."

"Yes, that is all true; but I do not wish you to agree with either; but to agree with the Bible. I have no desire to make a Presbyterian of you. I only wish you to be a Christian, and I am fully content to have you judge for yourself what the gospel teaches, without being influenced by the Presbyterian Confession of Faith or any other human composition. The Bible is the rule. If we agree with it, we are right; if not, we are wrong. You will understand it well enough to be saved, if you will study it prayerfully, and exercise your own good sense. You have to give an *account of yourself unto God*, and it matters little to you what other people believe."

"Why are you unwilling," says she, "to have me read your Confession of Faith?"

"I am *not* unwilling, Madam,—not at all, if you wish to read it, I will bring it to you, with pleasure, at any time you desire it. But I am only expressing my opinion, that it will do you no good at present. I think the Bible is far better for you to read just now. At another time, the Confession of Faith may be of service to you, but not now."

"I was not brought up in the Presbyterian church, sir. My father is a Universalist, and my mind is not settled about the doctrines of religion."

"Are you a Universalist too?"

"No, sir, I don't think I am; but I don't know *what* to believe," said she most mournfully.

"Do you believe the Bible is God's word?"

"Oh, yes, I believe that."

"Well, the Confession of Faith is *not* God's word (though in my opinion it substantially agrees with it); and I advise you to take the Bible and lay its truth upon your own heart, with all candor and with sincere prayer. If you get into the Confession of Faith, I am afraid you will not understand it so well as you can understand the Bible; and I am afraid your understanding alone will be employed, and not your heart; or at least, that you will have more of the spirit of speculation than of heart religion, and will leave your sins, your Saviour, and salvation too much out of sight."

"Oh, sir, I don't mean to do that."

"I think, Madam, that you know perfectly well, that the Bible demands of you a repentance, and a faith, and a love of God, which you do not exercise; and your first business should be, not to examine the Confession of Faith about a great many other doctrines, but to get your *heart* right,—and what that means, the Bible teaches you, and you painfully feel its truth."

"But, sir, I ought to know what a church believes, before I unite with it."

"Most certainly you ought. But you are not prepared at present to unite with any church. You do not think yourself to be a true Christian at heart —a true penitent—a true believer—a sinner born again, and at peace with God through Jesus Christ. Come to these things *first.* Get a *heart* religion; and after that you will be better prepared to examine the Confession of Faith. But don't allow your mind to be led away into a wilderness of doctrines, to the neglect of your present, plain duty. You are an unhappy woman, a sinner without pardon. You have no peace of mind. And first of all, yes *now* on the spot, you ought to give up your heart to Christ, penitent for sin and trusting to the divine mercy. Here lies our present duty. Don't you think so yourself?"

"Yes, sir, indeed I do," said she, sadly; "*I wish I was a Christian.*"

"I will send you the Confession of Faith if you desire it, but in my——"

"No, don't send it," said she, interrupting me, "I will not read it yet."

"You said your father was a Universalist, but

you did not think you yourself were one. I have no desire to say anything to you about that doctrine. It is unnecessary. If you will read the Bible with candor and common sense, and with humble prayer for the direction of your heavenly Father, you certainly *can know* as well as any one, what the Bible teaches about that. I leave that to your own judgment. If you find any difficulty on that or any other subject, I shall be happy to tell you hereafter just what I think. But I am sure you cannot mistake the meaning of God's word about the everlasting punishment of sinners."

"Do come to see me again," said she, with a sad earnestness. "I am not satisfied to rest where I am. I will try to follow your advice."

After a short prayer, I left her. In subsequent conversation with her, I discovered nothing to make her peculiarity or hindrance to repentance any more intelligible. I did not suppose that the religious opinions of her father were exerting any influence upon her mind, for it seemed to me, and to herself, too, that she had entirely abandoned them.

Just at this time, her father paid her a visit, and remained with her for more than a week. He probably noticed that she was unhappy, and probably knew the cause; but he said nothing to her on the subject of religion. He was one of the prominent men and liberal supporters of a Universalist church in the place of his residence; and as she afterwards told me, she longed, day after day, while he remained with her, to talk with him about religion, and about her own feelings; but he seemed to avoid all conversation which would lead to the subject, and she "could not muster courage enough," as she expressed it, "to speak to him and tell him how she felt." Every day she thought she certainly *would* do it, but every day she neglected it, and every night she wept bitterly over her neglect. Says she to me, "he is a very affectionate father, he has always treated me most kindly; but I could not tell him how I felt—my heart failed me when I tried."

The morning at last came when he was to leave her. He prepared for his departure, and she had not yet told him of the burden that lay on her heart. He bade her good-bye very affectionately, gave her the parting kiss, passed out at the door, and closed it after him. Suddenly, her whole soul was aroused within her. She "could not let him depart so." She hastily opened the door and ran after him through the little yard before the house, to the front gate. She flung her arms around him, "Father, oh, my father!" says she, the tears streaming from her eyes, "I want to ask you one question; I can't *let* you go till you tell me. I have wanted to ask you ever since you came here, but I couldn't. I am very unhappy. I have been thinking a great deal about religion lately, and I want to ask you one thing. Tell me, father, what you truly think—you *must* tell me—do you really believe that all people will be saved hereafter, and be happy in another world? *Don't deceive me*, father, tell me what you really believe."

"Elizabeth," said he, with evident emotion, which he struggled to conceal, "I think it is very likely that some will be *lost forever!*" and lifting his hand to his brow, he instantly turned away and left her. He could not tell his daughter, as she hung upon him in such distress, that dangerous falsehood which he professed to believe.

His tearful daughter returned into her house, the last prop knocked away, the last refuge gone! "Now," as she said to me afterwards, "she could look to nothing but Christ, and have hope only in sovereign mercy. My last deception was gone." And it was not long before she became as happy in hope, as she had been sad in her perplexities and fears. She was a firm and joyful Christian.

She united with the church, and for more than twenty years has lived as a happy believer. Her children have grown up around her; and some of them, the delight of her heart, are the followers of their mother's Saviour and their own.

But her father returned to his home and his former place of worship, professing still before the world to believe in universal salvation, a falsehood which he could not tell his daughter, when she wept upon his bosom.

After her hopeful conversion she wrote to her father, giving him a simple and affectionate account of her religious experience, thanking him for his kindness in telling her his real opinion, and entreating him to forsake a congregation where he himself knew he did not hear the truth—beseeching him to turn to Christ, that he might be saved from everlasting punishment. His reply to her letter was kind, but evasive. He made no response at all to the real burden of her letter. She then wrote to him again. In the most kind and touching manner she recapitulated her experience, told him of her sweet peace of mind, her joy and hope, and asked him whether he was willing that she should unite with the Presbyterian church, as she proposed to do, or would rather that she should be a Universalist. In his reply, he adverted to what he had said to her on the morning when he parted with her, and very plainly assured her that he would rather have her join the Presbyterian church than his own. But still he avoided saying anything about *himself*. Again she wrote to him, and appealing to the declaration of that morning, and to his letter, she affectionately entreated him to obey the truth as it is in Christ Jesus, and not go down to death with a lie in his right hand—a thing the more dreadful because he *knew* it was a lie!

But all this did no good. He remained in the Universalist church. Though for a time he appeared to waver, and occasionally for some weeks together would attend the Sabbath ministrations of another congregation, and sometimes wrote to his daughter in a manner which encouraged her to hope he would become a Christian; yet all this passed away, and the last time she mentioned her father to me, she told me with bitter tears, "He has gone back to the Universalists, and I am afraid he will be lost forever!" "Oh!" says she, "he *knows* better—they all know better—they *try* to believe their doctrine, but they don't believe it." I shrewdly suspect there is no little truth in her declaration.

The course of this man at first appeared to me very astonishing. I marvelled at it beyond measure. I could not doubt that he told his daughter the truth, when he said he "thought it very likely that some would be lost forever." But while entertaining such an opinion, and while unwilling that the daughter whom he fondly loved should be a Universalist, that he should himself still continue to be a supporter of that system of falsehood, appeared to me most surprising. But I have ceased to wonder at it. He only followed the inclination (as I suppose) of his wicked heart. He did not obey his conscience. He only strove to pacify it with a delightful deception. He did not love the truth. And with some dark and indefinite notion about the salvation of all, he strove to hide himself from the power of the truth, which he both feared and hated—hated, *because* he feared. Any man who will be wicked and hardened enough thus to trifle with truth, and thus to run counter to conscience, and thus aim to "believe a lie," may be left to do the same thing. Human depravity, fostered and indulged, has immense power, and will lead in strange ways to the eternal ruin of the soul.

Sinners are sometimes kept from repentance by a hindrance which they do not suspect. This woman was. She afterwards recollected, that idea would come floating over her mind, and lingering around it, "Perhaps all will be saved." And this it was that half stilled her fears, and half pacified her conscience, and threw a sort of dimness and doubt over the whole field of religion. On this account she lingered in her sins, and away from her Saviour. She knew not her own heart till it sunk within her, as her delusion fled. But she soon came to Christ after her delusion was dissipated by the words wrung from the conscience of her father on that memorable morning, "Elizabeth, I think it is very likely that some will be *lost for ever!*"

The Lost Child:

OR, AFFLICTION SANCTIFIED.

I RECEIVED a very polite and fraternal note from a neighboring clergyman, whose kindness and confidence I had experienced many times before, desiring me to attend the funeral of the only child of a gentleman and lady, who had formerly been attendants on his ministry, though at that time they had come to reside nearer to myself. Another duty called him to a distant part of the state, and he commended these afflicted parents to me. I had never seen them, and I believe they had never seen me; but the brief note which commended them to me, prepared me to have a high respect for them, and to sympathize in their sadness, as they were now bereft of the only child they ever had.

The person who brought me the note and engaged my services for the funeral, could tell me but little about them. They were not communicants of any church, though my clerical friend in his note gave me to understand that they were persons of a serious turn of mind, and at times felt some personal anxiety, one or both of them, on the subject of religion.

I felt no hesitation about my duty. Indeed I could not mistake it, and had no desire to avoid it. But I was burdened with the impression, that it was a difficult duty for me to discharge with acceptance and propriety. It is a delicate thing to go to strangers in the day of their deep sadness. A friend may carry the balm of consolation to hearts that have often opened to him, but how can a stranger dare to meddle with the tenderness of grief? I feared that their hearts would be shut up against me—*must* be from the very nature of the case, or would recoil from me as an intruder, if I should attempt at all, stranger as I was, to meddle with the sacredness of their sorrow, or should even try to lay the consolation of heaven's mercy upon the grief-spot of their smitten bosoms. And I was the more embarrassed, on account of what their messenger had told me respecting the child they had lost. It was a little gem of earth,—a most beautiful, intelligent and amiable little girl, about four years old, with a maturity of mind far beyond her years; and her parents were peculiarly cast down, now when death had snatched her away. I knew that I could sympathize with them, but I did *not* know that they could receive my sympathy. Affliction seldom resorts to a stranger. It seeks solace in solitude, or the sympathy of some long-tried friend. And I was not a little afraid, that their tender and hallowed sadness would shrink from me, if I should attempt even to comfort them. They had no faith, as I supposed; and I knew that nothing but the truths of Christianity could afford them anything better than a fictitious and deceptive comfort, worse than none. I knew that mere reason would be dumb over a corpse,—that no philosophy could grapple with grief and the grave.

At the hour appointed I went to their house. It was filled with people. I spoke with the parents for a few moments, and before the funeral services commenced there was put into my hands the following letter:—

"DR. SPENCER,

Rev. Sir:—We thought we should like to give you a few particulars in regard to our only child. She was of uncommon promise, and for her age, possessed a mind much matured. During her illness of two weeks she was a great sufferer, without murmur or complaint. Her mind continued perfect until the last, and she would often say, 'Mamma, comfort your little daughter.'

"Previous to her last sickness she had enjoyed unusual health with a heart full of mirth, tenderness and sympathy. She was a favorite, and beloved by all. We have never known her to speak an untruth. She loved to do right, and was very conscientious in regard to her conduct on the Sabbath. She loved to talk of God and heaven, and a few weeks since, while an uncle was very ill, she said, 'Mamma, when we die, if God would only take us in his arms and carry us right up into heaven, so we should not have to be put into the dark coffin, how happy it would be.' We trust she is now there."

* * *

I read this affecting note (signed by both the parents), and the funeral services were conducted in the usual manner. Before prayer, I aimed to say such things as I thought might be profitable to the assembled multitude, and such especially as I had some hope would bring at least a gleam of comfort to the crushed and bleeding hearts of these parents, now stripped of their precious treasure. It was a most solemn and tender occasion. The little coffin was placed near the folding doors, which opened between the parlors. I had looked into it just as I entered the room. Its slumbering tenant was lovely even in death. It looked as if it were asleep, and appeared more pure and beautiful than the flowers which were placed beside it, and on the coffin's lid. But that marble brow was cold; and those lily lips, which seemed as if ready to utter some syllable of love, would never speak again. I could not look upon it. I turned away and wept.

After the religious exercises were closed, I sat where I could see the countenances of the multitude, who came one after another and looked into the little coffin. I did not see one who turned away without eyes suffused with tears. Every one was affected. Old men, with stern and severe faces, wept over it. And when the parents came to take their last look, and the mother bent down over the coffin to give her last kiss to such a child, I felt that her heart must break. Tears streamed from her eyes; her whole frame shook like an aspen leaf, with the dreadful violence of her agitation. There were no noisy out-bursts of grief, but such a deep and dreadful sorrow as seemed too much for nature to endure. She retired from the coffin supported by her husband; and tear-dimmed eyes followed her, as she went up to her chamber—a childless mother!

Promising to call on them the next day, I left the melancholy scene; and this sweet child was conveyed to the tomb.

The next day I called at the house. Business had compelled the father to leave home, but the mother met me with a heavy heart. She could scarcely utter a syllable for some moments. She gave me her hand with a look of despair that horrified me!

"I have called to see you, madam," said I, "for

I sympathize with you in your heavy trial, and if I could, I would say something which shall comfort you."

Evidently struggling to conceal her emotions, she answered:

"I am glad to see you, sir. I feel very wretched. I never expected such a trial as this. My child was everything to me. Our hearts were wrapped up in her, and now she is gone! I do not know how to endure this. I cannot endure it—I feel that I *cannot!*" and she wept bitterly.

"It is *God*, madam, who hath taken away your child. I am sorry for you, my heart bleeds for you. I do not blame you for mourning, and God will not blame you for it. You cannot avoid it, if you would; and you would not, if you could."

"Oh, no, sir," said she weeping, "she was such a lovely child—so affectionate and intelligent, and—my *all!* She had a maturity of mind far beyond her years. I wanted you to know something about her before the funeral; and because we wished you to know something of her, we wrote you that little note."

"That letter," said I, "affected me very much. I shall answer it as soon as I have time. It was put into my hands just after I came in here yesterday, and as I glanced over it and found her expression about being taken right up into heaven without being buried, I could not repress my emotions. I could scarcely command composure enough to conduct the funeral exercises with propriety. I am sorry for you;—I can weep with you; but God alone can do you any good. Do you think you are submissive to His will?"

"I am afraid not, sir. I know His will is right; but I cannot feel reconciled to it as I ought. It is such a stroke to me, I know not how to bear it. I never knew what affliction was before. We were very happy. I am afraid we loved our child too much. I often thought how much I had to enjoy in my husband and my child; but now God has taken her away, and I am perfectly wretched." She sobbed aloud.

"My heart bleeds for you, my dear friend; but I want you to remember, that God only can comfort you, or make your affliction beneficial. You must not murmur. You must not rebel or repine. You are not forbidden to mourn. I do not blame your grief, and do not wish you to blame yourself for it; but I want you to be satisfied with God, and especially I want you to be profited by your dreadful trial. God *means* something by sending it; and I want you to ask Him *what* He means, and be led by this sad providence nearer to Himself, in faith that rests on Christ and will fit you for another world. Do you think you have *any* faith?"

"Oh, no, sir. My mind is *all* dark. I have no

comfort, no peace. It seems as if I could think of nothing but my child."

"I do not blame you for thinking of her. You cannot help thinking; but you ought to be led by this affliction to seek the Lord. Have you been praying to Him?"

"I have tried to pray, sir; but my prayers seem almost like mockery. My thoughts wander; and God seems to be *very far off.* I am entirely cast down. My heart seems broken, and I think there is no comfort for me in this world, now my child is gone."

"I assure you, my dear friend," said I, "I feel your affliction deeply and tenderly; and that makes me the more anxious for you, to have you fly in faith to that Saviour, to that God and Father, who I know has comfort for you, and will lay the balm of a precious solace upon that deep sorrow of heart, which no other friend can reach. Fly to Him, as a child to a father. He will not cast you off. He will love and comfort you; I know He will."

"I am very miserable," said she. "It seems to me that my trial is more than I can endure."

"God will enable you to endure it, and to profit by it, if you give up sin and the world, and betake yourself to Him in faith. He invites you to his arms; He wants you to lean upon Him confidingly and affectionately, as a child. He asks you to 'cast all your care upon Him,' drawn by the power of that blessed argument, for '*He careth for you.*' "

"I do feel as if I needed comfort," said she.

"God only can comfort you," I replied.

"My child was my treasure," said she.

"Prepare to follow her to another world, Madam."

"I wish I could. When you were speaking yesterday at the funeral, your words went to my heart. It was so sweet to think she is happy now, and may be hovering near us to do us good. I could have heard you speaking as you did of my angel child all night—any length of time. It gave me the only comfort I have, to think she is forever happy with God."

"Waiting there," said I, "to welcome *you* into heaven, and rush into your arms in a little while; if you will only give up the world, and, as a sinner to be saved, flee now to the Saviour who calls you. Do you mean to do so?" Mournfully she replied:

"I hope I shall try. The world all seems different to me now. I was happy; but now, all is dark to me, for this world and the other! I cannot think of anything but my lost child."

"*Not lost,* Madam, not *lost*; but gone before. Do not think of her as lost to you; but think of your *duty* to prepare to follow her."

"I feel entirely discouraged. If I try to seek God, it is in vain. My prayers are not answered. Everything is dark. I can think of only one thing."

"My dear friend," said I, "you *must* not let this affliction be lost upon you. Turn *now* to God with all your heart. He will pity you. He will hear your prayers and comfort your heart, if you will come to Him in faith. Do you intend to do so?"

"My thoughts have been directed to the subject of religion, but I cannot seem to have any faith. All is dark to me; and now, my loss is more than I know how to bear."

"You cannot bear it rightly, but by the help of God. 'In Me is thy help,' says He: and you will find help there, if you will only seek Him with all your heart. He has directed your attention to the subject of your salvation before; and now He has given you such an affecting call, that surely you ought to heed it. I hope you will. Go to Him—tell Him all your wants and sorrows. He is of infinite love and kindness; and you have no need to be discouraged. He will not let you sink."

Very much in this manner our conversation continued for some time. I strove to comfort her, for I felt that she had a very sore trial, in which I could not but sympathize with her grief. She was a perfect picture of woe, if not of entire despair. Her intelligence too, and her frankness and simplicity, had deeply interested me; and I especially strove to persuade her to make a just use of her bitter affliction. But it was very noticeable how her mind rested upon but one thing. Whatever I said, she would come round to that. Her lost child absorbed all her thoughts, all her heart. If I spake of God, her mind would turn upon her child. If I spake of submission, it took only a moment for her to get her thoughts turned back to her child. If I spake of her duty to improve her affliction, or of the kindness of God, or spake of Christ, or comfort, or prayer, or the Holy Spirit, or sin, or faith, or heaven, a single expression would bring round her thoughts to the same melancholy theme—her lost child.

I felt it to be no easy thing to deal with such a heart rightly. To soothe and comfort her crushed spirit, and at the same time to lead her to make a just use of her affliction, appeared almost impossible. If I should attempt to lead her mind off from her lost child, all a mother's heart would be against me. If I should attempt nothing more than to condole with her, she might indeed be soothed a little by the sympathy, but that soothing would not lead her to salvation. I strove, therefore, to find some hold upon her sensibilities, some link which should unite her sorrow and her Saviour; which should neither do violence to a mother's bleeding heart, nor peril her everlasting interests. And before I left her, one of her own expressions had, as I thought, furnished me what I desired. I resolved to employ the idea afterwards—it was the idea of her own child now in heaven.

Before I left her, I prayed with her, as she requested me to do, that their affliction might be sanctified to her and her husband.

As soon as I was able, I sent an answer to the letter which was given to me at the funeral; and in the answer I aimed to comfort and counsel my sad friends as well as I could.

Pressing engagements hindered my seeing her again, except once for a few moments, till nearly a fortnight after the funeral. It was Saturday when I called upon her again, and found her, if possible, more miserable than before. In answer to my inquiry, she replied:

"I feel perfectly miserable, and there is nothing that can comfort me. I feel my loss more and more every day."

"I am sorry for you, my dear child. Your loss is indeed great, and I do not wonder at your feeling it. I do not blame your sorrow. I should blame you, if you had none. God would have you mourn. Jesus wept at the grave of Lazarus, whom he loved. But God can comfort you, and I hope He will. The Holy Ghost is the Holy Comforter. Have you been praying to Him?"

"Yes, I have tried; but my thoughts are wandering. It seems to me that God will not hear such prayers as mine. My mind is all dark. I have tried to pray, but it does me no good."

"What have you been praying *for?*"

"I have prayed that our affliction may be sanctified to us."

"Do you think it will be?"

"I am afraid not. God does not answer me, and my heart appears to me to be very hard."

"Have you any comfort in praying?"

"No, none at all; and I am discouraged in *trying* to seek God."

"You need not be discouraged. If you seek Him with your whole heart, He will be found of you. He has promised that, and He will be true to his word."

"But my heart is so senseless. I try to believe, but it seems as if I had no faith. I read the Bible, but it is dark to me. I try to pray, but my heart is not in my prayers; and I am afraid God will never hear me."

"Do you think you have been led to know and feel that you have a *wicked* heart, and need God's help to make it different?"

"I *know* it, but it seems to me I do not *feel* it at all; and I wonder at myself."

"Do you wish to feel it?"

"Yes, I do. I have prayed to be enabled to do so. I know I am a sinner, and I wonder I do not realize it more. I think I never have had conviction enough."

"How much conviction does a sinner need, in order to be prepared to come to Christ? He needs just to know and feel that he cannot save himself. If he knows he is a lost sinner, he knows all the truth about himself that he needs to know; and he ought instantly to accept the offers of God, trusting Christ to save him. Do you think you feel your need of the atonement that Christ has made for sinners, in order that you may be forgiven and saved?"

"Yes, I do. I can do nothing for myself."

'Well, then, let Christ do everything for you. *Trust* Him to do everything for you. He *offers* to do everything for you. Come to him *just as you are*, with all your sin—with all your darkness—with all your unworthiness—with your cold and unbelieving heart—and let Him give you another heart. He waits to receive you, and your delaying is unnecessary. Your waiting to gain more distressful feelings about yourself, will not make you any better prepared to give up the world and trust in Him. Come to him now—not to be lost, but to be loved—not to be cast out, but to be comforted *and saved.* Come now, while the Holy Spirit strives with you."

"I *need* His blessing," said she. "I feel very miserable. God has taken away the only child I ever had; and I believe He has done it to show me my sins; but I am afraid it will be in vain to me. I cannot feel *anything*. My heart seems hardened."

"But, my dear friend, your child is better off than you; and your duty now is to prepare to meet her in heaven. God has spread a cloud of gloom over this world, to turn your heart to a better one. But you do not give God your heart; you are still hesitating, fearful, and unbelieving. If you remain thus, all your affliction will only be lost upon you. I am not a little afraid it will. Do you not know that the instances of conversion to Christ are far less than the number of mourners?—that very few persons are ever led to religion by such afflictions? Affliction goes everywhere—death goes everywhere. You see it all around you. 'Who has not lost a friend?' Parents die, and children die; and yet how seldom it is that the bereavement profits the living. Such trials do *Christians* good; but they seldom bring unbelievers to true religion. You *know* this is true; you see it to be so all around. And even now, when the only comfort you have is to think of the little gem you have lost, now a gem in heaven, I am afraid your affliction will not lead you to Christ."

"My heart," said she, "is very hard. I am miserable; but it seems to me I cannot feel my sins. I have tried to seek God, but something keeps me from thinking of anything but one."

"Give God your heart just as it is,—remember

just as it is, and let Him make it feel. 'Turn unto the Lord and He will have mercy upon you, and to our God for He will abundantly pardon.' You must have faith. You must *believe* what He says to you. You must trust His promises, and fall into His arms. Salvation is all of grace. Do not wait for feeling. Have the faith first, and let the feeling come afterwards. Receive Christ as your own, affectionately, and as a child; and then you may expect your hard heart will melt. The Holy Spirit strives to bring you to this. 'Now is the accepted time.' Flee to Christ to-day, and be prepared to follow your child to glory."

As her thoughts hung constantly around her child, I aimed, with all my might, so to connect the idea of her loss with the idea of her personal obligation to religion, that she should not be able to think of her child without thinking of her own salvation. I may not here record all my exhortations to her—it would tire the reader. But I strove to make every recollection say to her, "Prepare to meet your child in heaven." I hunted her soul with that thought, and linked the thought with every recollection. I made it come up with every sigh, and burn in every tear. I associated it with the last look she took of her child, and with that coffin-kiss, which I thought would break her heart. I wrote it upon the little grave, and made the green grass that grows over it say to her, "Prepare to meet your child in heaven." The past uttered it to her, the future uttered it. Love, hope, disappointment, grief, every little memorial, was made say to her, "Prepare to meet your child in heaven." I aimed to people the whole universe for her with that one thought, "Prepare to meet your child in heaven." I linked this thought with the morning, the evening, the bedroom, the books, with all this wilderness world. I painted to her, her lost one now bending over the battlements of heaven and looking down upon her, and saying, "Mother, Prepare to meet your child in heaven." I represented to her that lost child, now perhaps hovering around her as a "ministering spirit" sent forth from heaven, in some mysterious manner to minister for her as an "heir of salvation," and waiting to carry the tidings of her repentance on high, that there might be a new "joy in the presence of the angels of God."

After beseeching her in this manner to fly to Christ, and praying for her, I took my leave, saying to her with solemn tenderness,—"Prepare to meet your child in heaven."

The next morning I perceived that she and her husband were in church, and appeared very attentive to the sermon.

It was not possible for me to call upon her on Monday or Tuesday, as I had intended. Late in the evening of Tuesday, a messenger brought me the following letter:

"DR. SPENCER,

Rev. Sir:—I have taken the liberty of addressing a few lines to you. Allow me, in the first place, to *thank* you for your kindness and sympathy towards us, strangers as we were to you. I shall never forget your consoling words; they fell like balm upon a bruised and broken heart. The light and the joy of our home was taken; but the fond hope which your words inspired, that our dear child 'might be hovering over us, missioned from heaven in some mysterious manner to minister to our spirits,' seemed to animate and encourage me not to be weary in well doing. When I saw you on Saturday, I felt that I was still far from God. I had no heart to read the Bible, no heart to pray. I was overwhelmed with grief; my child was gone, and what had I to live for? It seemed that one thought had taken the place of every other; but I still continued to pray, although my lips uttered words which I thought my heart did not feel. On Sabbath morning, before entering the church, I prayed that God would bless to me the words that I might hear spoken. 'Faith and grace'—(alluding to the sermon)—"it was just what I most needed; but the door of my heart was closed, and they could not enter in. After dinner,

I took up a book, and one piece that I read, 'Waiting for Conviction,' made me feel that I was standing in just that position. I had been relying upon my own self-righteousness, waiting for something, I knew not what. I felt as if you were talking to me; every word came home to my heart. I went to my room and prayed, as I had never prayed before,—'God be merciful to me a sinner.' I was a good deal cast down, and it seemed to me as if I must not retire to rest that night, until I had made my peace with God. I passed a restless, weary night; the words kept sounding in my ears, 'Prepare to meet your child in heaven.' I could but cry, Lord have mercy! When I awoke near morning, after a short and restless sleep, I felt as if the work must be accomplished before another day passed over. During the day, I felt better, had some comfort in reading the Bible, felt that God had answered my prayers, unworthy as they were. He had convicted me of my sin; and I seemed to have more faith, but still unbelief held its sway. I prayed earnestly for more faith and grace; and as I sat alone in my room, the twilight hour, I thought over all of my past life. I had done nothing for God, and He had done everything for me. He had given me a most precious gift, and I had never once thanked the Giver, but went on in my own pride and self-love, building fond hope and joy for the far-off future; and in a little time she was stricken from my sight. It appeared to me that God had taken that means to bring the parents to repentance; and I felt that it was but right and just. While I thus sat holding communion with my own thoughts, recalling the blessed promises of the Bible, all at once such light, and love, and hope, shone into my heart, it seemed as if I must clap my hands and sing aloud a new song:

"His loving kindness—oh, how great!"

"I could kiss the hand that had smitten. The heavy load of sin is gone. Will you, dear sir, be kind enough to call and see me to-morrow. I have no words to thank you for your kindness. I am as a little child just entering upon a new world, and I am afraid my feelings will not last."

* * * *

In accordance with the request contained in this letter, I called upon her the next morning. She met me with a smile of gladness. Her downcast look was gone—not a trace left of that deep and settled melancholy, which had formerly rested upon her countenance and made her such an image of wo. Her joy and peace seemed to have transformed her into another being. She was perfectly happy. Peace filled her heart, and her countenance was lighted up with the signals of an ecstasy which she could neither repress nor conceal She was solemn, but "her joy was full." Smiles of peace unbidden would spread, like a beam of light, over her features; her step, her mien, the whole woman was changed.

"I wanted to see you," said she (with a look and in an accent of rapture), "I want to tell you how happy I am. I can bless God now. He has been very gracious to me, and I can praise Him for all He has done. I can see His goodness in all my affliction. I thought, yesterday, I must go and see you and have you rejoice with me."

"What makes you so happy?" said I.

"Because God has heard my prayers, and removed my dreadful burden of sin, and given me peace with Himself. I know it is not anything that *I* have done—it is the mercy and grace of God. He has heard me, and given me faith and love: I cannot be grateful enough."

"Do you think you have faith now?"

"Oh, yes, I have faith. I believe and trust Him, for He has shown me the way, and brought me to this delightful peace. I was very wretched, and could not feel reconciled; but now I see the hand of His kindness in it all. I see the leading of His Providence all along, in sending us here and directing us to you. I cannot be thankful enough. I feel very grateful to you for your kindness to us in our affliction. I was afraid to have you come when my child died. You were a stranger to us, and I did not know as you could enter into our feelings; but when I heard you speak at the funeral, my fears vanished; and when you came afterwards and talked to me, I thought God had sent us here, and taken away our child, on purpose to have us led to repentance. I thank you for all you have done."

"Do you *love* God now?"

"Oh, yes, I do. I cannot thank Him enough. I can submit to His will now, though my loss is so great. I see He meant it for my good."

"Does your heart rest on Christ alone to save you?"

"Yes, I trust Him entirely. I have nothing else to trust in. I know I am a great sinner; but He has heard me, and answered me. He has set my heart at rest."

"Have you this peace of mind and joy in God, all the time?"

"Sometimes, I am afraid I am deceived for a little while; but the most of the time I am very happy. At first, I felt as if I could not restrain my feelings. I did not want to come down to tea: I was afraid they would think me crazy, for I knew I could not conceal my joy, my looks would betray me, and I was afraid I should lose my happy feelings.

"I want you to see my young friend. I want you to tell her that she has only to come to Christ, that she 'need not wait to get ready' as you told *me* on Saturday. It all seems to me *so easy* now—only to come to God in faith—not wait to get ready. I wonder people do not see it. I wonder that I did not see it before. But I had not faith. Now I can see the way all clear; and this light and peace with God make me very happy. I feel my loss and cannot but weep; but I know God has done it for my good, and I am resigned and happy. I thank and praise Him for his kindness."

"Have you any doubts or fears to trouble you?"

"Yes, I have at times, for a little while; but when I go to God in prayer, my joy returns. Sometimes, I am afraid my feelings are not the right ones, and that I am deceived. I know my heart is deceitful; but I trust in God, and then I am happy. I feel as if I was a little child, and want to be led. I have only just begun to learn. I know but very little, and I am afraid these joyful feelings will not last. God has afflicted me, but now He comforts me."

"You recollect I told you on Saturday that *such* afflictions were very seldom of any benefit to unbelievers."

"I know you did, and it made me feel very sad."

"But you know it is true," said I.

"Oh yes, I know it is true, a great many have lost children, and never came to repentance; and that made me feel the more anxious to improve the time."

Again and again, when I saw her, she conversed

in the same happy strain, affectionate, grateful, and simple-hearted as a child. She was peculiarly desirous that other members of her family should have the same faith and peace of mind which made her so happy. She told them how she felt, with an earnestness, affection, and simplicity which could not be surpassed, and with the manifest impression fixed upon her mind that salvation was freely offered to them, and they had nothing to do but to believe it and accept the offer.

As I was talking with her at one time, in the presence of a young woman in whom she felt a deep interest, and to whom she had done me the favor to introduce me, I thought many of her expressions must reach the young woman's heart. I asked her,

"Do you still feel the same happiness that you have had?"

"Oh, yes, most of the time. Sometimes I have a little darkness, but it soon passes away and my happy feelings return. God answers my prayers. I go to him for everything. I have just begun. I am a little child, and want to be led all the time. I want some one to teach me whether my feelings are right. But I feel very happy."

Said I, "I wish to ask you one question. You have given some attention to the subject of religion before this time. It has often been on your mind, and you have tried to seek the Lord. And after your child died, you were for some time in great distress and darkness. Now I wish to ask you this question: What kept you so long in darkness—what hindered you that you did not come to Christ sooner?"

"Oh," said she, "I was *self-righteous:* I did not have *faith*: I was trying to do something for myself, *to get ready* to trust in God."

The eyes of the young woman filled with tears, her breast heaved with emotion, and I could not but hope that the truth, which I had elicited from the lips of her happy friend, would lead *her* to a happiness as precious. At least, she was taught, that she *need not "wait to get ready."*

Notwithstanding the severity of her affliction, this bereaved mother was uniformly happy. She seemed to live on high. In prayerful communion with God and in contemplation of heaven, she spent her days in peace. She could not forget her child, and she could not cease to mourn; but her grief for her loss was mingled with joy in God, and many times have I seen tears and smiles blended together on her expressive countenance. She was a most affectionate mother. She loved deeply and tenderly. Her peace of mind, her submission and joy, were not in the least the results of a stupid or a stoical heart; but they were the gift of God, and in the exercise of them she was no less tender and affectionate as a Christian than she was as a mourning mother.

Her deep and tender solicitude for her irreligious friends was a most interesting feature in her character. From the commencement of her seriousness, I had aimed to awaken in her heart an interest in the salvation of others. Several of her "nearest and dearest friends" were, as she said, still in unbelief. From the first, she manifested much interest in their eternal welfare; but before the time when she came to her own sweet hope in Christ, her thoughts seemed to be called back from them to herself, and she found an almost insuperable obstacle in her way, whenever she attempted anything for them, even in prayer. Her thoughts were drawn back, and her feelings were borne down by the sadness and gloom of her own mind. But after she came out of that gloom, her heart turned to the subject of *their* salvation with much tenderness and strength of affection. She was not only willing, but prompt and joyful to second any of my attempts to bring them to Christ.

A few weeks after she began to find Christ her refuge, she expressed some of her reflections in the following letter:

"Dr. Spencer,

Rev. Sir:—I will intrude upon your time but for a few moments. We have been looking for a visit from you for some days. It has been so pleasant to have you come in and see us, that it really seems as if you had almost forgotten us. I shall ever hold in grateful remembrance your kindness to me; and those consoling words which feel like balm upon my bruised and sorrowful heart, will never be forgotten. They were the first words that made me feel deeply; and through God I feel that you have been the instrument of opening my eyes—'whereas I was once blind, but now I see.' Oh, how beautiful is the plan of salvation! to be redeemed, to be bought with the price of a Saviour's blood, to be justified, adopted, and sanctified! to call God our Father! and when our hearts go forth to Him in prayer, to feel that He is so near to us! Oh, that I may be wholly His! My earnest desire is to be a whole-souled Christian, not a half undecided one. When I look at my poor sinful heart, so prone to wander, so vile, and so full of sin, I almost despair, sometimes, of ever attaining the only worthy end for which to live; but with God all things are possible, and I can but pray to be purified—'wash me, and I shall be whiter than snow.' I have spent many calm and peaceful hours in my retirement, communing with my own thoughts and with God, thinking of my angel child as she walks the golden streets of the New Jerusalem. Hers was a bright and joyous spirit on earth, and how much more bright and beautiful there. Heaven does not seem so far off as it once did.

"I often ask myself when the time comes for me

to mingle again with the world, if my heart will be as near to God as it is now. I hope that He will ever guide me. I must watch and pray. Prayer and the precious Bible must be my refuge. How beautifully the hymn,

'Jesus lover of my soul,'

warms the heart, and makes it feel indeed, that

'Thou, Oh Christ, art all I want,
All in all in thee I find.'

God has supported and directed me. He seems to know just what I most need.

* * * * *

"But it seems to me that I know too little of divine truth. I want to be fed with the bread of life, to drink deeper from the fountains of living waters. My health has been such that I have not been able to attend divine service, and I thirst for more knowledge of the Bible.

* * * * *

"'How beautiful are the feet of him that bringeth good tidings; that publisheth salvation.' I know, my dear sir, that you have often been made very happy, and have felt doubly paid for all the toil and trouble, when sinners have come to you with faith and joy beaming in their countenance, and told you that they had found their God. My request, therefore, will not afflict you, though it should add to your labors.

* * * * *

"I know your time is much occupied, and you will please pardon my intrusion upon you."

* * * *

I visited her often. It was delightful to witness her joy. She seemed to live in the sunshine of peace. Seldom were her skies overcast; and when a cloud did darken her heavens, it was only for a moment, and only served to make the returning light more sweet.

"I have sometimes a little darkness," said she.

"And what do you do then?"

"Oh, I pray to God, and the light returns."

"Do you *love* to pray?"

"Oh, yes, I always love to pray. It seems to me such a precious privilege. Whenever I am sad, thinking of my child, or my mind is downcast, I find that when I pray, God answers me and I am comforted. I just go to Him with my trouble. It is a precious privilege."

"Have you ever any doubt whether God has given you a new heart?"

"At times I have, for a little while. But the most of the time I cannot doubt; I have such sweet peace in thinking of God, Christ is so precious to me, and all my feelings are so different from what they used to be. I know I am still a sinner. I sin every hour; and I know my heart is deceitful; but I trust in Christ, and God comforts me with hope."

Such were her feelings week after week. Her joy was full. Her faith appeared to grow stronger, and while her humility became more deep, the tenderness of her love and her *confiding* became more and more peaceful.

When our communion season came, she did not unite with the church. She thought it best to defer the public profession of her faith for a time. But she was present at the administration of the ordinance of the Lord's Supper. A day or two afterwards I called upon her, and she adverted to it with a very manifest delight.

Said she, "I had a happy day last Sunday. When I saw those young persons come forward to unite with the church, I longed to be with them. I thought it would be such a privilege, to confess my faith in the Lord Jesus Christ, and aim to honor Him before so many people. And when the members of the church were partaking of the bread and wine, they all appeared so solemn and happy, I wondered that anybody *could stay away.* It was the happiest day I ever saw. I thought the Lord was there to comfort his people. It seemed to me that they had the peace of heaven; and I hoped the time would come, when I should myself be with that great company and partake of their joy."

"Such occasions," said I, "have been profitable seasons to us."

"Oh, I think they must be," said she. "Though I was only a spectator, I felt it was good for me to be there; and I did not wonder, when you said, that you scarcely recollected a communion season, when there was not at least some one sinner awakened to seek the Lord. It seems to me, that nobody could have witnessed the exercises of last Sunday unmoved. I should think that every spectator would be convinced of the presence of Christ, and the happiness of communion with him. I look forward with delight to the time when I shall come myself to that solemn spot, and give away myself to our Lord Jesus Christ."

In due time, she *did* come. Years have since rolled away, and she still lives a happy believer—one of the *few*, whom bereavement has called out of the world's allurements, and aided towards Christ and heaven.

If this publication should ever meet her eye, I am aware it may open afresh the fountains of her grief, and that is the only idea which makes me hesitate about giving this narrative to the world. But I am sure she will *know* that it is not in my heart to afflict her, by exposing to the world the sacredness of her sorrow, or by recalling to her mind a scene which grief burnt upon her memory; and I am sure she will pardon me the liberty I have taken, when she shares with me the hope, that some *mourning mother* will be led to Christ by this narrative of THE LOST CHILD—not lost, but gone before.

'Twas a gem fit for love, 'twas the gift of her God,
But no thanks did the gift e'er excite;
Death snatched it away—she sunk under the rod!
All her world was a chaos of night!

Then there whispered a voice from the land of the blest,
Oh my Mother, my Mother! on high
I wait to receive thee to this land of sweet rest—
Oh my Mother, prepare thee to die.

I'm not in the dark coffin, Christ spread his arms round me,
I awoke 'mid this light and this love,
Where the bright beams of heaven spread their glory around me,
For *I* died to allure *thee* above.

She heard it; she felt that attraction of heaven,—
It was peace: she can now kiss the rod;
She flew to her Christ—she's a sinner forgiven:—
They shall meet in the bosom of God.

This is one of the few instances that have come within my own knowledge, wherein the sorrows of mourning have been of any lasting spiritual benefit to an unbeliever. To God's people bereavements and sorrows are sanctified. This is general, if not universal. Our observation can behold it, and we often hear the testimony from their own lips. But to the 'children of this world,' their days of mourning are very much in vain. They can bury their friends, and with a depth and tenderness and bitterness of mourning weep over their loss; but in a few brief days their hearts turn back again upon the world, and they go on as carelessly and gaily as before. The place of the funeral is a very hopeless place for preaching the gospel to unbelievers. I recollect but two instances before this, in a ministry of more than twenty years, in which anything that I ever said at a funeral has been the means of arousing and leading to Christ a single impenitent sinner. The hope which irreligious persons so frequently indulge, that some future affliction, when it shall come, the loss of some loved and valued friend, will lead them to religion, is almost universally a hope of entire vanity and deception. They do not know their own hearts. Both observation and experience prove such a hope to be delusive. Bleeding hearts are not necessarily penitent ones. Among hundreds whom I have heard, at the time of their reception into the church, giving an account of the manner in which they had been led to religion, I recollect *only two*, who mentioned the death of a friend as the means of leading them to seek God. The member of a family dies, but the survivors do not become pious. Indeed, so common is this—such an ordinary historical fact, that scarcely a man among us can point to a single instance, where the doings of death and the effectual workings of the Holy Spirit to convert to Christ, have gone side by side. Indeed, unbelieving hearts crushed with a burden of sorrow in the dark and dreadful days of mourning, are more apt to be injured than benefited, by the bitterness of their sad experience.

I knew of a woman, many years since, whose attention had been earnestly directed to the subject of religion, and who, for some weeks, had been prayerfully attempting to seek the Lord; when she was suddenly summoned to the death-bed of one of her children in a neighboring state. She came home from the funeral of that child; and immediately after her return, several other relatives of her own family were brought, disfigured corpses, to her house, having been killed by the explosion of the boiler on a steamboat. No one could have been more shocked, or more deeply plunged into anguish than was she. "Now," says she (referring to her loss, a day or two afterwards), "I give up the world; it is nothing to me any longer." But when, by the lapse of time, her grief had somewhat lost its poignancy, her seriousness was all gone. Her grief had dissipated her religious anxiety; she had forgotten the subject of her salvation; and relapsing into her former indifference, she went on for months and months in her irreligion and prayerlessness, as unconcerned as ever.

Such things appear strange and wonderful to many people At the first thought, probably, such a thing appears wonderful to everybody. But I think it is a thing susceptible of a very intelligible explanation. Sorrow leads the mind one way, and seriousness about salvation leads it quite another. Grief for a lost friend is one thing, and grief on account of sin is quite another thing. When a sinner is seeking salvation, his thoughts are turned upon his sins, his soul, his eternity, his God and Saviour; but when he is overwhelmed with personal affliction and sorrow, his thoughts are turned upon his loss. Then, it is not his *sin* that troubles him,—no, he is just thinking of his loved-one dead, his child, his sister, or his father taken from him, and now buried in the deep, dark grave. His mind is now called off from the state, the guilt, and danger of his own immortal soul, from his need of Christ to save him, and of the Holy Spirit to 'renew a right spirit within him.' *Whatever* it may be, that leads him to forget his sins, does him an injury. Any diversion of his thoughts to a new channel, does him an injury. The channel may be *more* dark—more distressful—more dreadful to him; but his attention has become diverted to a new object, and that 'one thing needful' is at present crowded away into the back-ground of his contemplations, or forgotten entirely. And hence, the deeper his sorrow, the more dangerous its influence becomes. His affliction just makes him forget his sins, and his soul.

And thus it is, as I suppose, that we behold, all over the world, the mourning of unbelievers so generally unattended or followed by any religious benefits. Their thoughts are on their loss—their earthly loss. The death of their friend has spread a glooom over the world. Their house lacks an inmate,—their heart lacks a friend to lean upon, along the pilgrimage of life. Another star has gone out, and left a dark spot in their heavens, which once appeared so bright and beautiful to their eye. A seat is left vacant at the fire-side,—a friend is absent from the table,—a familiar voice is missed in the family-circle. But all these are earthly griefs. They are not spiritual ones to an unbeliever. The mourning unbeliever *never* much prized his now lost friend, as an aid to his holiness and salvation; —he prized him only for earthly reasons. He *never* loved the lost one as a companion to go hand in hand with him to Jerusalem, or along the vales of Palestine, amid the fragrance and beauty of 'the rose of Sharon and lily of the valley.' He *never* loved his companionship, because his lips were vocal with the melody of 'another country, even an heavenly,' which he hoped to reach;—but simply because his companionship made earth more pleasant, not heaven more near. And, therefore, when death has snatched away this now lost companion, only an earthly sorrow takes possession of the heart, just that 'sorrow of the world which worketh death.' And when he turns away from the grave of his buried friend, or, in the dark days that follow, thinks of him so mournfully, the whole effect of his sorrow is just to make the world more dreary; not the world to come, more gladsome and inviting. If he had lived with his friend *as a Christian*, it would have been very different with him now, when his friend is no more; and the death he deplores would have made his thoughts hang more fondly around the *religious* things, in which he and his friend used to aid and comfort one another. But he did not;—he was an unbeliever (*himself*, whatever his lost friend may have been); and, therefore, the death which has saddened him, just confines his thoughts to this dark and dreary *world*, instead of leading them towards the *world* of immortality.

God is infinitely willing to sanctify to *men* their sorrows, and bring the beams of gladness over the dark days of their mourning. But men misuse their times of sorrow. The sad history of thousands of hearts that have bled, demonstrates but too plainly this melancholy truth,—our piety seldom springs from the grave that our tears have watered.

The Stormy Night:

OR, PERSEVERANCE.

THE most remarkable instance of protracted and determined perseverance in seeking God, that has ever come within my knowledge, was that of a young married woman, whose seriousness commenced soon after I visited her at her own house, for the first time. The conversation that I then had with her, as she afterwards told me, "led her to make up her mind that she *would* seek the Lord, and would not stop, till she believed her salvation was secure." The one consideration, and so far as I could ever ascertain, the only one, which had any special influence to lead her to form this resolution and begin to act upon it, was taken from the assurance I gave her in my first conversation with her, that salvation was within her reach,—that she might be a Christian if she would,—that she would not seek the Lord in vain, if she only sought Him with all her heart. "You told me, sir," said she to me, years afterwards, "I should not seek God in vain. Your words were (I remember it well and always shall),

'*I know*, Mrs. E——, that you will be saved, if you seek God with all your heart.'"

She tried to do so. She came to my house for conversation with me about her salvation, almost every Sabbath evening for nearly two years. In the depth of winter, on a cold, stormy night, the wind blowing violently, the snow drifting into the path, in places more than two feet in depth (as I found on accompanying her home),—one of the most unpleasant and even terrific nights for a woman to be abroad; she came nearly half a mile to my house, alone. As I opened the door for her admission that stormy night, I uttered an expression of surprise, "why, Mrs. E——! are you here on such a night?" And I shall never forget the severe, *deserved* rebuke, which she unwittingly gave me, many months afterwards, in reference to that expression. "It stumbled me," says she; "I did not know what to make of it. You had invited us there, and I thought you would be expecting me. I thought you ought not to be *surprised* to see me there, if sinners were in danger of the everlasting wrath of God and might escape it, as you had preached that day. It was a long time before I could get over that stumbling-block. I thought, if you had *believed* what you preached, and felt about it as I did, you would *expect* to see me. I know it was a stormy night and I was afraid; but I kept thinking as I went, that the day of judgment would bring a worse storm, as you said once in your sermon—'hail-stones and coals of fire.'" This she said to me more than a year afterwards, and after she had attained hope in the mercy of God through Christ Jesus.

At the same time, she told me another thing, which added keenness to her unintentional rebuke. She said, that her husband (at this time an irreligious man), was very unwilling that she should venture out on that stormy night, and strongly urged her to stay at home, when he found she proposed to go. "But," says she, "he told me afterwards that my going to your house that night, was the first thing which brought him to reflection; for he thought there must be *something* about sin and religion which he did not know anything about, if I would go to your house in such a storm, all alone. I did not know it at that time; but when he told me afterwards, I remembered that he looked very cross when I came home, and I thought he was angry because I went. But I was not going to mind *that.* I knew I had done rightly, and I was not going to let anything turn me aside from trying to be a Christian. And don't you remember, three Sunday nights after that, he came to your house with me?"

Month after month, this woman's deep anxiety continued I never could discover why she lingered so long in her unbelief. Again and again, I aimed with all possible carefulness to tell her all the truths of the gospel, and to discover what error, sin or temptation, kept her from repentance and peace with God. But I never could discover her hindrance: and she never could tell me, then or afterwards, of any difficulty or temptation, which had troubled her, except the expression I made to her on that stormy night. And in justice to her I ought to say, that she did not mention that as having been a hindrance, though she called it a stumbling-block; but mentioned it casually and in another connection—not to find fault with me, and not to account for her continuing so long in unbelief. Far from this. She was one of the most modest of women, and one of the most affectionate and devoted friends I ever had. Nothing, I am sure, could ever have tempted her to find fault with me, or utter a syllable with any intent to censure me or wound my feelings. *Before* that memorable night of storms, when her presence surprised me, she had been for months an anxious inquirer.

It was a most painful and perplexing thing to discharge my pastoral duty to this woman. I could not understand her state of mind. She was frank, she concealed nothing, she told me all her heart, she was desirous of being interrogated. She was, moreover, an intelligent, well-educated woman, and trained in early life by religious parents. But I could not even conjecture what kept her in her unbelief, since, for so long a time, she had known the truth, and had such powerful strivings of the Holy Spirit. And what then could I say to her? how could I hope to do her any good?

She came to me so many times, and I had so many times told her all that I knew about the way of salvation, and so many times presented to her every motive of the gospel, and invited and urged her to cast herself upon Christ, that I did not know what more to say or do; and time after time I was half sorry to see her come into my house, and then ashamed of myself because my heart had such a feeling. I knew not what to do. At one time I was on the point of telling her that I had nothing more to say to her, and she need not come to me again. But I could not do it. She was so miserable, so sincere, so determined, docile, and confiding, that it was impossible for me to cast her off. I afterwards rejoiced that I had not done it. Her husband became pious, her sister, and others of her friends, all of whom began to seek God after she did; and yet, there she stood, the same unhappy, unconverted sinner. She did not advance, and she did not go back. Time after time I assured her that her lingering was unnecessary, and would gain her nothing,—that she had but to trust herself to the arms of Christ outstretched to receive her,—that 'without faith it was impossible for her to please God,' or gain an item of profit to her own soul. A hundred times I cautioned her most solemnly against putting any trust in her perseverance, for that she was persevering in the wrong course while in her unbelief, and the farther she went, the worse would be her condition. Time after time, the Bible in my hand, and she in tears before me, as a minister of God, and on his authority, I offered her a free salvation, and demanded her heart's faith, and instant submission to divine authority and unbounded love. Her mind, her conscience, her heart, I besieged with all the kindness of Christ. I explained to her such passages of the Scriptures as 'the marriage which a certain king made for his son,'—and 'the prodigal,' who, in a far country, 'began to be in want.' All would not do.

As far as I could discover, she had for many weary months a full conviction of all the great doctrines of the Bible, of the entire depravity of her heart, of her sin and danger under the law as a condemned sinner, of the impossibility of her salvation but by Christ, and of the full and free salvation offered to her in the love of God, on the ground of the great atonement. I have never spent half as much time with any other awakened sinner, or uttered to any other one half as many threatenings and promises of God, or kneeled with any other half as many times in prayer. But so far as I know, she never received any benefit from it all, unless that was a benefit which she one day suggested to me long afterwards, when she said, "if *you* had been discouraged with me, *I* should have been discouraged,—and should have given up trying to be saved."

She persevered. She became a child of hope and peace. She united herself with the people of God; and now, after more than thirteen years, she still lives in the enjoyment of Christian hope. Neither she nor I,—yea, nor her husband, will ever forget that *stormy night.*

Ministers ought never to despair of the salvation of any sinner. To despair of any one, is just the way to make him despair of himself. Many have been ruined in this way probably. We ought to *expect* sinners to repent,—and treat them accordingly. Who shall limit the Holy One of Israel? It took me long to learn the lesson, but I have learnt *never to give up a sinner.* We must urge the duty of an immediate faith and repentance, as the Bible does so continually; but we should be careful to enjoin this duty *in such a manner*, that if it is not immediately *done*, the individual shall not be led or left to cease seeking God. Many a sinner turns back, when just at the door of heaven.

The Choice:

HOLD ON OR LET GO

MANY months after the foregoing sketch was all written, together with the reflections I have made upon it as they are printed above, I had an opportunity for conversation with my persevering friend, and I made another attempt to learn, (as I had sometimes tried to learn before,) what it was that kept her in her unbelief for so long a time, in those dark days of her wearisome perseverance.

"You have asked me that," said she, "more than once before, and I never could tell you. I have often thought of it, but it always seemed mysterious to me. I believed the Spirit had led me, but I did not know how. But awhile ago, in one of my backslidings, I thought I found out something about it."

"Well, how was it?"

"I was in a cold state," said she; "I had lost all the little light I ever had. I knew I had done wrong. I had too much neglected prayer, my heart had become worldly, and for a good many weeks I was in trouble and fear, for I knew I had wandered far from God. Then I thought I felt just as I used to, before I had any hope, when I was coming to your house so much. And then I tried to recollect what I did to come to the light at that time, so as to do the same thing now. But I couldn't remember anything about it. However, while I was trying, one thing came to my mind which did me some good. You know your sermon that you preached just before I came to have any hope,—I don't remember the text,—but it was about wandering sinners lost on the mountains."

"No, indeed, madam, I have no recollection of it."

"Well, I can't tell you what it was; I can't repeat it; may be I can tell enough to make you remember. I know you represented us in that sermon as lost sinners, lost in the woods, wandering over mountain after mountain, in dark and dangerous places among the rocks and precipices, not knowing where we were going. It grew darker and darker,—we were groping along, sometimes on the brink of a dreadful precipice, and didn't know it. Then some of us began to fall down the steep mountains, and thought we should be dashed to pieces. (I know *I* thought so.) But we caught hold of the bushes to hold ourselves up by them;—some bushes would give way, and then we would catch others, and hold on till they gave way, broke, or tore up by the roots, and then we would catch others, and others.—Don't you remember it, sir?"

"Partly. But go on."

"Well, you said our friends were calling to us, as we hung by the bushes on the brink, and we called to one another, '*hold on—hold on.*' Then, you said this cry, '*hold on—hold on,*' might be a very natural one for anybody to make, if he should see a poor creature hanging over the edge of a precipice, clinging to a little bush with all his might,—if the man didn't see anything *else*. But you said there was another thing to be seen, which these '*hold on*' people didn't seem to know anything about. You said the Lord Jesus Christ was down at the bottom of the precipice, lifting up both hands to catch us, if we would consent to fall into his arms, and was crying out to us, '*let go—let go—let go.*' Up above, all around where we were, you said they were crying out '*hold on—hold on.*' Down below, you said, Jesus Christ kept crying out, 'let go—let go;' and if we only knew who he was, and would *let go* of the bushes of sin and self-righteousness, and fall into the arms of Christ, we should be saved. And you said we had better stop our noise, and *listen*, and hear *his* voice, and *take* his advice,—and '*let go.*'"

"Don't you recollect that sermon, sir?"

"Yes, only you have preached it better than I did."

"Well, when I remembered that sermon last spring, in my dark, back-slidden state, I tried to obey it. I 'let go' of *everything*, and trusted myself to Christ; and in a little while, my heart was comforted,—my hope came back again. And afterwards, when I was wondering at it, I thought, perhaps it was just so when you preached that sermon a great while ago, when I was first led to have a hope of salvation. But I never thought of it before; I don't know how I found peace and hope the first time, if this was not the way. I suppose we have to make our choice whether to 'hold on' to something which can't save us, or 'let go,' and *fall into the hands of the Lord.*"

The efforts of a legal spirit are directly the opposite of an evangelical faith. By nature every sinner resorts to the Law. It cannot save him. He must let go of that, and fall into the arms of Christ. *Faith* saves, and Jesus Christ is the sole object of faith.

The Neglected Bible.

In the month of February, 18—, I called at the house of a family, which I had several times visited before. I knew them well, and my purpose was to make another attempt to do them good. They were very poor, their home was very uncomfortable, their apparel dirty and ragged, and what was most mournful of all, these evils were manifestly occasioned by intemperance. The husband and father was an intemperate man, as all his acquaintance knew, and as anybody would know by the sight of him; and the wife and mother was an intemperate woman, as I was frequently told, and as her appearance but too plainly indicated. Such they had been for more than a score of years. They had several small children, who were miserably clothed and repulsively dirty, appearing to be little cared for by either father or mother. They had one daughter, the eldest of their children, a very worthy girl, of about eighteen years, who was a seamstress, supporting herself in a very respectable manner, and moving in respectable society. But she seldom or never went home. She had left her parents because she could not live with them any longer. She once told me, that she could not endure the pain of seeing her father, and especially her mother, in such a condition as they were; and when she had sometimes gone home to see them after she left them, they only complained of her, and reproached her for her pride, because she had dressed herself in a decent manner, and because she would not consent to board at home any longer. Her mother had once requested me to induce her to return to them; but after learning all the circumstances, and hearing the daughter's touching story from her own lips, I had no heart to do it,—I could not attempt it,—I told the poor girl, that in my opinion she was right in staying away. She could do them no good. She had tried it. She was only reproached if she called upon them. The treatment she received made her the more unhappy; and she once told me with bitter weeping, that if she went there at all, she "came away with such a feeling of shame, that it made her wretched for a month." It was a very delicate thing for me, and a very painful one, to mention the subject to her at all; but I trust I was enabled to do it in such a manner as to wound her feelings but little, and to gain her respect and confidence entirely. She certainly gained mine.

On the morning to which I now allude, I rapped

at the door, and the old woman opened it and looked at me without uttering a word. She did not even respond to my "good morning;" and when I enquired more particularly how she was, in as kind and respectful a manner as I could, she scarcely made any reply at all. She did not ask me to walk in; but as the door was open, and she did not forbid me, I passed into the house. Thinking that she might perhaps be a little disconcerted by my coming at a time inconvenient for her to see me, I told her as I went into the house, that "I would not hinder her long, I had called for only a minute, to see how she was."

"I am glad to see you," said she, with a low voice and a very sullen look. She appeared so different from what I had ever seen her before, so downcast and sad, that I thought she might be unwell, and therefore enquired particularly if she "was sick."

"I am well," was her brief and solemn reply, uttered in a low and sepulchral tone.

In order to make her feel at ease, if possible, I seated myself upon a chair. It was covered with dust; and her whole room, as I had often found it before, was so far from being decently clean, that I hesitated to sit down in it. Everything was in disorder. The floor had not been swept apparently for a week, —the ashes were scattered over the hearth-stone,—

the scanty furniture was most of it broken, and resembling one of the chairs, which had but three legs, and was lying on its back,—the ceiling was festooned with cobwebs, that had caught the floating dust, and as they waved to and fro in the wind, they appeared like a mournful token of the wretchedness, which seemed to have taken possession of her heart.

I made several attempts to lead her into some conversation, but it was all in vain—she spake only in muttered monosyllables. This surprised me. I had many times visited her before, and had supposed that my attention to her, my familiarity and kindness, had entirely won her esteem and good-will. Indeed I had supposed myself quite a favorite with her. Though I had sometimes reproved her very plainly, I had always done it affectionately, and she had always treated me politely, and as a friend. But now all was changed. She was cold and mute. She appeared very much as if she was angry, and moved about the room adjusting her little stock of furniture, as if she was too sad or too sullen to be conscious of my presence. She scarcely noticed me at all.

Most sincerely I pitied her. I saw she appeared very wretched. I thought of her poverty, of her better days, of her youth, of her children, of her sins and her soul. She was of a respectable family, and had received a respectable education in her youth. I had often thought in my previous conversation with her, that she possessed a superior mind. And now, to behold her in this miserable condition, and no prospect before her of any relief, a disgrace to herself, to her children, wretched and heartbroken; was too touching a thing to allow of any other feelings, than those of compassion and kindness. My heart bled for her. I could not have uttered a word of censure, even if my principles would have allowed it. I resolved to soothe and console her for a moment, if I could, before I left her. Said I:

"Mrs. B——, do you remember what I was speaking to you about, when I was here week before last?"

"*Yes,*" said she, with a low and sepulchral voice.

"You know I told you that you had no reason to be discouraged."

"I know you did," said she mournfully.

"I told you that I thought you a woman of superior sense, and capable even yet of doing a great deal of good to yourself and your family."

"What can *I* do?" said she in a tone of despair.

"My dear friend, I *told* you when you asked me that question the other day. With God's blessing, if you will seek it, you may do *anything* you wish—you may be respected and happy here, and be saved in the world to come."

I paused, but she made no reply. Said I:

"Have you thought of what I told you *then?*"

She gave no answer. Said I:

"Have you any disposition to try to seek God, and aim to gain everlasting life?"

Still she was silent. Rising from my seat, and stepping towards the door, I said to her:

"I am aware that I have called on you rather early in the morning, and I will not hinder you any longer now. If you will allow me, I shall be glad to call on you at another time."

I offered her my hand to bid her good bye, but instead of taking it, she placed her hand against the door to hinder me from opening it, saying in a firm and solemn tone, "*Don't go.*"

"I will stay longer," said I, "if you wish me to do so. I will do anything in my power for you, Mrs. B——, most willingly; but I suppose—" (lifting my hand to the latch)—

"*Don't* go," said she, placing her shoulder firmly against the door, to keep it from opening.

"What can I do for you?" said I.

She did not answer.

"Is there anything you wish to say to me, Mrs. B——? I hope you will speak freely to me. I assure you I will treat you with all kindness, and I think you know me well enough to trust me."

Still she did not answer. She stood like a statue of stone, her eyes fixed on the ground, her large frame slightly bending forwards, and her countenance strongly indicative of deep thought and melancholy emotions. She seemed lost in her own contemplations. I considered her for a short time in silence. She moved not—she spake not—she never raised her eyes upon me—she scarcely breathed. I knew not what to think of her. She appeared angry, and yet it was not anger. Her solemn look, fixed and indescribable, made her resemble one wrought up to an iron determination for some mighty purpose. Said I:

"Mrs. B——, you appear to feel unhappy this morning. What has occurred that troubles you? or can I assist you in any way?"

She drew a long breath, but remained as silent as ever, lost in thought, or in some wilderness of emotions. I did not know what to make of her. Evidently she was sober. At first I had thought she was angry, but her voice did not sound like it, in the few syllables which she had uttered. I could not leave her, for she stood motionless by the door, in such a position that I could not open it without swinging it against her, to push her out of the way. She held me her prisoner.

I knew not what to say; but concluded to make another attempt to find what was occupying her thoughts. Said I:

"Mrs. B——, I wish you would tell me what

makes you so unhappy. I should think you *would* tell me; I have always been a friend to you, and I think you have reason to confide in me."

"I know you have," said she, as unmoved and solemn as ever.

"Then tell me what is the matter? what troubles you?"

"I am a *great sinner!*" said she, slowly and with deep solemnity.

"That is true, and a much greater sinner than you think."

"I am *such* a sinner!" said she, with a countenance as fixed and cold as marble.

"Yes, I am glad you have found it out; for now you will see the necessity of fleeing to that Saviour, of whom I have spoken to you so many times, as your only ground of hope."

"I am *undone forever!*" said she, with a look of cold, fixed despair.

"You *would* be, if there was no mercy in God, and no Christ Jesus to save. But God is able and willing to save all sinners who repent of sin and forsake it, and put all their trust in Christ."

"I have sinned a great while!"

"And God has borne with you a great while, simply because He is 'not willing' that you 'should perish, but come to repentance.' Have you been praying to God to save you?"

"Yes, I prayed a long time last night; and I have been praying this morning till you came in."

"What did you pray *for?*"

"I prayed that God would forgive me."

"And do you think He will?"

"I am afraid not! I am a very great sinner."

"Jesus Christ, madam, is a very great Saviour. He will save all that come to Him in faith. The *greatness* of your sins cannot ruin you, if you will but repent of them and forsake them, trusting to the great Redeemer of sinners for pardon, through His atoning blood. 'The blood of Jesus Christ cleanseth from *all* sin.'"

"*Will* God have mercy upon me *now*, after all I have done?" said she, (for the first time lifting her eyes upon me, with a beseeching look.)

"Yes, He will; He *says* He will. 'Though your sins be as scarlet, they shall be as white as snow; though they be red like crimson, they shall be as wool.'"

"I have been an awful sinner! I am a poor creature, unworthy of anything but God's curse!"

"True, all true, madam; but Christ is infinitely worthy, has borne the punishment due to sinners, and is willing to save you."

"I wish I could think so," said she, with the same fixed and despairing look.

"You *may* think so; God thinks so."

"There is no mercy for me any longer!"

"So *you* think, but God thinks differently. You and He do not think alike. He thinks right, and you think wrong. You must fling away youı own thoughts and act on His. And that is what He means in that expression in Isaiah, 'let the wicked forsake his way and the unrighteous man his *thoughts*, and let him return unto the Lord, and He *will have* mercy upon him, and to our God, for he *will* abundantly pardon. For my thoughts are not your thoughts, neither are your ways my ways, saith the Lord.' Your *thoughts*, madam, your very sincerest and soberest thoughts, are to be *forsaken*. Your thoughts are wrong. Fling them away, and use God's thoughts. His thoughts are right. You think differently from Him, and therefore your thoughts are not to govern you. 'Let the unrighteous forsake his thoughts.' You think wrong about God, and wrong about yourself, and wrong about sin, and wrong about forgiveness. I do not mean that you think yourself a greater sinner than you are, for you have not yet seen the half of your guilt and danger; but you think wrong about God's readiness to forgive you. Remember that He says, 'Let the unrighteous forsake his thoughts.' And then, a little after, He says again, 'my thoughts are not your thoughts,' and goes on to say, 'for as the heavens are higher than the earth so are my thoughts higher than your thoughts.'

What does He mean by all this? He means that it does not belong to *you* to tell what God will do or will not do. If you undertake to tell, you will be sure to tell wrong, because you think wrong. You must let *Him* tell what He will do. And He is telling in that very passage about the forgiveness which you say you cannot think there is for you: 'Let him return unto the Lord and He will have mercy upon him.' But the sinner does not think so; and therefore God says it over again, as if He would beat it into the poor sinner's heart, 'let him return unto our God, for He will *abundantly* pardon.'" (She shook her head with a slow desponding motion, as I went on.) "You do not think so, but God does. He *tells* you 'my thoughts are not your thoughts, neither are your ways my ways.' Your thoughts this minute are, 'I am a great sinner.' God's thoughts are, 'I will have mercy upon her.' Your thoughts are, 'I have sinned too long to be forgiven.' God's thoughts are, 'I will abundantly pardon her.' I should like to show you that whole chapter. I want to read it to you. Have you got a Bible, Mrs. B——?"

Without uttering a word, she slowly moved from the door to the other side of the room, placed a chair beneath a high shelf, that was made of a single rough board, and hung up on rude wooden brackets, almost up to the wooden ceiling of the room. She then stepped up upon the chair, and reaching her hand upon the shelf, felt along till she found it, and took down her Bible. She stood upon the chair, and gazed upon it as she held it in her hand, with a fixed look. Then she slowly stepped down from the chair holding her Bible in her hand, and stopped and gazed upon it, motionless, and without uttering a word. It was covered all over with dust, soot and cobwebs, appearing as if it had not been handled for years. I thought her heart smote her, as she held it unopened and looked down upon it. I thought I could "see the iron enter into her soul." I did not disturb her. I was willing she should meditate and remember. There she stood, motionless as a stone, with her eyes fixed upon her Bible, and I did not think it was best for me to say anything to her,—the dusty, cobwebbed Bible was speaking! The tears gushed from the eyes, and fell in quick drops upon its blackened lid. Slowly she lifted her tattered apron, and wiped off the tears and the dust, and deliberately turning towards me she extended to me the book—"*there* is my *Bible*!" said she, with a bitterness of accent that I shall never forget. She turned from me, with both hands lifted her dusty, ragged apron to her face, and wept aloud.

I could not but weep too. It was a scene surpassing, I am sure the genius of any painter.

When she had become a little composed, I requested her to sit down by me, and then directing her eye to the expressions, I read and explained to her the fifty-fifth chapter of Isaiah.

I attempted some farther conversation with her, but she did not seem so much inclined to talk as to listen. At her request I prayed with her; and when I was about to leave her, I enquired:

"How long have you been in this state of mind, Mrs. B——, feeling that you are such a sinner?"

"Since last night."

"What led you to feel so last night?"

"It was a little book that I read."

"What book was it?"

"Sixteen short Sermons."

"Whose sermons were they?"

"I don't know. I came across the book somewhere about the house. I don't know where it came from."

"I mean who *wrote* the Sermons?"

"I don't know."

"Where is the book? I should like to see it."

"It is not here. I lent it this morning to Mrs. A——" (a near neighbor).

"Did Mrs. A—— want to read it herself?"

"Yes. She was in here, and would make me tell her what was the matter with me; and after I told her, she said she wanted to read the Sermons too,

So I lent it to her, a little while before you came in."

Taking leave of Mrs. B——, I went immediately to call on Mrs. A——. I found her in tears. She had become alarmed about her condition, as a sinner against God. She frankly expressed to me her convictions and fears, adding with great emphasis, "what *shall* I do?" Of course I conversed with her and explained the way of salvation. But she said nothing about the book, until, as I was about to leave her, I enquired what it was that had inclined her to attend to her salvation. "It was a little book that Mrs. B—— lent me this morning," said she; and taking it from under her Bible that lay on the table, she put it into my hand. Then I discovered that it was a Tract, bearing the title, "Sixteen short Sermons," one of the publications of the American Tract Society, which I had entirely forgotten if I had ever read it, so that I did not recognize it by the title.

After this, I often visited Mrs. B——, and had many an interesting conversation with her. In one of these conversations, she referred gently and humbly to her daughter, and not, as I had formerly heard her, with manifest anger and ill-will. She said, "I should like to see her,—I have not seen her for many months; but, I suppose, it hurts the poor child's feelings to come home, and find us—as we have been. I hope we shall not always be so." I immediately went to see her daughter; and alone, and in as delicate a manner as I could, I told her of her mother's altered feelings, and suggested the propriety of her going to see her. She wept bitterly and long. It was almost impossible to comfort her at all; and before I left her, I found it was not her mortification and shame about her mother, so much as her anxiety about her own salvation, which caused her distress. She had already heard of her mother's seriousness, and that was one of the causes of her own. But she did not go to see her mother. I pointed her to Christ as well as I could, and left her.

A few days after this, I called upon the daughter again. I went to tell her of her mother's happy hope in Christ, which she had just expressed to me for the first time; and to my no small joy and surprise, I found that the daughter had been led to the same sweet hope also. "*Now*," said she, the tears of joy coursing down her youthful and beautiful cheeks, "*now*, I can go to see *my mother*."

She did go. She opened the door, and found the old woman alone. "My *mother*," said she,—and she could say no more. In an instant they were clasped in each other's arms, both bathed in tears of unutterable joy.

That humble dwelling soon became as neat, as

grace had made its inmates happy. The daughter went home. She aided her mother in all her domestic duties, with a glad and grateful heart. She made their house as attractive as it had been repulsive. She made clothes for the younger children, and having assisted her mother to dress them up in a neat and respectable manner, the old woman attended them herself to the Sabbath school, and requested to have their names put down, "for," said she, "they will always be here every Sabbath, if you will be so kind as to teach them the Bible."

That house and its inmates were very different in June, from what they had been in February. Neatness and peace reigned, where there had been filthiness, and clamor, and contention, through year after year of misery. The whole appearance of the woman was changed. She did not look like the same being. She became dignified, lady-like, intelligent, easy in her manners, and, though always solemn, she was uniformly contented and happy. "It seems to me," said she, "that I need but one thing more, and my cup is full: if my husband would only quit his ways, and turn to God, it seems to me we should be happy enough." But he never did. He continued his intemperance. I exerted all my skill to persuade him to forsake his ruinous course; but I met him thirteen years afterwards, staggering in the street.

Eight months after the time when I found this woman so suddenly awakened to a sense of her situation, by "a little book that she had read," I baptized both her and her daughter, and they were received into the church the same day. Mrs. A——, her neighbor, who borrowed the book, was received and baptized at the same time. When the old woman presented herself in the church for the reception of baptism, her old neighbors and friends, who had been acquainted with her for a score of years, did not know who she was,—her appearance was so altered;—and I found it difficult the next day to make them believe that it was verily their old neighbor, whom they had pitied and despaired of so long.

There was nothing of any marked peculiarity in this woman's religious experience, unless it was her deep humility; her iron determination manifest always from the very beginning of her conviction; and after her conversion, her unbounded gratitude to God. "Who could have thought," said she, "that God would have mercy upon such a creature as I?"

That "little book," the "Sixteen Short Sermons," lent from house to house through the neighborhood, did good service in that season of a revival of religion, which I have always supposed originated from its influence, more than from any other one thing. However this may have been (and I believe there is a great deal of foolish error abroad among the churches in attempting to account for revivals of religion, and trace their origin), the name of Mrs. B—— stands recorded in my private book, the very first name in the list of the hopeful converts to Christ in that revival—a list containing more than Two Hundred and Fifty names.

As long as I continued to be her Pastor, Mrs. B—— always appeared to me to be a humble and happy Christian. There was uniformly an air of deep solemnity about her, of profound humility, and a cast of mournfulness too, whenever she adverted to her past life, or the time of her hopeful conversion. The remembrance of what she was, seems to have thrown a sombre shade over her character. Twenty years have passed away, and she still lives, enjoying the Christian confidence and affection of her church.

I have sometimes called upon her, since I ceased to be her Pastor, and removed to another and distant place. At one time I visited her after an interval of thirteen years. I did not expect she would know me. I knocked at the door—she invited me in—and taking a seat I asked some business-like questions about two or three of her neighbors. She responded readily to my questions, but kept her eyes fixed upon me, with a kind of curious and doubtful inquisitiveness. This questioning and answering and inspecting continued for several minutes, till I supposed that the nature of my questions had thoroughly concealed my identity. Finally I asked her,—

"Have you got a Bible?"

Adjusting her spectacles to her eyes with both her hands, she replied,—

"Ain't *you* priest *Spencer?* Them are the same eyes that used to look right through me. How *do* you do? I am glad to see you."

"I am no *priest*," said I.

"Well, we used to *call* ministers so when I was young. It is just like you to come and see me. But I didn't expect it."

I inquired whether she still kept her "Sixteen Short Sermons."

"O, yes," said she, "*that* is next to the Bible."

I told her that I should like to have that same book, and asked if she would be willing to give it to me. Said she,—

"I will give you anything else I've got; but I should be unwilling to spare that, unless I could get another just like it. I read it over every little while."

She produced the same old tract, which I had seen in her house more than seventeen years before. It bore the marks of age, and of much service. It had become almost illegible by use, and time, and dust. "It has been all around the neighborhood," said she. "I have lent it to a great many folks; and sometimes I have had hard work to hunt it up, and get it back home again."

I gave her two new ones of the same sort, and also the whole bound volume which contains it; and after carefully examining the two, leaf by leaf, "to see if they were just like it," as she said, she finally consented to part with her old, time-worn, rusty tract. "I thought," said she, "I never should part with that book,—but these new ones are better; I can read them easier, and I can lend them to more folks. Some people will read these, who would not read one so dirty and old as that."

I felt half guilty for taking her old companion, and was sorry I had ever asked for it. As I parted with her and came away, I noticed that her eyes kept fixed upon the "Sixteen Short Sermons," that I held in my hand. I hope yet to be permitted to return it to her.

There were two things in the character of this woman worthy of very special notice,—her determination and her dependence. So firmly was she fixed in her resolution to abandon the habit, which had so long been her sin, and the cause of her misery, that after her first seriousness on that memorable night, she never once tasted the cup of her shame. She would not see anybody else do it,—she would not go where it was,—she would cross the street to avoid passing the door where it was sold, —she would not even *look* at it. And so entire was her dependence on God to keep her from it, that she gave the memorable description of her course,—"*drink anything?* no! if I ever *think* of it, I immediately go to prayer." I recommend her example to every reader of this book:—"drink anything? no! if you ever *think* of it, immediately go to prayer."

No Escape.

IN conversation with a young man, who desired to unite with the church, he surprised me very much by a reference which he made to his former "detestation of religion," as he called it, and by mentioning the manner in which he was first led to any considerable concern in reference to his salvation. I had known him with some intimacy for several months, had frequently conversed with him as a serious inquirer, and afterwards as one who entertained a hope in Christ. But he had never before mentioned to me so definitely the means of his awakening, and his previous opposition to religion.

He belonged to a pious family; his parents and several of his brothers were members of the church; he was a moral and staid, industrious, intelligent young man, always attending church, and was a teacher in the Sabbath school. I had not supposed that his feelings of opposition to religion had ever assumed the strong character which he described to me now; and I had never known the means of their alteration. I happened to ask him,—

"Mr. H——, what was it that first called your attention definitely to religion, when you began to make it a matter of your personal concern?"

"I found there was no escape, I could not get away from it."

"What do you mean, when you say 'there was no escape?'"

"Why the subject met me everywhere. Where-ever I went there was something to make me think of it."

"Yes," said I, "there are things to bring it to mind all around us and always, if we would heed them. God has filled His world with things suggestive of Himself."

"Oh, sir," said he, "I don't mean *that* at all. It is true, that *now* almost everything makes me think of God and my duty; but I mean things that were done *on purpose* to catch me. It seemed to me that I was pursued everywhere. There was no getting away. If I went to church on Sunday; you never let us off with a descriptive or literary sermon, like a college professor; you always had something about faith, or repentance, or depravity, or the duty of sinners to fly to Christ. If I went to my store on a week day, thinking I should escape *there*, because I had something else to attend to; my partner would have something to say to me about religion, or something to say in my presence which I knew was meant *for me.* If I met you in the street; you were sure not to let me pass without bringing up that subject in some way or other. If I went home to dinner or tea; religion would be talked of at the table. If I was spending any part of the evening in the family after I left the store; it was the same thing again: religion, religion would come up; every one had something to say which made me think of religion. If I went off to bed, (as I did many a time to get out of the hearing of it;) my sister had put a tract upon my pillow. I could not bear all this. I often avoided everybody and went to my room, where I could be alone, and think of what I pleased; and *there* the first thing to meet me would be some religious book, which my mother or some one else had put in the place most likely to attract my attention; and perhaps left it open at some passage marked on purpose for me. After several of my young associates had become Christians, and began to talk about religion; I avoided them and sought other company, and pretty soon *they* began to talk religion too! I was provoked at it!"

"Did these people, who endeavored to influence you, treat you rudely or impolitely?"

"Oh, no! That was the worst of it. I hoped they would. If they had been meddlesome and impudent, I should have had something to find fault with, and should have told them to mind their own business, and keep their religion to themselves. I should have said, that religion makes men ungentlemanly, and unfit for society,—and so should have excused myself. But there was none of that. There was little said to me. All that was done, was only calculated to make me think *for* myself, and *of* myself; and so I could not complain. But religion came up before me on all sides; whichever way I turned, morning, noon, and night, it was there. I could not escape it."

"Did you have a strong *desire* to escape it?"

"Yes, I did. I turned every way. I avoided Christians. One Sunday, I stayed away from church;—but that contrivance *worked the other way*, for I could think of nothing but religion all the morning, and so in the afternoon I went to church, to see if I couldn't forget it there. When I came home I went into an unoccupied room, because they began to talk about the sermon in the parlor; and the first thing that met me was *the Bible*,—laid open at the second chapter of Proverbs, and a pencil-mark drawn round the first six verses. "This is some of mother's work," said I. Finally, I resolved to sell out my store, and get away into some place where I should not be *tormented about religion* any longer. I began to make arrangements for selling out."

"Well, sir, what altered your mind?"

"Why, just as I was in this trouble to get away from religion, resolving not to live any longer in such a place as this; I began to think what I was after,—why I desired to get away. And then I soon found out it was because I desired to get away from the truth, and away from God. That alarmed me, and shamed me. I thought, then, that if there was no escape from men here, there could be no escape from God anywhere. And though it cost my pride a hard struggle, I made up my mind that I was all wrong, and I would attend to my salvation. Then I began; but I don't think I ever should have begun, if I had not been hunted in every place where I tried to escape."

"Did you have any more temptation to neglect religion after that?"

"No. I immediately took my stand. I went among the inquirers openly. Then I was disappointed to find how little I cared any longer for the world, for what people would say, and all such things, as I used to think would be great trials to me. And I believe *now*, there is very much gained by getting a sinner to *commit himself* on this matter. Then he will not wish to get off."

"What way do you think is most likely to succeed for inducing any one 'to commit himself' to attend to his religion?"

"Oh, I cannot answer *that*. Any way is good, I

suppose, which will lead people to *think.* Judging from my own experience, I should suppose that no irreligious person in the world could put off religion any longer, if his way was hedged up as mine was, so that he could not avoid *thinking* of the subject."

Such was a part of my conversation with him. He united with the church; and I have some reason to suppose, that since that time he has aimed to "lead people to think," in such a manner that there could be "no escape."

Thoughtlessness is the common origin of unconcern. We do a far better office for men when we lead *them* to think, than when we think for them. A man's own thoughts are the most powerful of all preaching. The Holy Spirit operates very much by leading men to *reflection*—to employ their own mind. I should hesitate to interrupt the religious reflections of any man in the world, by the most important thing I could say to him. If I am sure *he* will *think*, I will consent to be still. But men are prone to be thoughtless, and we must speak to them to lead them to reflection.

But the instance of this young man contains, as I think, a most important lesson. It appears to show, that Christian people may easily exercise an influence upon the minds of the worldly; and I have often thought such an influence is the very thing which the church needs, more than almost anything else. There is many a member of the church having faith, having benevolence, and sincerely desirous of the conversion of sinners, who never has once opened his lips to commend religion to the careless, and has never in any way attempted to lead them to serious reflection. It is not too much to say, that this is *wrong*. Surely it *cannot* be right for the people of God to wrap their talent in a napkin and hide it in the earth! In *some* mode, almost every Christian in the midst of us is able to influence the thoughts of the careless every day. By conversation, by timely remarks, by books, by Tracts, and by a thousand nameless methods, they have opportunity to impress religious truth upon indifferent minds. There is too much neglect of this. The irreligious often notice this neglect; and whenever they notice it, they are very apt to have a diminished esteem for religious people, if not for religion itself. A minister cannot go everywhere and speak to every body in the community, but private Christians can. Such Christians are meeting the ungodly daily, they know them, they associate with them, work with them, trade with them, and it would be easy for them to awaken many a sinner, whom a minister cannot reach. Such exertion is one *great want* of the church. There are few irreligious persons in the midst of us who are compelled to say, "there is no escape."

The Date of Conversion.

In a very remote and rural part of my parish, several miles from my own residence, and by the side of an unfrequented road; there lived a married woman, whose state of mind on the subject of religion interested me much, the first time I visited her. I thought I discovered in her a sort of readiness to obey the Gospel, if I may use such an expression. She was about thirty years of age, full of vivacity, enthusiasm and kindness, simple, beautiful, graceful; and when she became animated in conversation, her clear blue eye beamed with intelligence and sweetness of disposition, which flung an indescribable charm around all that she uttered. She and her husband had been religiously educated. She was a woman of refined manners, and to me she appeared the more interesting, because she evidently never suspected herself of any refinement at all. Her politeness, which I have seldom seen equalled, was not the politeness of the schools, but of nature: not the polish of art, but the prompting of simplicity and an affectionate disposition. In all things she appeared unaffected, natural, simple. She was willing to appear just what she was, and therefore always appeared to advantage. Her manners would have graced the most refined society. She made no pretensions under the promptings of pride or vanity, uttered no apologies for her appearance, and felt no bashfulness in the presence of a stranger. Too far removed from any school to be able to send her children, she taught them herself; and her three little boys, for intelligence, kindness and propriety of manners, might have served for models to almost any other in the parish. I found the little things a short distance from the house, plucking the wild flowers in the woods, to entwine in their mother's hair, which they claimed the privilege to adorn in that manner, and which might be seen thus adorned, according to their taste, almost any day, from the early spring-time till the frost had nipped the last blossom of the year. Eight summers had not passed over the head of the eldest. They were the children of nature—simple, fearless, artless. The frank, gentle and affectionate demeanor of these little creatures, especially towards one another, gave me, as I thought, some insight into the character of their mother. I judged of her by her little pupils, and afterwards found that I judged justly. I took them as bright miniatures of herself. And I did not think the less of *her*, when I perceived the evident pleasure and exultation (if I may not say *pride*), which she had in them.

I visited her as her minister. I was a stranger to her. She was evidently glad to see me at her house, and the more so as she had not expected it. After making some inquiries about her husband and her children, I inquired of her,—

"Are you and your husband members of the church?"

"No sir," said she with a downcast look.

"Neither of you?"

"No sir."

"And why not? Are you still living without religion?"

"I suppose we are. I have wished a great many times that I was *fit* to be a communicant."

"And why are you *not* fit?"

"Because I have no saving faith. I could not go to the Lord's table without faith."

"No, but you ought to go *with* faith. Jesus Christ is offered to you in the Gospel, to be your Saviour. Your duty is to believe in Him. And are you still, at your time of life, an unbeliever?"

"I suppose I am," said she, with a pensive look.

"And are you going to continue so?"

After a long pause, during which her thoughts seemed very busy, she replied, with an accent of sadness,—

"Indeed, sir, I cannot tell."

"Are you *willing* to continue so?"

"No, sir, I am not satisfied with myself. I think about religion very often, but—"

"And do you pray about it very often?"

"No, sir, not *very* often, since I was a child."

"Have you prayed to-day?"

"No, sir."

"Did you pray last Sabbath?"

"No, sir. I read my Bible. I sometimes pray, but my prayers are not answered."

"What do you pray *for?*"

"I have prayed for forgiveness and the Holy Spirit; but it was all in vain to me."

"And so you ceased to pray."

"Yes, sir. I thought I could *do* nothing without the Holy Spirit."

"But, my dear madam, it was the Holy Spirit that led you to prayer. *God* was calling to you at those times when you were constrained to pray."

"I have never thought so, sir."

"Then He has been more kind towards you than you have thought."

"I wish I *was* a Christian."

"You may be one, if you will; but not without earnest prayer. Will you seriously attend to your salvation, beginning *now?* With the Bible to guide you, and the Holy Spirit to pray for, will you *at once* begin to seek the Lord?"

A long pause followed this question. She seemed to be lost in thought, and I did not choose to disturb her thoughts. She appeared downcast; but after a little while, I thought I perceived a sort of obstinacy manifest in her countenance, and fearing that she was about to utter some objection, I suddenly rose to take my leave.

"What!" said she, "are you going?"

"I *must* go, madam."

"Shall I ever see you again?" said she, beseechingly.

"Do you *wish* to see me again?"

"Yes, sir, I *do*," said she, emphatically.

"Then I will come to see you as soon as I can. But before I come, I hope you will have made up your mind fully, and will have turned to Christ."

A month afterwards I called upon her. She appeared much as before. At times she had prayed, but not daily. I talked to her plainly and affectionately, prayed with her and left her.

I had now little hope of doing her any good. However, about three months afterwards, being in that neighborhood, I called upon her. I could find little alteration in her feelings or habits, except that she seemed to have a more tender spirit, and was more accustomed to prayer. But nothing I could say appeared to make much impression upon her. She assented to all the truths of religion. She had known them from her childhood, when her religious parents taught her. A pensiveness and solemnity hung around her; but she had no deep anxiety. In various ways I strove to affect her; but it was all in vain, till I appealed to her conscience and sensibilities as a mother. I said to her,—

"You have three precious children intrusted to you, and your example will have great influence over them. They will be very much what *you* make them. If you are irreligious, they will be very likely to remain so too. If they see you living a life of faith and prayer, the example will not be lost upon them. You ought to be able to teach them religion. But how can you teach them what you do not know yourself? Allow me to say,—and I am glad I can say it,—I have been delighted to notice your conduct towards your children, In my opinion, *few mothers do so well.* I think you are training them wisely in all things *but one.* May I say it to you, I know of no children of their age who please me so much. In their excellence I see your own; and this compels me to respect and love you the more, and be the more anxious that you should train them for heaven. I am very sorry that you are *an irreligious mother!*"

She burst into tears; and rising suddenly from

her seat, turned her face towards the window and wept convulsively. I left her without uttering a word.

It was more than six months before I could see her again. As I called upon her after this long interval, she told me that she had tried to repent and flee to Christ, had prayed daily, but her heart remained the same, and she was amazed at her stupidity. "I am insensible as *a stone*," said she. "It seems to me I feel nothing. I wish to love God, and be a Christian; but I am fully convinced that I have no power at all over my hard heart. And yet I have some faint hope, that God will have mercy upon me, after all my stubbornness and stupidity, and will yet grant me the Holy Spirit. Is it wrong for me to have such a hope?"

"Not at all, my dear Madam. I am glad you have that hope. Hold on upon it. Only let all your hope be in God through Jesus Christ. Let nothing discourage you for an instant, while you attempt to obey the Gospel. I believe God has good things in store for you. You may say, 'will he plead against me with his great power? no, he will put strength in me.'"

"Oh that I knew where to find Him," said she.

"He is on His throne of grace," said I. 'Then shall ye go and pray unto me, and ye shall seek me, and ye shall find me, when ye shall search for me with your whole heart, and I will be found of you, saith the Lord.' "

"I *do* seek, sir; but why does not God give me the Holy Spirit?"

"He *does* give it, Madam. He calls you. He strives with you. He shows you your sin, your stupidity, your strange heart."

"But, sir, do you think the Holy Spirit is sent to one alone? and when there is no revival?"

"Strange question for you to ask! *Yes*, my dear friend, most unquestionably. Is the offer made only to a multitude? Is it not made *to every one* that asks Him?"

"I know it is. But it seems to me that it would be too much to expect God would regard me *alone*, when there are no others inclined to turn unto Him."

"Then your unbelieving heart does an injustice to His kindness. He is a thousand fold better than you think Him. He 'waits to be gracious unto you.' He 'calls and you refuse.' Because you do not know of others disposed to seek God, you have little courage to seek Him, though you know that His promises are made, and invitations given to each individual sinner like yourself: *to you*, as much as if you were the only sinner in the universe."

"But, if others were attending to religion, if my husband and neighbors were, I should have more expectation of succeeding."

"Madam, I am not sure of that. I will not too much blame you for thinking so; but see here; you do *not know* how many others feel just as you do, and wait for *you* just as you wait for *them.* You mentioned your husband. I am going to see him; and I have not an item of doubt, but before I have left him he will confess to me that he is waiting for *you.*"

"Why, I never thought of that," said she with surprise.

"I suppose not. But it is time for you to think of it. You and he are waiting for one another. Which shall begin first? I would not afflict you, or say an unkind word to you; I have not a feeling in my heart that would allow me to do it; but I tell you seriously, you are *a hindrance to your husband.* He may be a hindrance to you. I suppose he is. But you are a hindrance to him."

"I do not *intend* to be a hindrance to him."

"But you *are,* and you will continue to be, more or less, as long as he thinks you to be an unconverted sinner, living in your indifference and stupidity."

"What shall I do?"

"I will tell you what to do. First give your own self to the Lord. Did you ever talk with your husband on the subject of religion?"

"Oh yes, a great many times."

"Have you lately? and have you told him how

you feel about your own heart, your sin and your salvation?"

"Oh, no sir, I have not said anything to him about *that.*"

"So I supposed. And now I will tell you what to do. When he comes in, and you and he are alone together, just tell him plainly and affectionately, how you feel, what you have done, and what you intend to do. Open your whole heart to him. When he hears you talking so, *he* at least will know of one sinner who intends to seek the Lord. And thus, you will hinder him no longer."

This was quite an unexpected turn of thought to her. She sat in silence for a little time, as if meditating the matter, and then inquired,—

"Did you say you would see my husband *to-day?*"

"Yes. And he will tell me you are a hindrance to him, just as you say he is a hindrance to you."

"But, sir, I did *not* say exactly *that.*"

"True, madam, you did not. I have expressed the idea a little more plainly than you did, and much less politely. You said it in your kind way, and I in my coarse one. I have not essentially altered it. You *did* mention what an *encouragement* it would be to you, if your husband were attending to his salvation. He feels precisely so about his wife, in my opinion. And what I want of you both is, that you should encourage and aid one another."

"I should be *very* glad, if he was truly a Christian."

"He would be very glad, if you were truly a Christian. But will you do what I have just told you? Will you tell him your feelings?"

After a short pause, with her eyes fixed on the ground, and a look of ineffable solemnity and tenderness, she replied emphatically,—

"*Yes*, my dear pastor, *I will.*"

"Good-bye," said I, and reaching her my hand, instantly left her.

I soon found her husband in the field, at work among his corn; and shaping the conversation according to my previous intent, it was not long before he said to me,—

"Well, if my wife thinks it is time for her to attend to religion, I shall certainly think it is time for *me*, when my poor health reminds me so often of my end."

"I have been talking with her, and I assure you that, in my opinion, she would certainly be quite ready, were it not for one thing."

"What is that?" said he, with surprise and concern.

"That one thing is yourself. It is you who are a hindrance to her. You do not follow Christ, and she has not the encouragement of your example."

"That need not stand in *her* way"

"But it does stand in her way. She follows your example. She naturally looks to you as a guide, and her affectionate disposition catches your feelings. As long as you remain an irreligious man, your influence tends to make her remain an irreligious woman. You may be assured of this. You yourself just told me, that if she thought it was time for her to give her heart to religion, you should certainly think it was time for you; and is it not natural that she should think so too? You are the husband. She looks to you as a guide. She looks to you *more* than you look to her. She feels your influence more than you feel her's. Thus you are a hindrance to her, when you ought to be a help."

"She never said anything to me about it."

"And did you ever say anything to *her* about it?"

"No, nothing in particular. But I have been thinking about religion a good deal, as I told you when you came here in the winter; and I do not feel contented. I am not prepared to die, and the thoughts of it make my mind gloomy."

"You *may* have such thoughts as to make your mind glad. The gospel is 'good tidings of great joy,' and 'for all people,'—*for you*. And when you go home, I want you to talk with your wife on this subject, as you know you ought to do; and tell her what you think. Will you do so?"

"I will think about it."

"But will you *do* it?"

"I can't say, I can't say."

"Well, aim to do your duty in the fear of God; aim to lead your wife and children to the kingdom of heaven." I left him.

This man was of a very sedate and cautious disposition. He was amiable, but he was firm. He was no creature of impulses. His wife had more vivacity, more sprightliness, more ardor, while she was by no means deficient in decision of character. I hoped that the vivacity of the one would stimulate the slowness of the other, and that the thinking habits of the man would steady and temper the ardor of the more impulsive woman.

Without much hope of being able to influence them at all, I called upon them again the next week—sooner probably than I should have done, but for a sort of curious desire to know the result of their next meeting after I left them. The wife met me at the door with evident gladness. "I am very happy to see you," said she, "I have something to tell you. My husband is serious, and I *do hope* he will become a Christian."

"And I suppose he hopes you will become a Christian."

"I wish I *was* one, but I am as stupid as ever. My husband is much more like a Christian than I am."

"Then his seriousness has not done you the good you expected from it."

"No, and I am astonished at myself. But I must tell you. After you went away last week I did not know what to do, I felt very strange about speaking to him as I promised you I would. I did not know how to *begin.* I thought of it a long time. At last I came to the conclusion to begin as soon as he came in, and tell it all over, just as it was. So when I heard him coming through the gate, I went out and met him there under the tree. Says I, 'Mr. Spencer has been here talking with me, and I want to tell you, my dear Luther, how I feel.' He stopped and looked at me without saying a word, and I told him all about myself, since the time when I was a little child. He listened to it all, looking at me and then on the ground; and when I had got done, I asked him if he did not think we ought to live differently. I was *so delighted* when he answered right off, 'Yes, I do.' I could hardly keep from weeping for joy, it was so different from what I expected. I said, 'My dear Luther, let us not neglect salvation any longer.' Says, he, 'I don't mean to; I am determined to do all I can to lay up treasures in heaven.' After dinner we had a long talk. Almost the whole afternoon he sat here reading the Bible, and talking with me. Sometimes he did not say a word for a long time, but would read and then stop and think.

As soon as he went out, I went alone and prayed, and then for the first time in my life I was glad to think I *might* pray. In the evening he sat here with me and the children, without saying much, only he asked me some questions about the Atonement and the Holy Spirit and faith in Christ. And when it was time for the children to go to bed, I whispered to him, 'shall we not have family prayer?' He got right up, without saying a word, took down the Bible, told the boys to wait a little while, and then turned to the third chapter of John, and read it loud. Then we all kneeled down and he made a prayer. *Such a prayer!* I could not help weeping. After we rose from our knees, and were sitting in silence a little while, our second boy went to him and put his little arms around his neck. 'Father,' says he, 'I wish you would pray so *every* night.' He looked very serious; and when the boy waited for an answer, looking right in his face, he told him, 'I am going to do it every night and every morning too.' Since that time I have been more happy than I ever was before. I know I am not a *Christian*, but I hope God will have mercy upon us, and lead us to Christ."

Such was her simple story; and she told it in a manner that would have affected any heart. Her little boys clustered around her, wept at seeing her weep, and I should have despised myself, if I could have avoided weeping with them. Her husband soon came in from the field, and after some little conversation, I prayed with them, and left them.

Months passed away before I saw them again. They then appeared much alike. They had no hope, but they did not seem unhappy. They only hoped, that God would yet bring them to repentance. If now they had no faith, it did not seem to me that they had any slavish fear; and I could not say a word to discourage or alarm them, for I certainly did hope for them, since God is 'a *rewarder of them that diligently seek him.*' After this I left them to themselves.

Just before a communion season, which came about six months after my last interview with them, I was very agreeably surprised by an unexpected visit of this man and his wife, who called upon me at the time publicly appointed for conversation with those who desired to unite with the Church. They had come on that account. They believed that God had led them to faith in His Son, and they wished to commemorate the Saviour's death at his table. I had much conversation with them. They could not tell when their faith or hope *commenced;* and that was their greatest trouble, and the only ground of their hesitation about making a public profession of religion. They had been very much alike in their feelings. For months they had been happy, not by the belief that they were Christians, but in the exercises of the means of grace, and in the hope that God would lead them in his own way and time to religion. In this confidence they had rested, and loved to rest. The Bible, and prayer, and religious conversation were their delight. And it was not till they had passed month after month in this happy manner, that the idea occurred to either of them, that they were the children of God. The wife thought of this first, and the thought made her unhappy. "I was afraid," said she, "of a false hope, and I *tried to feel* as I *used* to, when I was afraid of being lost forever." She mentioned her fears to her husband, and was astonished to find that he had the same fear about himself; because he too had almost half hoped, that he was reconciled to God; but had been banishing the hope as a snare of the great adversary. Then they wanted to see me; and as I did not visit them, the wife proposed, that they should come to see me that very day, for she "wanted to know whether she was a Christian or not." After much conversation, her husband told her that no man could tell her that, for God only could read the heart, and it would be better to examine themselves alone for a while. And a week or two afterwards, he objected to coming to me at all on such an errand, because the Bible says, 'examine *your own selves* whether ye be in the faith, prove *your own selves*.' Said he, "let us pray, 'Lord search me and know my heart, and lead me in the way everlasting.'"

Week after week, their peace of mind grew more uniform and sweet. They found, as they thought, that they loved God, that they trusted in Christ for pardon, that they hated sin, and found their greatest felicity in the divine promises, and in the thoughts and duties of religion. Both alike, they were determined to serve their Lord and Master as long as they should live. And because they found, as they believed, the evidences of religion in themselves, they came to the conclusion that they were Christians.

But when they came to me, the husband said, "We have, after all, one great trouble. We are not fully sure that we have had the gift of the Holy Spirit. We have never been sensible of any *sudden change*, and we have had no strong feelings of distress on account of sin, or of great joy on account of having faith. If I have any religion, I want to know when it *began?*"

"Can you tell, sir, when your corn *begins* to grow?—or when your wheat *begins* to come up? Could you tell, my dear madam, when those beautiful violets and pinks under your window *began* to come up?"

She smiled upon me, with a countenance radiant with new intelligence and joy, and burst into tears.

Said her husband, after a serious, thoughtful pause, "I know my corn *has* come up, and I know my wheat *does* grow."

"Very well," said I; "I have no more to say."

The wife turned to her husband, after a few minutes, saying, "I *should* like to know *when* I began to love God: and, Luther, it seems to me that we have been Christians ever since that first night when you prayed."

They united with the church, though uncertain of the date of their conversion. He became a very staid and thoughtful Christian. She was a Christian of light and smiles. Both were contented and happy. "I am glad we live in this retired place," said she to me, a year afterwards; "we can enjoy religion here, and nobody comes to trouble us. We have some kind and pious neighbors a little way off, who are a great comfort to us; but my Bible, my boys, and my flowers are enough to make me happy. I would not give up my little home, my cottage, and my woods, for the richest palace in the world:"—and tears of joy coursed down her cheeks when she said it. Adverting to her former trouble, she said,—"I have come to the conclusion, that it is *best for me* that I have never yet been able to fix the time of my conversion; I am afraid I should trust too much to it, if I could. Now I trust to nothing but to continued faith, and to living in happy fellowship with my God, my Heavenly Father. My husband is happy too, and what can I want more, except the conversion of my children?" As she said this, she turned away, and wept.

Her husband died in peace, as I have been told; and his precious wife, now a widow, has unspeakable comfort in two pious sons,—her joy, and her earthly crown. They will soon be her eternal crown in the kingdom of heaven. I cannot doubt it.

These instances of conversion are here given, as examples of an extensive class. In making my first visit to the families of my congregation, I met with a number of persons, who appeared to me to have some readiness to give their attention to the gospel call. They were not anxious, not alarmed, or, in the common acceptation of the term, serious. They evidently did not consider themselves the subjects of any special Divine influence, or as having any particular inclinations towards religion. But they appeared to me to be candid and conscientious, and to have a kind of readiness to obey the gospel. There was an indescribable *something* about them, I know not what, which made me have more hope for them than for others.

To the names of about twenty such persons I attached a private mark in my congregational book, (containing the names of all my congregation,)—a mark to indicate to *me* their state of mind, and prompt me to visit them again as soon as possible, but the meaning of which no one but myself could understand. If I may say so, they seemed *ready to become Christians*,—I know not how to describe their state of mind by any more just or intelligible expression. If, in the time of a revival of religion, they had said the same things which they now said, had presented the same appearances, and manifested the same impressions, no minister or Christian, as it seemed to me, would have hesitated to ascribe their impressions to the influences of the Holy Spirit. And, therefore, why should I not *now* have that opinion respecting them? and why not *treat* them in all respects, as I would have done in the time of a revival?—and why not *expect* the same results?

These were serious and troublesome questions to my own mind. By conversation with older and more experienced pastors, I aimed to get some instruction on this subject; but all I could learn did not satisfy me, indeed it did not seem to do me the least good. I found I must teach myself what nobody appeared able to teach me. And, however just or unjust may have been the conclusion to which, by continued and intense reflection, my mind was at last brought; I retain the same opinions now, after a score of years has passed away, which I formed at first. I believe those persons had their cast of mind through the influences of the Divine Spirit. Almost every one of those, to whose name I attached my private mark, within the space of two years became hopefully converted to Christ.

I often visited them, conversed with them, and entreated them to be reconciled to God. And the greatest obstacle (as it seemed to me), that I had to encounter, was their uniform impression, that God had not given them the Holy Spirit, and that it would therefore be in vain for them to attempt to seek the Lord. It was an exceedingly difficult thing to convince any one of them, that the Holy Spirit was present, and that their serious impressions, and occasional fears, and occasional prayers, were the effects of a Divine influence, and the very substance of a Divine call. But I had myself been led to this conclusion. I thought that they themselves ought to be convinced of this, and ought not, through ignorance and error, to be left to misimprove the day of their merciful visitation, waiting for a revival of religion. In almost every instance, (indeed, I do not remember a single exception,) the commencement of an earnest and hoping attempt to gain salvation, originated in the conviction, which I strove hard to impress upon the mind, that the Holy Spirit was already striving with them, as really as if there was a revival all around.

To the name of the woman whom I have mentioned in this sketch, I attached my mystic mark the first time I ever saw her; and to the name of her husband, the first time I ever saw him. And on this account, I was led to see them the more frequently. I am very certain, that I was not at all the instrument of their *conviction*, (or that of the conviction of twenty more like them;) whatever assistance in other respects, the truths which I uttered may have been to them, in leading them to Christ. / Probably many, very many sinners, who *never think of it*, are visited by the Holy Spirit. Probably not a month passes, when there are not strivings of the Spirit with unconverted sinners in all our congregations. And if such sinners, instead of allowing every trifle of the world to dispel their serious thoughts, would only cherish them, conspiring with the Holy Spirit; there is every reason to believe that they would become the happy children of God. Oh, if they but knew how near God is unto them, and how infinitely willing He is, in His kindness and love, to lead them into the ways of salvation; they would not suffer these seasons of promise to pass by unimproved: especially the young, whose kindness of heart has not yet been all poisoned, or all blasted by the world, would not so often turn a deaf ear to the *still, small voice of the Spirit.*

"Their happy song would oftener be,
Hear what the Lord has done for me."

My Old Mother:

OR, CONSCIENCE IN TRADE.

A YOUNG man, who at that time was almost an entire stranger to me, called upon me at a late hour in the evening, and, after some general conversation, said that he wished to talk with me in reference to a matter which had troubled him for some time. He came *to me*, as he said, because a few days before he had heard a member of a neighboring church railing against me, and among other things, saying that I was stern and severe enough for a slave driver. "So," says he, "I thought you would tell me the truth right out."

He was a junior clerk in a dry goods store—a salesman. He had been in that situation for some months. He went into it a raw hand. His employer had taken some pains to instruct him in its duties, and had otherwise treated him in a very kind manner. But he was expected, and indeed required to do some things which he "did not know to be quite right." He stated these things to me with minuteness and entire simplicity. He had been taught by his employer to do them, as a part of the "necessary skill to be exercised in selling goods," without which "no man could be a good salesman, or be fit for a merchant."

For example, he must learn to judge by the appearance of any woman who entered the store, by her dress, her manner, her look, the tone of her voice, whether she had much knowledge of the commodity she wished to purchase; and if she had not, he must put the price higher, as high as he thought she could be induced to pay. If there was any objection to the price of an article he must say, "we have never sold it any cheaper," or, "we paid that for it, madam, at wholesale," or, "you cannot buy that quality of goods any lower in the city." With one class of customers he must *always* begin by asking a half or a third more than the regular price, because, probably, through the ignorance of the customer, he could get it; and if he could not, then he must put it at a lower price, but still above its value, at the same time saying, "that is just what we gave for it," or, "that is the very lowest at which we can put it to you," or, "we would not offer it to anybody else so low as that, but we wish to get your custom." In short, a very large portion of the service expected of him was just this sort, and as I soon told him, it was just to *lie*, for the purpose of cheating.

Whenever he hesitated to practice in this manner behind the counter, his employer (ordinarily present) was sure to notice it, and sure to be dissatisfied with him.

He had repeatedly mentioned to his employer his "doubts" whether "this was just right," and "got laughed at." He was told, "everybody does it," "you can't be a merchant without it," "all is fair in trade," "you are too green."

"I know I am green," said the young man to me, in a melancholy tone. "I was brought up in an obscure place in the country, and don't know much about the ways of the world. My mother is a poor woman, a widow woman, who was not able to give me much education; but I don't believe *she* would think it right for me to do such things."

"And do *you* think it right?" said I.

"No,—I don't know,—perhaps it may be. Mr. H." (his employer) "says there is no *sin* in it, and he is a member of the church; but I believe it would make my old mother feel very bad, if she knew I was doing such things every day."

"I venture to say, that your mother has got not only more religion, but more common sense than a thousand *like him*. He may be a member of the church, (the church always has some unworthy members in it, I suppose) but he is not a man fit to direct you. (Take your mother's way and refuse his.")

"I shall lose my place," says he.

"Then lose your place; don't hesitate a moment."

"I engaged for a year, and my year is not out."

"No matter; you are ready to fulfil your engagement. But what *was* your engagement? Did you engage to deceive, to cheat and lie?"

"Oh, not at all."

"Then certainly you need have no hesitation, through fear of forfeiting your place. If he sends you away, because you will not do such things for him, then you will know him to be a very bad man, from whom you may well be glad to be separated."

"He says he will have his business done in the manner *he* chooses."

"Very well: you have no objections to *that;* let him do his business in the way he chooses: but he has no right to make you use *your tongue*, in the way he chooses: and if he complains of you, because you do not choose to lie for him every hour in the day; just tell him,(that you have not hired out your conscience to him,)and you will not be guilty of committing any crimes for him. Ask him, if he expects you to *steal* for him, if he should happen to want you to do it."

"When I told him I thought such things wrong, he said, 'that is *my* look out.'"

"Tell him it is *your* look out, whether you please God, or offend Him—whether you do right or wrong

—whether you serve the God of truth, or the father of lies."

"If I should say that, he would tell me to be off."

"Very well; *be* off then."

"I have no place to go to; and he knows it."

"No matter; go anywhere—do anything—dig potatoes—black boots—sweep the streets for a living, sooner than yield for one hour to such temptation."

"He says, 'everybody does so,' and 'no man can ever get along in the way of trade without it.'"

"About everybody's doing so, I know better. That is *not true.* Some men are honest and truthful in trade. A man may be honest behind the counter, as easily as in the pulpit. But if a man can't be a merchant without these things, then he can't be a merchant and get to heaven; and the sooner you quit that business the better."

"And in respect to his declaration, that 'no man can get along in the way of trade without such practices,' it is false—utterly false! And I wish you to take notice of men now when you are young, as extensively as you can, and see how they come out. You will not have to notice long, before you will be convinced of the truth of that homely old maxim, 'honesty is the best policy.' You will soon see, that such men as he, are the very men *not* to 'get along.' *He* will not 'get along' well a great while, if he does not alter his course."

"Oh, he is a keen fellow," said the young man smiling.

"So is old Satan a keen fellow; but he is the greatest fool in the universe. His keenness has just ruined him. He is an eternal bankrupt, and can't 'take the benefit of the Act.' He is such a known liar, that nobody would believe him under oath. And your employer's keenness will turn out no better. He may, indeed, probably prosper *here.* Such men sometimes do. But the Bible has described him—'they that will be rich, fall into temptation, and a snare, and into many foolish and hurtful lusts which drown men in destruction and perdition.' He 'will be rich;' that is what he wants; his 'will is all that way. And he has fallen into the 'temptation' to lie, in order to get rich. And this is a 'snare' to him—it is a trap, and he is caught in it; and if he does not repent and get out of it, he will be 'drowned in destruction and perdition.'

"But I was going to speak of his worldly prosperity. I am no prophet, nor the son of a prophet. I do not believe, that God will work any miracles in his case. But I *do* believe, *that man will fail!* Mark him well; and remember what I say, if you live to notice him ten or twenty years hence. In my opinion, you will see him a poor man; and probably, a despised man."

"What makes you *think so?*" said he, with great astonishment.

"Because he is not honest,—does not regard the truth. His lying will soon defeat its own purposes. His customers, one after another, and especially the best of them, will find him out, and they will forsake him, because they cannot trust his word. He will lose more than he will gain by all the falsehoods he utters. I know a dozen men in this city, some of them merchants, some butchers, some grocers, some tailors, whom I always avoid, and always will. If I *know* a man has lied to me once, in the way of his business, that ends all my dealings with him; I never go near him afterwards. Such is my practice; and I tell my wife so, and my children so. And sometimes, yea often, I tell them the *names of the men*. If any of my friends ask me about these men, I tell them the truth, and put them upon their guard. And thus their custom is diminished, because their character becomes known. This is one reason why I think Mr. H—— will not prosper.

"But whatever the mode may be, his reverses will come: mark my words, they will come. God will make them come."

With great depression, he replied,—"I don't know what I *could do*, if I should lose my place: I don't get but a little more than enough to pay my board, —my mother gives me my clothes, and if I lose my situation, I could not pay my board for a month."

"Then," said I, "if you get so little, you will not lose much by quitting. I do not pretend to know much about it, but in my opinion, Mr. H—— *wrongs* you, does you a positive *injustice*, and a *cruel* one, by giving you so little. And if you quit, and cannot pay your board till you get something to do,—tell *me*,—I will see to that." (He never had occasion to tell me.)

"If I quit that place so soon," said the young man, "it will make my old mother feel very bad; she will think I am getting unsteady, or something else is the matter with me. She will be afraid that I am going to ruin."

"*Not a bit of it*," said I. "*Tell* her just the truth, and you will fill her old heart with *joy:* she will thank God that she has got such a son,—and she will send up into heaven another prayer for you, which I would rather have than all the gold of Ophir."

The young man's eyes filled with tears, and I let him sit in silence for some time. At length he said to me,—

"I don't think I can stay there; but I don't know what to do, or where to look."

"Look to *God* first, and *trust* Him. Do you think He will let you *suffer*, because, out of regard to His commandments, you have lost your place? Never. Such is not His way. Ask *Him* to guide you."

"I am pretty much a stranger here," said he, with a very dejected look; "I know but few people, and I don't know where I could get anything to do."

"For that very reason ask God to guide you. Are you accustomed to pray?"

"Yes, I have been at times, lately. Some months ago, I began to try to seek the Lord, after I heard a sermon on that subject; and ever since that time, off and on, I have been trying. But I didn't know what to do in my situation."

"Will you answer me one question, as truly and fully as you are able?"

"Yes, sir, if I think it is *right* for me to answer it."

"The question is, has not your seriousness, and has not your trying to seek God, sometimes been diminished, *just when* you have had the most temptation in the store, leading you to do what you thought wrong,—even if you did it for another?"

He sat in silence, apparently pondering the question for a few moments, and then replied,—

"Yes,—I believe it has."

"'Quench not the Spirit,' then," said I. I then entered into particular conversation with him about his religious feelings, and found that his convictions of sin, and his desires for salvation, had rendered him for some weeks particularly reluctant to continue in an employment, where he felt obliged to practice so much deception. And I thought I could discover no little evidence in the history he gave me of his religious impressions, that the way of his daily business had been hostile to his attempts to come to repentance. And after I had plainly pointed out to him the demands of the gospel, and explained, as well as I could, the free offers of its grace and salvation, to all which he listened with intense attention and solemnity, he asked,—

"What would you advise me to do about my *business?*"

"Just this: go back to your store, and do all your duties most faithfully and punctually, without lying. If your employer finds fault with you, explain to him mildly and respectfully, that you are willing to do all that is right according to the law of God; but that you cannot consent to lie for anybody. If he is not a fool, he will like you the better for it, and prize you the more; for he will at once see, that he has got one clerk, on whose veracity he can depend. But if the man is as silly as he is unconscientious; he will probably dismiss you before long. After that, you can look about you, and see what you can do. And, rely upon it, God will open a way for you somewhere. But first and most of all, repent and believe in Jesus Christ."

The young man left me, promising soon to see me again. He did see me. He was led to seek the Lord. He became a decided Christian. He united with the church. But he did not remain long in that store. His mode did not please his employer.

However, he soon found another place. He established a character for integrity and promptness, and entered afterwards into business for himself. He prospered. He prospers still. It is now thirteen years since he came to me at that late hour in the evening; and he is now a man of extensive property,—of high respectability,—has a family,—and is contented and happy. I often hear of him, as an active and useful member of a church not far distant. I sometimes meet with him. He is still accustomed to open all his heart to me, when we are together; and it is very pleasant for me to notice his engagedness in religion, his respectability and happiness.

His employer became bankrupt about seven years after he left him, and almost as much bankrupt in character, as in fortune. He still lives, I believe; but in poverty, scarcely sustaining himself by his daily toil.

I attribute this young man's integrity, conversion and salvation, to his "old mother," as he always fondly called her. But for the lessons which she instilled into his mind, and the hold which she got upon his conscience, before he was fifteen; I do not believe I should ever have seen him. In my first interview with him, it was evident that the thought of his mother touched him more tenderly than anything else; and to this day, I scarcely ever meet him, and speak with him of personal religion, but some mention is made of his "old mother."

The instance of this young man has led me to think much of the dangers to which persons so situated are exposed; and I think I find in his history the clue to an explanation of a melancholy fact, that has often come under my notice. The fact to which I now refer is simply this,—that many young men are, at times, evidently the subjects of the alarming influences of the Holy Spirit, who, nevertheless, never become true Christians. And this young man's history goes far to convince me, that the Holy Spirit is quenched and led to depart from them, by some unconscientious proceedings in their business. If this young man had yielded to his employer, who can believe that he ever would have yielded to the Holy Spirit?

It was not strange that this young man should have felt a great anxiety about his earthly prospects and prosperity. He was poor. His "Old Mother" was poor. He had no friend to lean upon. In such a situation I could excuse his anxiety; but, in such a situation, it was most sad, to have the influences which were around him every hour of the day, turning his anxiety into a temptation to sin. Before I knew him, he had almost come to believe, that falsehood was a necessary thing in the transaction of business. He had noticed the eagerness of his employer to be rich. He had been sneered at and ridiculed as "too green," simply because he chose to act conscientiously; and this was a trial and a temptation very dangerous for a young man to encounter. It was a difficult thing for me, with all I could say, to pluck him out of this snare of the Devil. And I deem it quite probable, that large numbers of our young men are kept from seeking God, by an undue anxiety about worldly things,—an anxiety, fostered and goaded on to madness, by the spirit, example and influence of their employers. By this unwise and uncalled-for anxiety to be rich, the heart is harassed, the conscience is beclouded by some smooth sophistry, the Holy Spirit is resisted, and heaven forgotten; and all this, at that very age, when the heart ought to be happy, and when, as the character is forming, it is most important that God's word and God's Spirit should not be unheeded. By this anxiety to be rich the bright morning of youth is overhung with dark clouds of care, and the immortal soul is grappled to the world as with chains of iron! No young man should feel himself qualified or safe, in entering upon the business of the world, till his hope is fixed on Christ, and his unalterable determination is, to obey God, and gain heaven, whatever else he loses. And it would be well for every such young man, when surrounded by the influences of an eager and craving covetousness and its thousand temptations, to hold the world in check, and be led to prayer, by the remembrance of his "Old Mother."

One Word to a Sinner.

I HAVE known few seasons of greater coldness and less promise in respect to the prosperity of religion, than was the time when a young woman called upon me, to ask what she should do to be saved. Her call somewhat surprised me. I had not expected it. I had never noticed any particular seriousness in her. But now, she was evidently very much awakened to a sense of her duty and danger, and was evidently in earnest in seeking the favor of God.

After some conversation with her, and giving her such instruction as I thought adapted to her state of mind; I asked what it was that had induced her to give her attention to the subject of religion now, any more than formerly. She replied, "it was what you said to me one evening, as we were coming out of the Lecture-room. As you took me by the hand, you said, '*Mary, one thing is needful.*' You said nothing else, and passed on; but I could not forget it." I had forgotten it entirely, but it had fastened one thought deep in her mind.

The sermon, which I had just preached, and to which she had listened, had been of no avail to her; but she could not forget the personal address to herself, "Mary, one thing is needful." She is now, as I trust, in possession of that "one thing."

How much more efficacious is a message than a proclamation—a personal than a public address—a letter than a newspaper. The one is to the heart, but the other scarcely appears designed for it. The one is *to us*, peculiarly, especially; the other to everybody—to us indeed, as we form a part of the multitude, but that is very seldom what the heart wants or likes. One word to a sinner is often more effectual, than a score of sermons. Indeed, the secret of convicting sinners lies just in this—leading them to a *personal* application of the truth.

Yet let us not despise sermons. They are the appointment of God, and the great means of conversion. The sermons, which Mary had heard, were probably the very things which *prepared* her to be awakened by a private word, and without which, that word, probably, would have been in vain. Still, it is quite probable that the sermons would have been in vain without that private and personal monition, "Mary, one thing is needful."

"Nobody said anything to Me."

The title which I have given to this sketch, is taken from the lips of a young man, who afterwards became a member of my church. He had called upon me for conversation upon the subject of his religious duty; and after conversing with him, and saying such things to him as I thought appropriate to his state of mind, I asked him how it came about that he had not given his prayerful attention to the subject of religion before.

"Nobody said anything to me," says he.

"Yes," I replied, "*I* have said a great many things to you."

"I know you have in *sermons;* but I mean, nobody said anything to me in *particular*, before yesterday."

"Who said anything to you yesterday?"

"Henry Clapp," said he, (naming a young man who had recently entertained a hope in God.)

"What did Henry say to you?"

"As I met him in the street," says he, "he stopped me, and told me he had something to say to me, and asked me if he might say it. I said yes, he might. And then he said, 'It is high time for you to begin to seek the Lord.'"

"And what did you answer?"

"I hardly had time to answer at all, for he passed right on. But I said to him, when he had got a few feet from me, 'So it is, Henry.' He turned back his face partly toward me, looking over his shoulder, and answered, '*do it then*,' and went right on."

"Have you seen him since?"

"No, sir."

"You say, nobody said anything to you before. If he, or some one else, had spoken to you before, do you think you would have begun before?"

"I believe I should."

Such was the opinion of this young man. To this opinion he adhered long after. The last time I spoke to him on that subject, he said to me that he believed he "should have sought the Lord *years before*, if anybody had spoken to him about it."

Here, then, was a young man, living in the midst of a Christian community till he was more than twenty years old, a regular attendant at church, known to scores of Christian men and women; and yet, "nobody said anything to him!" The first sentence that was uttered to him was not lost upon him.

There are few points of duty more difficult for wise and engaged Christians to decide, than it is to decide what they shall say, or whether they shall say anything, to the irreligious persons whom they are accustomed to meet. Many times they are afraid to say anything to them on the subject of religion, lest they should do them an injury by awakening opposition or disgust.

No man can teach them their duty. What may be the duty of one, may not be the duty of another. The question depends upon so many things, upon character, upon intimacy, upon time, place, occasion, age, and a thousand other circumstances, that no wise man will ever attempt to lay down any general rule upon the subject. But if a Christian's heart longs for the conversion of sinners as it ought, he will not be likely to err. If he speaks to an unconverted sinner, in love, and alone, and without disputation, and in humility, and in the spirit of prayer, his words will do no harm. He may not be able to do good, but at least he can *try*. The unconverted in the midst of God's people, meeting them every day, their friends, their associates, and neighbors, certainly ought not to be able to declare, "*nobody* said anything to me,"—"no man cared for my soul."

Family Prayer.

A MAN of my congregation, about forty years of age, after quite a protracted season of anxiety, became, as he hoped, a child of God. There was nothing in his convictions or in his hopeful conversion, so far as I could discern, of any very peculiar character, unless it was the distinctness of his religious views and feelings.

But this man did not propose to unite with the church, as I had supposed he would deem it his duty to do. One season of communion after another passed by, and he still remained away from the table of the Lord. I was surprised at this, and the more so on account of the steady interest in religion, and the fixed faith in Christ which he appeared to possess. I conversed plainly with him, upon the duty of a public profession of his faith. He felt it to be his duty, but he shrunk from it. He had a clear hope, was constant at church, was prayerful, but he hesitated to confess Christ before men. All the ground of hesitation which I could discover as I conversed with him, was a fear that he might dishonor religion, if he professed it, and a desire to have a more assured hope. What I said to him on these points appeared to satisfy him, and yet he stayed away from the Lord's table, though he said, "I should feel it a great privilege to be there."

In aiming to discover, if possible, why a man of such clear religious views, of such apparent faith, and so much fixed hope in religion, should hesitate on a point of duty which he himself deemed obligatory upon him; I learned, to my surprise, that he had never commenced the duty of family prayer. He felt an inexpressible reluctance to it—a reluctance for which he could not account. He wondered at himself, but still he felt it. He blamed himself, but still he felt it. This cleared up the mystery. I no longer wondered at all at his hesitation on the matter of an open profession of religion. I had not a doubt, but his fears of dishonoring religion, and his waiting for greater assurance of hope, all arose from the neglect of family prayer. I told him so, and urged that duty upon him, as one that should precede the other. His wife urged it; but yet he omitted it. Finally, I went to his house, and commenced that service with him. He continued it from that time, and from that time his difficulties all vanished. Before he united with the church, he said to me, "it was a great trial to me to commence praying with my family, but now it is my delight.

I would not omit it on any account. Since I have commenced it I find it a joyful duty. It comforts and strengthens me." He had now no hesitation in coming out before the world, and openly professing his faith in Christ.

Neglect of one duty often renders us unfit for another. God 'is a rewarder,' and one great principle on which he dispenses his rewards is this—through our faithfulness in *one* thing he bestows grace upon us to be faithful in another. 'To him that hath shall be given, and he shall have abundance.'

Doctrines Reconciled:

OR, FREEDOM AND SOVEREIGNTY.

I CASUALLY met a member of my church in the street, and the nature of some conversation which was introduced, led him to ask me, if I recollected the conversation I had with him, at the time when he first called upon me for conversation upon the subject of religion. I had forgotten it entirely. He then referred to the period of his trouble, before he entertained any hope in Christ, and mentioned the particular subject about which he came to consult me. But I had no recollection of what I had said to him. He then stated the conversation in his own way, and I afterwards solicited of him the favor to write it down for me, which he kindly did, (omitting the name of the minister he mentioned,) and I here transcribe it from his letter, which lies before me.

"At a time when my thoughts were led, as I trust, by the Holy spirit, to dwell more than had been usual with me, on God and eternity in their relations to myself, and I was endeavoring to get light from a more particular examination of the doctrines of the Bible than I had ever before made; great difficulties were presented to my mind by the apparent inconsistency of one doctrine with another. I could believe them, each by itself; but could *not* believe them all together; and so great did this difficulty become, that it seemed to me like an insuperable obstacle in a narrow path, blocking up my way, and excluding all hope of progress. But I was still led to look at this obstacle with a sincere desire, I believe, for its removal.

"While in this state of mind, a friend solicited me to converse with a minister of much experience and high reputation for learning. I visited him in his study, and was cordially invited to make known my feelings, with the promise of such assistance as he could render. I then asked, if he could explain to me *how* God could be the ever-present and ever-active sovereign of all things, controlling and directing matter and spirit, and man be left free in his ways and choice, and responsible for all his actions. He replied, that he thought he could explain and remove this difficulty; and commenced a course of argument and illustration, the peculiar mode and nature of which I have now forgotten, but in which my untrained mind soon became utterly lost and confused, as in a labyrinth. And when, after his remarks had been extended many minutes, he paused, and asked if I now apprehended the matter; I felt obliged to confess to him that I did not understand anything about it. He then (without any discourtesy, however,) intimated that my mind was not capable of mastering a logical deduction of that nature; and I retired somewhat mortified, and in much doubt whether the fault was in myself, the subject, or the reasoning I had heard.

"A short time after this, I called upon another well-known minister, who had invited any to visit him who were desirous of conversing on religious subjects. After a little general conversation, I repeated to him the same question that I had before addressed to the other minister, adding that I had been told that it could be clearly explained, and asking him if he could thus explain it to me. After a moment's pause he made this reply,—'*No*,—nor any other man that ever lived. If any man says he can *explain that*, he says what is not true.' This short and somewhat abrupt answer, spoken with great emphasis, produced a remarkable effect upon my mind. A sense of the incomprehensibility of God seemed to burst upon me with great power. His doctrines now appeared to me as parts of His ways, and His ways as past finding out. I felt as if I had suddenly and almost violently been placed on the other side of the obstruction, which, with others of its kind, had blocked up my path. And although they were still there, and still objects of wonder and admiration, they were *no longer in the way*.

"After a few moments, my instructor added, that he thought he could convince me of the *truth* of the the two doctrines I had named in connection; and by a short and simple course of argument, beginning with God as the Author of all things, he made more clear and distinct to my apprehension the entire sovereignty of God over all His works; and also on the other point, beginning with every man's consciousness of freedom of will, he showed me the indisputable evidence on which that truth rests. And then alluding to the axiom, that all truth is consistent with itself, and separate truths with each other, he left the subject to my reflections.

"I may be permitted to add, that I do not pretend to judge of the wisdom of the *modes* adopted by these two ministers, as applied to other minds than my own,—but in my own case I very well know, that the most labored reasonings and explanations could not have been half as effectual in resolving my difficulty, as that plain, direct answer before quoted.

"Although years have elapsed since these conversations occurred, the one last mentioned is still vivid in my memory, and its permanent usefulness to me is frequently realized, when vain speculations on subjects not to be understood intrude themselves upon my mind."

Things hidden belong to God : things revealed belong to us. Little is gained by attempting to invade the province of God's mysteries. Every man will *attempt* it. Such is human nature. Mind will not willingly stop at the boundaries, which God has for the present prescribed for it. But in vain will it strive to overpass them. 'We know in part. When that which is perfect is come, then that which is in part shall be done away.'

There is one great reason *why* we cannot know everything—simply because we are not God. The only real religious utility, which grows out of the attempt to understand things not revealed to us, is to be found in the fact that such an attempt may humble us: it may show us what inferior beings we are, how ignorant, how hemmed in on every side; and thus compel us to give God His own high place, infinitely above us, and hence infinitely beyond us.

If I am not mistaken, those men, those ministers, who so strenuously aim to vindicate God's ways to man, to make clear what God has not revealed, do, in fact, degrade our ideas of God more than they illuminate our understandings. They make God appear not so far off, not so much above us. If they suppose that they have shed any light upon those unrevealed things which belong to God, it is quite probable that they suppose so, very much because they have levelled down his character and ways towards the grade of their own. Thus they may lead us to pride, but not to humility; they have not brought us nearer to God, but have done something to make us feel that God is very like one of ourselves; they have not given us more knowledge, but convinced us (erroneously,) that we are not quite so ignorant and limited after all. This is an unhappy result. It would be better to have the opposite one, to make us feel that God is God, and therefore inscrutable. 'He holdeth back the face of his throne and spreadeth his cloud upon it.' Better far to show a sinner 'the cloud,' and hold his eye upon it, and make him stand in awe, and feel his own ignorance and insignificance, than to make him think (erroneously,) that there is no 'cloud' there.

Somewhere the human mind *must* stop. We cannot know everything. Much is gained when we become fully convinced of this; and something more is gained when we are led to see clearly the line, which divides the regions of our knowledge from the regions of our ignorance. That dividing line lies very much between *facts* and *modes.* The facts are on the one side of it, the modes are on the other. The facts are on *our* side, and are matters of knowledge to us (because suitably proved); the modes are on *God's* side, and are matters of ignorance to us (because not revealed). "*How*" God could be an efficient and sovereign Ruler over all things and yet man be free to will and to do, was the question which troubled this young man, when he first began to seek God. It was not a question of *fact*, but of *mode*, ("how?"), and therefore, not a thing of duty; and therefore, a thing of difficulty to him, if he chose to meddle with it.

Now what should I say to him? It seemed to me, to be at once honest and wise to tell him *the plain truth*,—"*No*,—nor any other man; no man ever did explain it, or ever will. If any man *says* he can explain it, he says what is *not true*." That was the fit answer, because the true one. The young man in his account of that answer, very politely calls it "somewhat abrupt;" but he might very justly have called it by a less gentle name, *blunt*. In my opinion, that was the very excellence of it—that is the reason why the answer answered its purpose. It was the truth condensed and unmistakable. At a single dash it swept away his army of difficulties. It showed him that he had been laboring at an impossibility—at a thing beyond man—a thing with which he had nothing to do, but believe it and let it alone, and let God take care of it. He says, "a sense of the incomprehensibility of God seemed to burst upon me with great power. His doctrines now appeared to me as parts of His ways, and His ways as past finding out." Again he says, "the most labored reasonings and explanations could not have been half as effectual in resolving my difficulty, as that plain, direct answer." Its excellence consisted in this—it *was* plain, just the whole, blunt truth. *He* says it was "permanently useful," to keep him from "vain speculations." Its utility was just this: it led him to give God the place which belongs to Him, and take his own.

His trouble undoubtedly was, that he could not see "how" the doctrines he mentioned were reconcilable. But they did not *need* any reconciling. They do not quarrel. *God is an efficient sovereign over all.* That is one of the doctrines; and it was easily demonstrated to his entire satisfaction. Anybody can demonstrate it. *Man is free and accountable.* That is the other doctrine; and it was easily demonstrated. Anybody can demonstrate it. Both the doctrines are *true*, therefore, and hence they need no reconciling. There is no inconsistency betwixt them. That is enough.

If any one choose to atttempt to go beyond this, and by any metaphysical explanation of God's sovereign efficiency on the one hand, and man's freedom on the other, explain "*how*" the two things *can* be true. he will flounder in the mud—he will 'darken counsel by words without knowledge.'

An unconverted sinner is not reconciled to God, and this is the very reason why he is not reconciled to the doctrines of God. In my opinion these doctrines ought *always* to be presented in such a manner as to indicate their high origin, as to show they are *like* God. *Then*, an unconverted sinner will be apt to see that he dislikes the doctrines, just because he dislikes God; and thus his convictions of an evil heart will become more fixed and clear; or, at least, he will perceive that the doctrines are just such as he ought to *expect*, because they precisely accord with their Infinite Author. Let him be reconciled to God, and he will find little trouble with the doctrines. But let him be reconciled to God *as He is*, an incomprehensible sovereign, an infinite mystery to a finite mind, 'the high and lofty One, who inhabiteth eternity.' If he is reconciled to false notions of God, all his religion will be likely to be false. A comprehensible God is no God at all, for what is comprehensible is not infinite. Let men beware of 'intruding into those things which they have not seen, vainly puffed up with their fleshly mind.'

I Can't Pray:

OR, THE TWO SISTERS.

I HAPPENED to be seated in the library of a literary Institution with an intimate friend, when two young ladies entered the room, whom he introduced to me as sisters, who had come from a distant State to be pupils under his care. I had never heard of them before. The elder one appeared to be about twenty years of age, and the other, perhaps two years younger. My friend was soon called out of the room for a few moments, and I was left alone with them. I thought the opportunity too good to be lost, and felt it to be my duty to speak to them, on the subject of their salvation. In a brief conversation upon common topics, which I endeavored to shape in such a manner as to prepare the way for my design, I was much pleased with them. I thought they manifested more than an ordinary share of talent, and I was particularly pleased with the frankness and simplicity of their manners, and more than all with their manifest sisterly affection.

I inquired whether they were members of any church. They were not. "And do you think you are yet living without any religion?" said I. "We are not Christians," was the answer. Their mother was a member of the church, and they told me that they had themselves "studied religion," as they expressed it, "a great deal," and "thought about it very often," but they said, "we are not Christians." "And why not?" said I. The question appeared to confuse them a little, and I endeavored to relieve their embarrassment by some general remarks, such as demanded no specific reply. I asked permission to call and see them.

A little more than a week afterwards I had an interview with them. I was still more pleased with them than I had been before. They were frank, gentle, simple-hearted, and without affectation. But in respect to their religious inclinations I found little to please me, and still less in respect to their religious opinions. Their minds appeared to be stored with a species of metaphysical ideas on the subject of religion, which I could not reconcile to the Bible or to common sense, but to which they tenaciously adhered, as being in accordance with the teachings which they had always heard from the pulpit. As I entreated them to give their attention to their salvation immediately, all I could say appeared to be warded off, or its truth rendered vain by a single idea. That idea would constantly come out in some such question as "how *can* we seek God with such hearts?" or, "how can we do anything without the Holy Spirit?" or, "what can *we* do if God does not give us the right motives?" This was their one difficulty. They maintained with true metaphysical courage and acumen, that they could do nothing, and any attempt to seek the Lord must be useless, because their hearts were wrong, and they could not therefore "seek Him with the right feelings," as they expressed it. No act, no attempt, no thought of theirs, "could possibly be acceptable to Him," or of "any avail" for themselves. They clung to this idea constantly and tenaciously.

I supposed at first, that this was only a casual thought which had occurred to them; but in a second interview, I found them just the same as in the first. The idea which hindered them from any serious attempt in religion, had become interwoven with all their religious thoughts and feelings,—had been entertained so long and employed so often, that now it came up spontaneously, and spread itself over every thought about personal religion. They presented it so naturally, so easily, and in such varied shapes and connections, that I began to despair of having any influence over them. However, I resolved to try.

I took care to assure them of the deep interest I

took in them already, which I certainly could do with entire sincerity, for they had won my esteem, and it made me sad of heart to see two such estimable girls entangled in the snares of such a deception. I aimed to win their confidence; and before I left them, having now learned their cast of mind, and their peculiar religious difficulty, I assured them most affectionately that they were mistaken in many of their notions, and that they certainly might find the favor of God, if they would seek it in the Bible way. To give some practical point and direction to their thoughts, I desired them to read carefully and with prayer the fifty-fifth chapter of Isaiah, as proof of the truth of what I told them, and especially as a specimen of the manner, in which their heavenly Father calls to them and counsels them in His infinite 'kindness and love.' They both promised to *read* it, but I noticed that they did *not* promise to *pray* over it, as I had requested them to do.

They were very much alike in all their ideas about religion. Their hindrance was the same. I resolved, therefore, to converse with each one separately after this, because I perceived that they mutually hindered each other;—for when one of them would say, "I can't seek the Lord with such a heart," the other would often reiterate the same idea in some other form, manifestly supported and confirmed in her strange notion. Urged separately to attend to their salvation, I hoped their error might be corrected. And as I had discovered a greater susceptibility, as I thought, in the younger sister, I determined to commence with her.

Consequently, I soon afterwards called upon her, and asked to see her alone. She met me very affectionately. But I had scarcely uttered a single sentence in respect to her duty, before she asked suddenly, and with much animation,—

"Shall I call my sister?"

"Oh, no," said I, "I wish to see you alone. You may say some things which I should not wish your sister to hear."

This reply appeared to give her some little confusion, mingled with sadness; but she made no objections to my proposal, and soon recovered her composure. I urged her to her religious duty, as faithfully and affectionately as I could. She listened to me apparently with candor and with some emotion, as in the language of Scripture I enjoined upon her repentance, and faith in the Lord Jesus Christ for justification unto life eternal. But the old hindrance was still in her way. The following is a part of our conversation:

"I suppose you are convinced of the *necessity* of religion?"

"*Oh, yes*, sir! I *know* its necessity but I do not feel it,—I cannot feel it."

"Do you feel, that you are a sinner,—without Christ, an *undone* sinner, and have a wicked heart opposed to God?"

"I *know* I am; but I don't feel it as much as I ought to."

"What do you mean by saying, 'as much as you ought to?'"

"I mean, not enough to be able to seek the Lord, or repent."

"Are you really giving any definite attention to your duty towards God, to your salvation?"

"At times, I have thought about it a great deal."

"Are you willing to seek the Lord *now*, in obedience to His word, and as well as you know how?"

"I have felt for a long time, that I should like to be a Christian; but it is rather the conviction of my head than the feeling of my heart. My reason teaches me it is wise to make my peace with God; but I suppose such has not been the desire of my heart. My attention has been called to the subject very seriously, and I have felt it deeply at times; but the Spirit has forsaken me, and I have gone farther off than ever. Once I could have given my heart to God a great deal easier than I could now," said she, with deep sadness.

"I have no doubt," said I, "that is true, entirely true. It *has* become more difficult for you, and will be the more difficult still, the longer you delay. You ought to seek the Lord *now.*"

"If I could seek Him, sir, with an acceptable heart, I would not neglect it."

"And so, becoming worse and worse, going farther and farther off, you let your life run on, living without God and without hope, making no attempt to gain eternal life. My dear girl, this is all wrong. Salvation is to be *sought,*—if there is an item of truth in the Bible, it is to be sought. You may obtain it, if you will. Salvation is offered to you,—it is free,—it is fully within your reach; the gospel calls to you. If you will seek God with all your heart, I know you will not seek in vain. God has said this to you to induce you to seek Him: 'Hear, and your soul shall live. I will make an everlasting covenant with you. Let the wicked forsake his way, and the unrighteous man his thoughts,'—(you *think* wrong, remember,)—'and let him return unto the Lord, and He will have mercy upon him, and to our God, for He will abundantly pardon.' And all this, God says *to you*, and says it just in connection with his command, 'Seek ye the Lord, call ye upon Him.' You must seek Him. You must turn to Him with repentance and prayer. He gives you the fullest encouragement to do so. Let his word sink deep into your heart, my dear girl: 'Then shall ye go and pray unto me, and I will hearken unto you; and ye shall seek me, and ye shall find me, when ye shall search for me with all your heart, and I will be found of you.' That is the way which the God of all love calls on you to take in order to be saved; and you do not obey Him; you are not *trying* to obey Him!"

"Why, sir, I have been taught, that I must *submit to God first*, or He will not hear any prayer I could make. I have heard my *minister* say so."

"I am not teaching you, *not* to submit to God (as you call it). He commands you to seek Him, and tells you how to do it, and I want you to 'submit' to His command."

"I think," said she, "that praying before submitting to God, would only be hypocrisy."

"Then you should do *both*. He certainly commands you to *pray*."

"Not with such a heart as *I* have got," said she, emphatically, and with an air of triumph.

"Yes, He *does*," said I. "Here is His command in the Bible,—it is addressed *to you*,—to every sinner on earth,—'Call ye upon Him while He is near.' He does, indeed, command you also to repent; but if you choose *not* to repent, that sin does not alter His command to you *to pray*. His command lies on just such a heart as you have this moment. Your impenitence and unbelief are no excuse for you."

"How can I have any power to pray to Him, and seek Him rightly?"

"The Bible answers your question: 'to as many as received Him, to them gave He power to become the sons of God.' The Bible offers Christ to *you*, a guilty sinner. You are to *receive Him* as your own Saviour, in order to have 'power' to become a child of God. You are to 'deny yourself, and take up your cross and follow Christ.'"

"But," said she, with much agitation, "I cannot *ask* God to receive me as *His child.* I cannot plead with my whole heart for His blessing, as I would ask my earthly father for a gift which he could bestow."

"Do you *never* pray?"

"No, I *never prayed.* It seems to me it would be nothing but mockery for me to pray. *I can't pray.*"

"You cannot be saved *without* prayer. If you will not ask God's blessing, you cannot have it. 'Ask, and ye shall receive,' is God's direction and promise. You foolishly invert the order, and thus 'handle the word of God deceitfully,' hoping to 'receive' *first*, and then 'ask.' If you would be saved, my dear girl, you must do as God bids you."

"But I *can't ask* with all my heart, and anything short of that would be as bad as sacrilege."

"You are wrong, my child,—all wrong. It is true you ought to seek the Lord with all your heart, as he requires; but it is *not* true, that your praying is worse than neglecting prayer, and it is not *true*, that you have any ground to expect His blessing *before* you ask it. You think wrong. 'Let the wicked forsake his THOUGHTS.' You and God do not think alike. Your false notions hinder you from becoming a Christian. God commands you to seek Him by prayer. You may think what you will about 'mockery,' still He tells you to pray, in order to your being saved; and while you do *not* pray, you do not take the way which His mercy points out to you."

"I *can't pray*," says she, with an accent of vexation and despair.

"You say you can't pray," said I. "God thinks you can. Just as soon as He has said to you, 'Seek ye the Lord,' He goes on to tell you *how* to seek Him,—'call ye upon Him.' *He* thinks you can pray. In that passage He tells you to pray even *before* He tells you to repent. 'Call ye upon Him' comes *first*: it stands before the command to repent,—'let the wicked forsake his way.' God knows that if you do not pray, you will not repent. I do not say that you ought to pray with an impenitent heart, but I say you ought to *pray*, be your heart what it may. And what an awfully wicked heart you must have, if you cannot even pray."

"Oh, I can't *pray*, I have such a heart!"

"You refuse to pray, because you have such an evil heart. That evil heart is the very reason why you have need to pray the more earnestly. Your evil heart, instead of being an argument against prayer, is the strongest of all possible reasons why you *should* pray. You infinitely need God's help, and you should ask for it."

"I *can't* pray! It would be hypocrisy!"

"Perhaps it would; but it is *rebellion* to neglect it."

"Well, hypocrisy is worse, sir."

"I do not know *that;* in such a case as this," said I, "if you pray with such a heart as you have now, you will at least *try* to obey God in the form; but if you do not pray at all, you are a rebel both in heart and outward conduct. Which is the worst—to try and come short, or to stand here before God and say you will not try at all?"

With vexation of spirit she replied, "I *can't* pray; my heart is all wrong."

"How do you expect to get a better one?"

"I know God must give me a new heart, if I ever have it."

"Do you want Him to give you a new heart?"

"Oh sir, I *wish* he *would*," said she, weeping.

"Why then don't you tell Him so, in earnest prayer?"

"I *can't* pray, it would be insincere."

"Are you insincere to *me*, when you tell me with

so much emotion, you 'wish God *would* give you a new heart?' Do you tell me what is not true?"

"*Oh, no sir!*" said she earnestly, "I hope you don't think I would utter a falsehood to you?"

"Not at all, my friend; but if you spoke the truth, you do sincerely wish God would give you a new heart. Where then would be the insincerity of telling *Him* so; of *asking* Him for what you sincerely desire?"

She paused a long time, pondering this question, apparently with mingled thoughtfulness and vexation; at length she replied,—

"I can't *pray*, I have not the right motives."

"How do you expect to get the right motives?"

"I never *shall* have, if God does not put them into my heart!"

"Do you *want* Him to put them into your heart?"

"Yes, *I do*, above all things," said she, earnestly.

"Why then don't you ask Him? If you are sincere in wanting Him to do so, you can sincerely ask Him to do so."

"But I *can't* pray, sir; the prayers of the wicked are an abomination to the Lord."

"So *you* say," said I.

"Does not the *Bible* say so, sir?"

"No, my child, nowhere."

"Why, sir, I thought it did."

"It does not. It says, 'the sacrifice of the wicked is an abomination to the Lord,' but the meaning of that is, that when the wicked offer sacrifice, and at the same time do not intend to abandon their wickedness, it is an abomination."

"Well, sir, the Bible requires good motives."

"Certainly it does; and it requires you to pray to God, 'create in me a clean heart, and renew a right spirit within me.' You need good motives, and for that very reason you should pray."

"But I *can't* pray. It is *not* prayer, such as the Bible demands, if I should ask God for another heart."

Said I, "The *common* complaint of the Bible against sinners is not, that they pray with bad motives; but that they do not pray at all. It censures the wicked, because they 'cast off fear, and restrain prayer,' as you do; while it makes promises to those who seek God by prayer."

"I *never* prayed," said she, with manifest fear and vexation of spirit. "*I can't pray*, till I have the right feelings."

"You must pray, my dear girl, in order to *get* the right feelings. So the Bible teaches you, and you pervert it. You say you must have the right feelings *first*. The Bible tells you to pray for them, if you would ever have them. In Jeremiah, xxix. 12, 13, God says, 'Then shall ye call upon me, and ye shall go and pray unto me, and I will hearken unto you; and ye shall seek me and find me, when ye shall search for me with all your heart, and I will be found of you, saith the Lord.' The praying, the seeking, is *first.* The finding comes afterwards. 'Ask, and ye shall receive,' says God. 'Give to me, and then I will ask,' is your answer."

"But, sir, I certainly have no heart to pray. I *can't* pray! God would frown on any prayer I could offer."

"So *you* say, but He has not said so. He will frown upon your *refusing* to pray. It seems to me perfectly clear, that God is far more kind to you than you think Him, more kind than you are to yourself. He says to you, in your weakness and all your want, 'In me is thy help.' You demand of your poor heart to be holy first, *before* it can have any encouragement at all, even to pray for help. Your cold heart does him an injustice. He is more kind than that. He encourages you to come to Him, and call upon Him, with just such a needy and imperfect heart, as you have this moment, to come to Him by Christ in all your unworthiness and fear, and tell Him your wants, and beg for mercy and Divine assistance. He stands ready to hear you, to forgive and love you, and bestow upon you that better heart you long for, if you will ask. And you abuse His kindness by your unbelief. He is far better than you think Him. He invites you to come to Him in Christ Jesus, and ask Him what you will. You demand of your poor heart more (in one sense,) than God demands of it. You demand of it faith and holiness *aside* from any Divine help, and without prayer; while he *offers* you help, to aid you to holiness and faith. I do not understand him, as inviting you to Christ, only *after* you have a good heart, but as inviting you *now*, just as you are."

"Oh!" said she, quite overcome with her emotions, "I wish I had a right to come."

"What do you mean, my dear girl? You talk inconsistently, absurdly. You want a right heart *first*, and then you will consent to pray for a right heart."

"I know, sir, my mind is wrong; but it does seem to me, I *cannot* pray with such a heart."

"That is only a deceitful *excuse*. If you do not *love* to have such a heart, you will pray God to give you a better one."

"Oh, I am such a sinner! How can such a creature pray?"

"Others just like you *have* prayed, and God has answered them. You can do the same thing, if you will."

"But my very heart is too wicked!"

"You do not more than half believe what you say. If you really believed you had such a wicked heart, you would cry for mercy with all your might."

"I *would pray*," said she, "if I had such motives that God would hear me."

"That is the very essence of self-righteousness," said I. "You expect to be answered, not because you shall have cried, 'God be merciful to me a sinner;' but because you shall have gone to God with such good motives, with a heart so much better, that he will hear and answer you *on that account*. You wish to be able to stand up and offer the Pharisee's prayer, 'God, I thank thee that I am not as other men are.' You are unwilling to be the poor publican, and smite on your breast, despairing of your wicked heart, and cry, 'God, be merciful to me a sinner.' You won't consent to be a beggar. Your heart is too full of pride and self-righteousness to consent to let you be an infinite debtor to Divine mercy, as an undone and helpless sinner."

"Why, sir," said she with amazement, "do you think I am self-righteous?"

"I *know* you are. You have shown it in almost every sentence you have uttered for the last half hour. You justify yourself. You justify your prayerlessness even. You think to pray with such good motives, some time or other, as to meet acceptance. Rejecting Christ, you rely on the good motives you hope to have, as the ground of your acceptance. And that is all self-righteousness."

After a solemn pause she asked,—

"What *shall* I do? I am undone."

"Seek the Lord," said I, "call upon Him; fly to Christ, as you are—remember, *as you are.*"

"*Will* He *hear* me?"

"Yes; He *says* He will. 'Ask, and ye shall receive.' Believe His promise of the 'Holy Spirit to them that ask Him.' You have no need to be hindered, my dear child, for an hour. Give God your heart as it is. Go to Him as you are, a poor, undone sinner, and beg for mercy. And *believe* He will not cast you off. God loves you, and waits to save you. He offers you all the benefits of the blood of atonement and of the aids of the Holy Spirit—'the Holy Spirit to *them that ask Him,*' remember. And what more can your wicked heart need?"

She seemed to be melted into tenderness.

"And now, my dear girl, *will* you *pray?* Will you begin this night?"

"I *ought* to," said she trembling.

"Then, *will* you?"

"Yes, sir, *I will,*" said she emphatically.

"Good-bye," said I, and instantly left her.

During this interview she became greatly troubled. Evidently she was tost with conflicting emotions. She began to perceive that her excuse of a wicked heart would not answer her purpose; and at times I thought her affectionate disposition on the very point of yielding to the kindness of God.

I now had some hope that she would seek the Lord. She had promised to *pray*, and thus had yielded the very point in which all her opposition practically centered. But on considering the whole matter more carefully that evening at home, I came to the conclusion that she would not pray as she had promised; but that when she was alone, the influence of her old difficulty would return upon her and overthrow the urgency of all that I had said.

Early the next morning, therefore, I called upon her. She was taken by surprise. Said I,—

"Did you *pray* last night, my dear girl?"

Her eyes filled with tears. She was silent. (She told me some days afterwards, "I felt my very heart sick within me, the moment you asked me if I had prayed.") I repeated the question,—

"My child, did you keep your promise? Did you pray last night?"

Her whole frame was agitated. The question seemed to pierce her heart.

"No sir, I did not!" said she faintly, and covered her face in her handkerchief, in convulsive agony.

"And why not? Why didn't you pray? You make my very heart sorry, when you tell me you neglected it!"

"I did try," said she weeping; "I did try. I kneeled down, but I could not open my lips to utter one word! My heart was so cold and wicked, I did not dare to speak one word to my heavenly Father."

"Your heart is far more wicked than you think; and if you wait to make it better, you will wait forever! But God is a thousand-fold more merciful and kind than you think. Give yourself to Him. Just trust to Christ, bad as your heart is."

"Oh, sir, it is hard to learn to *trust!* I have tried to trust myself in Christ's hands. How *can* I trust?"

"Suppose," said I, "you were here on this island, and you knew the island was going to sink under you, and you must get off or sink with it, and you could do nothing at all to save yourself, and then a boat should come to save you, and you had every reason to believe it would hold you up from sinking and take you off safely, and land you where you wanted to go,—would it be 'hard to trust' to it? No, no; you would instantly go on board and stay on it, and take care not to fall off. You would trust it willingly, fully, joyfully. Just so commit yourself, a helpless sinner, to Christ, and not sink into perdition. He will take you, and land you safe in heaven, if you will ask Him and trust Him."

"I am afraid I have not such a sense of my sin, as to seek God *earnestly.*"

"What, then, will you do?"

"I don't know, unless I wait for it."

"And will you get it by waiting?"

"I suppose," said she, "a just sense of sin is the gift of the Holy Spirit."

"I suppose so, too; and therefore you must pray for the Holy Spirit. It is promised as a gift to them that ask. You are not to *wait.* 'Behold, now is the day of salvation.' Give your bad heart to God."

I left her more solemn and docile than ever before. Her stout heart trembled.

The next day but one, I called upon her. She was in her class. I sent for her to meet me in a private room. I asked her,—

"Have you trusted yourself to Christ yet?"

She shook her head. Her eyes filled with tears.

"What have you been waiting for?"

"Oh, my dear friend, I don't know. It seems as if I *cannot* offer myself to God in such a manner that He will accept me. I try with all my power. But my thoughts wander when I try to pray. My heart is *all* unbelief and sin!"

"You must pray for God's help, and *trust* Him to help you."

"Oh, sir, if I go to God I am afraid He will not accept me. There *never was* such a sinner."

"You need not fear an item, my dear friend. He has *promised* to accept you. Go to Him by faith in his Son for all you want. His very throne shall crumble, sooner than you shall be cast off."

I left her in tears, apparently in a subdued and tender agitation.

Four days afterwards I saw her again. She met me with a smile of gladness.

"Oh, I am glad you have come. I have wanted to see you very much." Grasping my hand, she began to speak to me of her feelings,—"I want to tell you a great many things about myself," but her emotions choked her utterance. I asked her,—

"Can you pray *now*, my dear girl?"

"*Oh, yes, I can pray now with my whole heart.* But, sir, it seems to me I do not come fully to Christ, though I *know* I want to."

"Do you still love sin and the world too much to give them up for Christ?"

"No, sir, I think not," said she, solemnly.

"There may be some darling sin you do not renounce. Perhaps you love the world too well. Weigh well the matter. Count the cost. 'Choose this day whom you will serve.' If you choose the world, it will cheat you. If you choose the God of love, He will save you."

"I do want to be a Christian," said she, tenderly. "I pray my God for this with all my heart."

"And what has made you so much more earnest?"

"I have felt so ever since I heard your sermons on the text, 'Go thy way for this time.' I was afraid I was like Felix, to tremble and yet delay."

"Do you intend to delay?"

"No sir, indeed, I do not *intend* to," said she, the tears gushing from her eyes.

The next morning I found her in deep solemnity. Her weeping eyes told of her agitated heart. I asked,—

"Are you willing now to give up all and follow Christ?"

"Oh, sir," said she, with the utmost earnestness, *I do not think there is any other desire in my heart*, except that I may be a Christian."

"Do you now love God?"

With some thoughtful hesitation she replied,—

"I am afraid, sir, to venture an answer to that question."

"You need not answer it. I will not embarrass you. But see to it, that you trust all to the sovereign mercy of God, offered to you in his Son. I can say no more than I have said already. I have told you all. My work is finished. I leave you with God. See to it, that you make an entire commitment of yourself, for time and eternity, to your Lord and Redeemer."

On the evening of the next day I had a long interview with her. It was delightful to hear her expressions. Among other things she said to me,—

"*I feel* that I am now *at peace*. I *trust* my God. I *love* to trust Him. The Saviour is everything to me. I know He will fulfil all His promises. Oh, my dear friend, I have had a dreadful struggle! but I have had strength given me to persevere. Now the love of God is very precious to my soul. I never expected this happiness."

"Do you love to pray?"

"*Oh yes;* prayer is sweet to me now. I can *tell all my wants to my heavenly Father.*"

After some farther conversation, I said to her,—

"You seem to have come into a different state of mind within a few days. You do not talk as you did. How have you brought yourself to this? to feel so differently?"

"Oh, sir! it is nothing that *I* have done! I *just prayed to God with all my heart and in full faith, and he did every thing for me.*"

She appeared to be a very happy Christian. Her joy was full. Her life was prayer.

The elder sister, who so much resembled the younger in her difficulty about prayer, I visited generally at the same times and as often as the younger. I had almost precisely the same things to say to her; and a few days afterwards she also entertained "just a little hope," as she expressed it.

These sisters were deeply interested for each other. Each would say to me frequently, "I want you to see my sister." Their anxiety for one another was beneficial to them, and their thoughts of their absent mother, whom they often mentioned, appeared to me to constrain them to more earnest endeavors to lay hold on eternal life. They both have hope in Christ, and I trust will both have heaven. I first saw them in the month of May, and on the seventh day of the following September, having returned to their distant home, their native place, they both came for the first time to the table of the Lord, happy Christians in the dew of their youth.

I have given this sketch, in this extended form, as illustrating the propriety of continued solicitation at the door of a sinner's heart. Here were two young ladies without any special seriousness, worldly, presenting no hopeful appearance, but presenting a cold discouragement, calculated to damp every hope, and stop every effort to do them good, and coming out so sadly in the words, "I never prayed in my life."

But one conversation was followed up by another; they were scarcely left a day to themselves, and the influences of the world, their strange hindrance of speculative error was assailed in every form, and overthrown again and again by declarations of Scripture and arguments of reason;—and their whole history shows, that vigorous and persevering attempts to convert sinners, have as much prospect of success, as any well-directed attempts in any ordinary matter. Not that man can reach sinners' hearts, but that God may be expected to reach them, when minister or any other man shall diligently knock at their door, with the voice of God's urgent and affectionate truth.

The reluctance of these young women to pray may have been fostered, (I suppose it was,) by the fogs of a metaphysical theology, in which they had been educated, and which they probably misunderstood. But it *originated* in a consciousness of a home-bred depravity. "I can't *ask* God to make me his child," said one of them; "I *know* my heart does not want it." But there was a propriety in urging them to prayer, because God commands men to pray, and because I expected they would be rendered more sensible of their opposition to God, and their need of his aid, when they should attempt its performance. And so it turned out. Their conviction, which *had* been superficial and speculative only, became more deep, more practical. While superficial and speculative, their depravity was an excuse to them. When rendered deep and thorough by a sincere attempt to pray, it became experimental, it was no longer an excuse, but only made them cry for mercy with all their might: "I prayed to God in full faith, and with all my heart, and He did everything for me." A just conviction of sin makes no excuse; but it will pray.

I might have avoided this girl's excuse by urging her to repentance and faith: I chose to meet it by urging her to prayer. It was her inability to pray in any manner to meet her own approval, which had contributed more than anything else to convince her of her deep-seated depravity, and alienation from God; and I did not wish to diminish this conviction, by leading her thoughts from the thing that caused it. It would have been dangerous to turn her thoughts into a new channel. I aimed to conspire with the Holy Spirit. It was important that she should realize the necessity of the direct help of the Divine Spirit *personally*, *practically*, and therefore more deeply, than by her speculation she ever could; and she was more likely to *have* such a realization through endeavors to pray rightly, than by any other means. In her speculation she *thought* she knew full well her wickedness and helplessness; but these were the very things she did *not* know. She found them out just when she endeavored to pray. Then, a full sense of her undone and helpless condition burst upon her. She could do nothing but cry: "I just prayed to God with all my heart, and in full faith." And then, as she expressed it, "*He* did everything for me." "Go thou, and do likewise."

I Can't Feel.

FROM early spring down to the autumn of the year, a very sedate and contemplative man had been accustomed to call upon me, in respect to his religious thoughts and anxieties. At first he seemed to have *thoughts* only, but they ripened by degrees into anxieties. He began by asking about theories, or doctrines, apparently without any idea of making an application of the truth to himself. He had points of difficulty which he wished to have explained, and then he found *other* points; and these gradually changed in character from abstract questions to those of the application of the truth. From the first, I tried to lead him on to the personal application; but months passed away before he appeared to have much sense of his sin, or much anxiety about himself.

But he came to this; and after quite a struggle of mind, as it appeared to me to lead himself to believe in salvation by personal merit, he gave that up; he said to me, "I have become convinced that sinners are saved, not by their own goodness, but because they are pardoned on account of Jesus Christ. Faith in Him is the only way for them."

After this, I had conversed with him several times, when he appeared to me to be not far from the kingdom of God; but I was as often disappointed, for he would come back to me again in as much trouble and unbelief as before. Again and again I had answered all his inquiries, teaching him out of the Scriptures; had brought up to his mind all the doctrines of truth, the divine promises and directions, sin and salvation; but all in vain. He had become very solemn, and seemed to be entirely candid and really in earnest. His Bible had become his constant study; he was a man of prayer; he attended upon all our religious services with manifest interest; he appeared to have a deep sense of his sin and danger. But he had no hope in Christ.

I finally said to him one evening,—

"I do not know, my dear sir, what more can be said to you. I have told you all that I know. Your state as a sinner lost, exposed to the righteous penalty of God's Law, and having a heart alienated from God; and the free offer of redemption by Christ; and your instant duty to repent of sin and give up the world and give God your heart; and the source of your help through the power of the Holy Spirit assured to you, if you will 'receive' Christ: all these things have become as familiar to you as household words. What more can I say? I know not what more there is to *be* said. I cannot read your heart. God can, and *you* can by His aid. Some things you have said almost made me think you a Christian, and others again have destroyed that hope. I now put it to your own heart—if you are not a Christian, what hinders you?"

He thought a moment,—said he,—

"I can't *feel!*"

"Why didn't you tell me this before?"

"I never thought of it before, sir."

"How do you *know* this hinders you?"

"I can think of nothing else. But I am sure I shall never be converted to God, if I have no more feeling than I have now. But *that* is my own fault. I know *you* cannot help me."

"No sir, I cannot; nor can you help yourself. Your heart will not feel at your bidding."

"What then *can* I do?" said he, with much anxiety.

"Come to Christ, *now.* Trust Him. Give up your darling world. 'Repent: so iniquity shall not be your ruin.'"

He seemed perplexed—annoyed—vexed; and with an accent of impatience, such as I had never witnessed in him before, he replied,—

"That is *impossible.* I want the feeling, to *bring* me to that; and I *can't* feel!"

"Hear me, sir," said I, and heed well what I say. I have several points:

"1. The Bible never tells you that you must *feel*, but that you must *repent* and *believe.*

"2. Your complaint that you '*can't feel*,' is just *an excuse*, by which your wicked heart would justify you for not coming to Christ *now.*

"3. This complaint that you '*can't feel*,' is the complaint of a *self-righteous spirit.*" (He started—rose upon his feet, and stood as in amazement.)

"How is it?" said he.

"Because you look to the desired *feeling* to *commend* you to God, or to make you fit to come, or to enable you to come."

"Yes, to *enable* me," said he.

"Well, *that* is *self-righteousness*, in the shape of self-justification for *not* coming, or the shape of self-reliance, if you *attempt* to come. That is all *legalism*, and not the acceptance of a gracious Christianity. You cannot be saved by *Law.*

"4. Your complaint is the language of the most *profound ignorance. To feel* would do you no good. Devils feel. Lost spirits feel.

"5. Your complaint that you '*can't feel*,' tends to lead you to a *false religion*—a religion of mere self-righteous feeling. Religion is duty."

"But, sir," said he, "there is *feeling* in religion."

"But, sir," said I, "there is *duty* in religion; and

which shall come *first?* You *ought* to feel: you ought to *love* God; and *grieve* that you are such a senseless sinner."

"I know I am a sinner; but I can't feel any *confidence* to turn to God, to *draw* me to Him."

"You are like the prodigal in the fifteenth of Luke, when he thought of saying to his father, 'make me as one of thy hired servants.' Poor fool! Say *that, to his father?* Why, the very idea is a libel on his father's heart! But he did'nt think so. Poor fool! he knew no better. And you are a greater fool than he. He went *home.* And where he met his father, he found his heart. He could "*feel,*" when he found his father's arms around him, and felt the strong beatings of his father's heart. Do as he did. Go home and you will feel, if you never felt before. You will *starve* where you are; your 'husks' will not save you."

As I was uttering this he hung his head, cast his eyes upon the floor, and stood like a statue of stone. I let him think. There he stood for some long minutes. Then turning suddenly to me, reaching to me his hand, says he,—

"I am very much obliged to you; good night."

I let him go.

About a month afterwards I met him riding alone in his wagon, and he insisted upon my taking a seat with him, for he had "something to say" to me, and he would "drive wherever I wanted to go." I was no sooner seated in the wagon than he said to me,—

"The human heart is the greatest mystery in the world; inexplicable, contradictory to itself; it is *absurd.* Man is a riddle. Who would imagine that when a sinner really wishes to feel his sins more, and wishes to have the love of Christ in his heart, it is because he is not willing to give up the world. He says, (as I said to you that last night,) "I *can't* feel," as an excuse for holding on to it. I found as soon as I was *willing* to "go home," as you called it, the *road* was plain enough."

"Were you hindered *long* with that want of feeling?"

"No; I never thought of it till that night. It came upon me like a flash; and then, just as I was thinking it was a good reason in my favor, you dashed it all into shivers."

"And can you 'feel' now?"

"Oh, yes; I have no trouble about that. I find, if a poor creature will turn to God, in the name of Jesus, he will learn to *feel* as he never felt before.

Sinners, not willing to give up the world, and wanting an excuse for their irreligion, exclaim, "*I can't feel.*"

Willing to be Lost.

I RECEIVED a letter from an individual in a neighboring State, an entire stranger to me. Omitting some names and dates, I here give some liberal extracts from it. It appears to me, that the religious experience which the letter describes, is one of the best possible refutations of the strange theological opinion to which it refers; and, perhaps, desponding affections in other people may receive some solace by knowing something of the experience of my correspondent, as recorded in the Letter.

* * * * * *

"SIR,

"I am troubled and perplexed, in reference to my spiritual state. Will you allow me to throw off all restraint, forgetting for the time that I am a stranger? With a grateful heart I tell you my dear parents were very godly persons, and we, their children, were educated most religiously. My blessed father, now gone to heaven, was a great admirer of Dr. Hopkins and Dr. Emmons. The great doctrines they inculcated were among the first lessons I learned on religious subjects; but truly, sir, I could not comprehend them, and the views they gave me of God, were truly undesirable. As I knew nothing about the filial love which glowed in the breast of my father, the ideas I entertained of my Creator filled me with dread, and I grew up *afraid* of this holy sovereign. After my marriage, I attended upon the ministry of one who called himself a Hopkinsian; but surely Dr. Hopkins would never have acknowledged him as a disciple. He used to tell me I must be willing to 'be led into sin, if the glory of God required it;' that I must 'go down to the potter's house,' and there become *willing* to see God *form* me into a 'vessel of wrath,' if he saw it most for His glory to do so. Well, as such doctrines were furnished me as 'the sincere milk of the Word,' I need not tell you I could not 'grow thereby.'

"In the year 18—, I indulged a faint hope that my heart was renewed; but so weak was my faith, that my days were divided between hope and *fear*. I really loved the society of devout, heavenly-minded Christians. I saw myself a vile sinner, despaired of making myself any better, and was brought to see that all I could do was to give my whole self to Jesus in all my *sinfulness*. This I did over and over again; but to you I confess, I never, never felt *willing* to go to perdition, though I saw God would be *just* in sending me there. But, oh sir, I shrunk from justice, and cried for mercy, mercy. Well, from that time to the present, (more than twenty years,) I have known nothing like the 'assurance of hope.' Though I am as certain that I love the prosperity of the Redeemer's kingdom, as I am of my own existence; yet *fear* so predominates in my heart, that I am at times ready to give up all hope of my adoption. Let me give you a single instance out of a thousand. If seated in the house of God, listening with delight and rapt attention to the preached word, joining with all my heart in the prayers and praises of that sacred place, and feeling in my very soul that to go—

> 'Where congregations ne'er break up
> And Sabbaths never end,'

is the heaven I desire; if my ear catches the sound of distant *thunder*, all is over with me,—my mind is filled with painful forebodings, and lines like the following are darted through it:—

> 'Quite weary is my patience grown,
> And bids my fury go,
> Swift as the lightning it shall pass,
> And be as fatal too.'

Trembling, sick, unable to sit up,—vomiting generally follows. Now the dreadful question comes, is not 'my house founded on the sand?' It is not *dying* that I fear so much, but the thought of dying *unprepared.* I feel no heart-rising against God, His love, or His government, but *heart-sinking* fear.

"Now do we not read, 'great peace have they who love thy Law,—perfect love casteth out fear,—the Lord will keep him in perfect peace whose mind is stayed on Him?' Here now is my trouble. *Afraid* of a holy, *righteous* God; sensible I deserve His anger, I sink beneath the *fear* of it. The other day I was meditating on my strange state of mind, and I thought I would go again, as the Hymn says:—

I'll go to Jesus, though my sins
Have like a mountain rose;
I know his courts, I'll enter in,
Whatever may oppose.'

When I came to the verse,—

'Perhaps, he will admit my plea,
Perhaps, will hear my prayer;'

the word, *perhaps*, troubled me. I consulted a book, in which the author has explained that *perhaps.* He says, 'there is no perhaps in the matter. God says there is none. "Hear, and your soul shall live." He says, 'the *Hymn* is right; because it represents what a sinner feels when he is resolving to go to Christ. But let him fling his "*perhaps*" to the winds; the sceptre of Immanuel shall be shivered into pieces, the throne of the Redeemer Jehovah shall sink, sooner than such a sinner perish.' This was enough for my poor heart. All I could do was to weep, and read, and weep again. It seemed to me that if I had ten thousand souls to save, and each as sinful as I felt mine to be, I would lay them all into the arms of Jesus, and not doubt about their acceptance. I thought I could never feel depressed again with fear. Those blessed words were so precious, my heart rested on the ability and *willingness* of Jesus to save me.

"But alas! sir, we have been visited with a tempest since that time, and again my poor house has fallen! Oh! tell me, if I cannot bear a *little storm*, how am I to view the terrors of the last great day? In all the simplicity of a child I ask you, dear sir, what I shall do? I cannot go to the world of despair. But if, after all, I must receive the merited reward of my sins, I will have *nothing* to do with the wicked men in that dreadful place, nor can I ever blaspheme the name of Jehovah Jesus."

* * * * *

"The lines have fallen unto me in pleasant places; I have a goodly heritage. God has given me a good, kind, faithful shepherd, whose ministrations I have enjoyed seven years. He is an excellent man. We all love him much. But for some reason he will not let me tell him of my fears, or, at least, he is pleased to treat them so lightly, that I do not often say much to him on the subject. He is a man of great energy, was never afraid of anything, and appears ever prepared for death, however sudden it may come. But his views on some points are very different from Dr. Emmons."

* * * * *
* * *

Such was the letter. I thought it furnished melancholy proof of the unnecessary perplexity and torment of spirit, which false theological principles will sometimes produce. This person was evidently annoyed, plagued, tormented for years, by the influence of an extravagant doctrine. The same has happened to others. An eminent clergyman, to whom I read that letter in my study, said to me, "Change the names and the dates, and that case is precisely my own."

The minister, who taught the doctrine, and insisted upon it with so much plainness and strength, probably went far beyond anything which Hopkins or Emmons would have said, though he deemed himself one of their disciples in theology. This is common to all *followers of men:* the scholar becomes worse than the master.

It is often difficult indeed to know how to deal with the troubles of mind which result from strange doctrines. The doctrine *will* come up before the heart which it has once tormented, and will stand as a wall of adamant, to keep from the heart that hope which otherwise the gospel would infuse into it. Or, if the strange doctrine is of an opposite character, and has led to a false hope, it will be very apt to come back again to do its old mischief, after the delusive hope has once been dissipated by the truth. And in the case of such doctrines and despondencies as this letter mentions; it is not easy for us to determine whether we shall reason or ridicule. A woman, who for a long time had been serious, perplexed and distressed, but who never had attained any hope in Christ, once went to her minister, the Rev. Dr. S——, of H——, and told him, that she now believed she had become a Christian.

"What makes you think so, Madam?"

"Because," said she, "I am now willing to be damned. I have tried a long time to come to such a state of mind, and never have succeeded; but *now*, I am willing to be damned, if God pleases to cast me off."

"Well, Madam," said the Doctor coolly, "if *you* are willing to be damned, and *God* is willing you should be, I don't know as I ought to have any objections." Probably this ridicule was quite as effective to correct a strange notion, as any didactic instruction could have been. However this may have been, to the above letter I returned the following answer:—

"MY DEAR FRIEND,—

"It is rather an awkward business to write a letter, when you do not know whether it is a man or a woman to whom you are writing. But I am placed just in that position. Your initials do not indicate your sex.

"The only thing, beyond the ordinary range of strictly religious matter, which (as I judge from your letter), you have any special need that I should write to you, is a few words to call your attention to *the influences of physical condition upon religious sensibilities.* 'Thunder' will sometimes kill goslings, turn milk sour, and spoil the tanner's calf-skins, when they are at a particular point in the process of being manufactured into leather. And it is not a miracle, if 'thunder' sometimes makes you sick. Though it may be a very humiliating idea to us, that we are sometimes under the influence of external physical causes in the sacred sensibilities of our religion, yet it is true. The east wind has shaken many a religious hope. We have not yet 'spiritual bodies' superior to the power of matter's contact, and we are greatly liable to have our comforts and griefs of mind swayed by the elements, especially when a timid or peculiarly sensitive soul is connected with a body not made of iron. The outward things of nature, such as 'storms,' and 'thunder,' and 'waters,' which you mention (or even our imagination at work upon them), may have upon us a more powerful effect than our intellectual or spiritual pride is willing to confess. Women more than men are liable to this, (and from your hand-writing, I *suppose* you to be a woman.)

"So far as your religious impressions have been moulded by Hopkins or Emmons, you may be unfortunate; but I see nothing in your case which is very uncommon, or which need greatly perplex you.

* * * * *

"It seems you have resort to Hopkins and Emmons, and to another book which you mention. All this may be very well, but you are quite too much *affected* by a *speculative spirit.* Be a child: not a philosopher, but a child: not a servant, but a child: not an angel, but a child,—just a *humble child.*

"Let me lift the curtain a little, and give you a glimpse of what lies within; when I say that *speculation* never humbles *spiritual pride.* You are startled. I do not wonder at it, though the words are not '*thunder.*' But you may be assured there is in the suggestion more truth than poetry or politeness.

"I hope you are a Christian; but a little more simplicity would not hurt you, and a little less pride would do you good."

* * * * *

* * *

Not many days had elapsed before I received

from my unknown correspondent the following letter:—

*   *   *   *   *

"You have taught me a lesson I shall not soon forget. Oh! sir, you *have* 'lifted the curtain.' I did 'not know what manner of spirit I was of.' You have read me rightly,—'a little more simplicity would not harm you, a little less pride would do you good.' Here is truth condensed. I really think I feel the force of it as keenly as you *meant* I should. The night I received your most welcome letter I had little to do with sleep, and the only prayer I could utter was, 'God be merciful to me a sinner.' Sir, I *thank* you, *sincerely* thank you for turning my eyes in the *right* direction. Why did I not know my heart better? 'Who can understand his errors? Cleanse thou me from secret faults.'

'Show me my sins, and how to mourn
My guilt before thy face.'

"In regard to my leaving you in the dark in respect to myself, I am much mortified, and can only say it was inexcusable carelessness. As I sat down to write, I felt as though I was talking to one whom I knew personally. * * * I beg you to forgive me, and be assured I shall be more careful in future. I feel so much obliged to you for writing, and especially for your *faithfulness*, that I am not sorry for obtruding my unworthy self upon your notice, however much mortification it has occasioned me. * * * Oh, sir, you *have done me good.*" * * *

To this I returned the following answer:—

"My Dear Madam,—

"I have just received your last letter, and seize a moment to respond to it. I am greatly rejoiced, if my letter afforded you profit or satisfaction; but I am quite sorry it kept you awake. That condition of nervous excitability, which forbids your sleeping, or forbids your loving 'thunder,' is not to be fostered or indulged. It will do your religion (if you have any,) no good; and it certainly will not lead you to it, if you are still an unbeliever. Perhaps you have not sufficiently considered, that *nerves* are poor counsellors. You would do well not to ask their advice. You had better ask Paul, or David, or Jeremiah even, if you must have the liberty to utter 'Lamentations.' And more: I am not willing to speak evil of anybody, but I can assure you, that these same creatures, called *nerves*, are the greatest liars in the country. Do not believe them, when they tell you that you are a Christian, or when they tell you that you are a reprobate. They will tell lies on both sides, and they don't care which. I did hope that you would be able to perceive their mischief, by what I said to you about the goslings and sour milk, and calf-skins. But you have not mentioned it in your letter. What I mean is simply this: that 'thunder' has an inexplicable effect upon some such things, with which religion has nothing to do; and if it has an inexplicable effect upon *you*, you need not link that effect with your religion: your sickness is caused by the 'thunder,' not by your depravity. 'Thunder,' winds, storms, 'waters,' may assail your timid nerves, and set them again at their old work of lies; but your *religion* has nothing at all to do with the matter. If old Elijah were alive, he could tell you something about this.

"You speak of seeing me, but you 'fear the water.' I should be happy to see you, madam, but I am in duty bound to tell you that you would be greatly disappointed. You might be benefited, indeed, but the *way* of the benefit would be very different from your anticipation. I know a man, who once travelled more than a thousand miles for the purpose of seeing a minister, whom he believed to be able to give him some light on the subject of personal religion, and all the good he received from him was just nothing at all; and yet this was the best possible good, for the experiment *convinced him fully that his help was not in man.*

'Let me lift the curtain a little farther. Faith,

you know, is the way of salvation,—is an essential in every part of religion. Sometimes we are *drawn* to faith, and sometimes our miserable hearts must be *driven* to it. Now, though I believe you are an amiable woman, (and none *too* amiable after all, *at times*,) yet somehow or other you are not easy to be drawn,—you must be driven. And your temptations, and fears, and plans, and efforts, every one of them, just tend to draw you away from the exercise of a naked, simple faith in God,—even many a one of your prayers has had the same effect, because you trusted the *praying* to do you good, instead of trusting God's answer to do you good. And for the proof of this, I call upon your own recollections, extending over years of fear and hope.

"One thing more. There is an *order* in the snares and temptations of the devil. He has three classes of temptations. You have got beyond the first, and perhaps the second; but you are not safe from the third. Yea, you are very much exposed to it, and the more so, probably, because you do not know or even suspect what it is.

"*First.* Satan employs *the world*,—just aims to keep sinners satisfied to love earthly things, and pursue them. If he cannot do that,—if they cannot be made to live on without any kind of religion, —hunting for riches, honor, pleasure, ease, or some such thing, then,—

"*Second*, Satan aims to lead them into a *false religion*, into deception, into some delusion, which shall lull them into a false peace to their ruin. (You have been quite sufficiently aware of this,—indeed you have feared it too much.) But if he cannot do this,—if they have too much knowledge of the Bible, and too much of the influences of the Holy Spirit to be led into a false hope, then the old liar shifts his ground; and,—

"*Third*, aims to drive them *to despair*. This is his last effort, and, I do believe, the most devilish one of all. It is most like him, for it is at once the *most false* and *most miserable*.

"But I must stop. 'Satan hath desired to have you, that he may sift you as wheat;' but I trust the Master hath 'prayed for you, that your faith fail not.'

"I want you to think of these three classes of temptations, and to oppose *faith* to each one of them. Just fling your faith into the face of the devil, however he may come to you. Especially, my dear friend, think of this third and last device of the adversary, which you have commonly too much overlooked, and let faith triumph over despair."

* * * * *

* * *

The following is her reply:—

"How shall I sufficiently thank you, dear sir, for your last kind letter? I cannot make you know how deeply your condescension is felt and appreciated. You will allow me now to tell you all my heart—I mean the little part of it that I know.

"You say 'nerves are poor counsellors,' and that 'they are the greatest liars in the country.' Now it has been *my* way to set down all the mischief you ascribe to *nerves*, to a *wicked heart.* Here I have found much trouble; but you have in a measure convinced me that I have got to learn *how* to use the shield of faith. Oh, sir, my eyes are open. Now I see that 'simple, naked faith in God' is what I need; and, if I am not wholly deceived, my resolution is taken. I will give Satan the lie, and believe God. He has said, 'come unto me,' and 'whosoever cometh I will in nowise cast out.' Now I will not be driven from a firm, practical belief of this *blessed, faithful* promise. This doubting, half dead, half alive way of living, is to be abandoned at once and forever. Not in my own strength may I attempt this; but lifting a tearful, trusting eye to Jesus, I will strive to maintain a 'cheerful courage,' and God helping me, I need never yield to one of either 'class of temptations,' employed by the great adversary. But if my sinful heart will sink in fear and dismay, amidst all the great and precious promises made by Him who is unchanging truth, then I will just bring this wicked heart the sooner to Jesus, that he may renew and sanctify it.

"How well I know what you mean when you tell me that 'all my plans and efforts, every one of them, just tend to drive me away from the exercise of a naked, simple faith in God—even many a one of your prayers has had the same effect.' Oh, I plead guilty.

* * * * *

"I do not know how it is, but you seem to know me at this distance better than I know myself. * * When I read in your last letter, 'and none too amiable after all, at times,' I laughed and cried both.

* * * * *

"The last time I wrote you my heart was too full to say what I wanted to. Indeed I did not quite know what you meant, by saying what you did in regard to the effect of 'thunder' on 'goslings, milk, and the tanner's work.' The fact is, I was so taken up, or rather 'cast down' by the closing part of your letter, that I did not think much about this. Yes, dear sir, I was truly 'cast down but not destroyed.' You did not intend I should be; but now I will just tell you the whole truth of the matter. I felt distressed, and the question I wanted you to answer was this: can there be any filial love in the heart that is so *full* of *slavish fear?* Well, I did cherish a secret hope that you would, in your kindness, send me a little soothing *salve*, but behold a *probe!* Oh, you pierced the festering wound, and I bless the

Lord for all you said. Your words, as you say, were not 'thunder;' no, no; they were something very different from mere *sound.* You have been so faithful to me, I want words to tell you how much I thank you for it all."

* * * * *
* * *

This letter was answered, and I afterwards received the following reply:—

* * * "But now let me tell you how much good you have done my poor soul. For *long years*, my time was spent betwixt hope and fear, fear greatly predominating. When I united with the church, instead of feeling 'joyful,' I was just able to stand on this precious promise, 'my grace is sufficient for thee.' Often I was led to see my sinfulness in such a light as to *hide* the Saviour from my view. Sometimes I was afraid to pray, lest I should be struck *dead* in the act. Sometimes I could look only at the *power* and the *justice* of God, and could see in Him only the stern law-giver; and, feeling a deep sense of my *guilt*, I have *trembled* where I ought to have *loved.* But since I read * * * * and your letters, especially the *second*, I have been made to see that 'faith is,' indeed, 'everything.' Now I can look to Jesus; and I feel so happy in realizing that he is *all* I need. I am so sinful, but He is so

holy, He is *worthy*, He has made *all* the sacrifice the broken, righteous law demanded; and now, as I am a *sinner lost*, I am the one for whom He died, the one He came to seek and to save. All I *can* do is just to *believe*.

"Hitherto I have read the Bible, especially the promises, for somebody else. I could apply the *greatest* of them in a most comfortable manner, to Christians about me, but feared to apply one of them fully to myself, lest I should be lost at last! But now I find much enjoyment often in studying the character of God the Father, in the face of Jesus Christ. Did He not say, 'he that hath seen *me* hath seen the Father'? Now I do so love to look at God in Christ my Redeemer. Oh, why did I so long refuse to trust *alone* in Jesus? I have indeed been a 'fool, and slow of heart to believe.' Nor do I yet know much about it, though I do feel encouraged to persevere in withstanding every temptation to 'despair.' For now I say to Satan, if I am a sinner, utterly lost, and have no hope of making my heart any better, then I must go to an Almighty Saviour, even to Him 'who is able to save to the *uttermost*.' Think of this word *uttermost*. I will believe God. I will love the Saviour, whom I would embrace in the arms of *faith*. He is all my hope. For a little while at a time, I can *let go* every cord of self-dependence, and just *fall* into the arms, the strong arms of Jesus, and there would I ever lie. Sometimes I do so want to go to heaven, that I may once feel just as sorry for sin as I want to feel, and love the Saviour as much as I ought. And will a whole *eternity* be long enough to praise Him? to tell the saints and angels how *much* I owe to Him, who washed me in His own blood? Sometimes I love to look forward to the time when all the redeemed will be gathered *home*, and hope to meet you there, and will tell you, as we sit on some 'green and flowery mount,' all the Saviour hath done for my sinful soul.

* * * * *

"I will not close this letter without telling you, the last thunder shower we had I did not feel *half* so much afraid as usual. I kept thinking all the time, I will give my body and my soul to Jesus. I will 'put that *cloud*,' *all* of it 'into *his hand*.' He can *hold* the *lightning*, and he can and will 'direct it, under the whole heaven.' But now you have put *another* comfort into my heart: you say, 'learn to hear in the thunder the voice of your own Father—a voice not threatening to *you*, but to your *foes*."

* * * * *

* * *

I answered this letter also, and in a few days I was gratified with the reception of the following sentences in her answer:—

* * * "I applied to you for aid in reference to *reconciliation* to God. And now, the way of salvation by *faith in Jesus Christ*, looks so much plainer than it *ever* did before, I feel sometimes as if I could not ever let go the thought, that Christ *alone* is the way. 'I am the way.' Oh, my Saviour, take me.

"You do not know how sinful a heart I have yet. *I* do not know. But Jesus knows just how much I need his pardoning love,—how much grace I need to keep me from falling into sin and destruction. I look back, and try to think what I have been doing to please *Satan* and grieve my Redeemer, while in the dark and cold speculations arising from the perusal of such sermons as Dr. Emmons' 'Pharaoh' sermon, 'for in very deed for this cause have I raised thee up.'

"But I turn away now, and just try to 'be a *child*,' not a servant, but a child: not a philosopher, but a child,—just a humble child."

* * * * * *
* * *

Extravagant theological opinions are apt to be adopted by those very persons to whom they are most unappropriate and most misguiding. This woman was an example. She was the last woman in the world to have any need of the stern theology of Dr. Hopkins and Dr. Emmons, (whom she perhaps misunderstood.) By natural disposition she was greatly inclined to fear; and being of delicate sensibilities, nervous, imaginative, poetical, and peculiarly affectionate, the severities of her adopted theology were the last things to profit her. They made her miserable only. They did not reach her heart. The 'kindness and love' of the gospel were the very things for her. Her heart, her affectionate heart, was (if I may say so), precisely adapted to them. This was her experience afterwards. She yielded to *love* what she never yielded to *terror*,—she was *drawn* where she could not be *driven*,—*faith* accomplished for her what *fear* could not accomplish,—she found simplicity better than speculation; and she then exchanged perplexity and despondency, for the calmness of trust and the sunshine of hope. The *Law* was before her mind when she tried to be "willing to be lost." No wonder that she despaired. She received relief, not by directing her eye downwards into that abyss of midnight, her own dark heart; but by being brought to look away to Christ and his glorious grace. Christ is light. Faith is the eye that sees Him. Christ would have sinners willing to be saved. False theology, despondency, and the Devil, would have them willing to be damned.

The Bird of Paradise.

Among my parishioners, there was a poor woman who had once seen better days. She had moved in the most respectable society, the wife of a man of wealth, who formerly held an important official station in the state, but who was now reduced to poverty; and, trembling with the weight of three score years and ten, had greatly lost the powers of his mind. She was many years younger than her husband. Neither of them was a follower of Christ. Indeed, after their early years, they had never paid anything more than a formal and fashionable attention to even the outward duties of religion. For years after their marriage, they lived in splendor; and when his extravagance had squandered his fortune, they were under the necessity of occupying the crazy old house where I first became acquainted with them. Through the benevolence of some wealthy relations, who were very kind to them, their temporal necessities were so provided for, that they did not suffer.

Earnestly I strove to interest their minds in the

subject of religion. The old man appeared to me to be as stupid as any sinner can be; and he remained so, I believe, to the day of his death,—a victim, as I thought, of the foolish love of mere earthly ostentation and pleasure. Not so, his far younger wife. She listened to me with attention, and apparent interest, as I spread the subject of religion before her mind, on my first visit to her house; and when I called upon her again, a month afterwards, I found she had commenced reading her Bible with evident anxiety and prayer. The questions she asked me, and her tearful attention to my answers, clearly indicated the interest she felt in this great subject, which, she said, was "almost new" to her thoughts; for, she had "scarcely given a thought to it in twenty years." Said she, "Pleasure occupied my mind at first, and after my husband's failure, it was all I could think of, to contrive how we should live."

She bore her reverses with commendable fortitude,—labored hard to support herself and her husband, kept her little old cottage a pattern of neatness, and on the whole she won the respect of the few neighbors that knew her. There was nothing about her, as a woman or as an inquiring sinner, which appeared to me uncommon or peculiar. There was, indeed, as I thought, some little manifestation of a nervous excitability, when she mentioned to me her wicked heart, her struggles in prayer, and her despondency about "ever gaining the forgiveness of God;" but this I never should have thought of again, had it not been for what occurred afterwards.

About a week after I had seen and conversed with her at her house, not for the first or second time, and when I began to hope that she was 'not far from the kingdom of God,' she called upon me. She came to tell me of her hope in Christ, and how happy she was now, in the belief that God had forgiven and accepted her. She trusted, as she said, that God had "heard her prayers, and had sent her an answer of peace."

By way of examining her state of mind, in order to know what to say to her, I asked her a few questions, which she answered in a manner quite satisfactory to me. I found in her nothing to make me distrust her,—indeed nothing but the contrary, till I asked her,—

"How long have you had this hope and 'this delightful happiness,' which you mention?"

"Since last Thursday night," was her reply. (It was now Tuesday.)

"What *then* led you to believe that God had 'heard your prayer, and sent you an answer of peace?'"

"It was what I saw," said she, with some little hesitation, as if reluctant to answer.

"What did you see?"

"It was," said she, hesitating,—"it was a great light," and she spake it solemnly, and with evident sincerity, but some excitement.

"Indeed!" said I. "And where did you see it?"

"In my room."

"What was it?—what caused it?"

"I don't know what it was, but it was *wonderful!* I shall never forget it."

"Did it frighten you?"

"Oh no, not at all."

"Was it moonshine?"

"No, not at all like it."

"Did it shine in at the window? or through a crack?"

"Neither; it was just in the room."

"What did it look like?"

"It was very wonderful, the sweetest light I ever saw. It was brighter than any sunshine; but it was so mild and soft that it did not dazzle the eyes. It was *perfectly* beautiful—most enchanting."

"Well now, Mrs. L——, just tell me all about it; I want to know how that was, the time, and all about it."

Seeming to arrange her thoughts, she replied,—

"I had been sitting up a long time after Mr. L—— went to bed, reading my Bible and trying to pray, and I almost despaired of mercy, because my heart was so wicked and obstinate. I felt as if I *could not* go to bed that night, without some proof that God would have mercy upon me. I was terrified with the thought of his wrath, but I felt that I deserved it all. Finally I went to bed. I had been lying in bed about half an hour thinking of my condition, and all at once, the most beautiful light I ever saw shined all over the room. It was a strange kind of light; brighter than day, brighter than any sunshine; but a great deal more beautiful and sweet. It was mild and so soothing, it filled me with perfect peace, a kind of sweet ecstacy, like a delightful dream. Then, in an instant, as I was thinking how delightful it was, there appeared the most beautiful creature that I ever saw. I was perfectly enchanted and carried away with the beauty of it, its colors were so sweet and mingled, and its form so graceful. It was a bird. He had a rainbow in his bill, and a crown of glittering, soft-shining gold upon his head; he was resting on a globe of the softest blue, the most enchanting color that ever was. I never before conceived of anything so beautiful. His color, and his figure, and the crown of shining gold upon his head, the rainbow he held in his bill, and the blue globe he stood on, and the bright sweet light which filled the room, were all of them more beautiful and lovely than anything I ever thought of before. I was amazed and perfectly happy. '*What is it?*' says I, 'what *is* it?' 'Why it is the bird of Paradise,' says I. 'My precious Father has sent it to me from heaven, I will not despair any longer.' Then, I thought how happy I am; God has heard me and had mercy upon me. I have been perfectly happy ever since."

She appeared to be in an ecstacy of delight.

"What makes you so happy?"

"Because, I think God has forgiven me, and because *now* I love Him and trust Him."

"How do you feel about *sin?*"

"Oh, I hate it. It displeases God, and separates me from Him."

"What do you think of Christ?"

"He is a precious Saviour. I love Him and trust in Him."

"For *what* do you trust Him?"

"For everything—for pardon, and peace, and heaven."

"Do you think you are holy now?

"No; I know that I sin every hour. But God is gracious to me and fills me with joy."

"Do you rejoice because you are so good?"

"No; I rejoice because God has been so good to me."

"What have you done to gain his favor."

"*I* have done *nothing* only turn to Him."

"Did you turn to Him of yourself?"

"No; I *tried*, but my heart would not yield, and I prayed for the Holy Spirit."

"How do you expect to be saved?"

"By the *mercy of God*, through my Saviour."

"How do you know He is *your* Saviour?"

"Because I trust in Him, and He has promised to save all that come unto Him."

"Have you any *doubt* about your forgiveness?"

"No, sir, not much,—none that troubles me. I know my heart is deceitful; but I trust only in Christ, and then I am safe."

"Do you think the appearance which you saw on Thursday night, was something sent by God?"

"Yes, I suppose it was."

"How do you know but the devil sent it?"

"I never thought it *could* come from anything but God."

"For what purpose do you think He sent it?"

"To give me peace."

"What *reason* have you to think it was sent to assure you of God's favor?"

"I don't know what reason I have to think so, only I was made so happy."

"Does the Bible teach you that God gives such visions as an evidence of His favor?"

"I think not."

"Do you think it was a miracle?"

"I don't know. I thought God sent it."

"What o'clock was it when you saw the light?"

"About one o'clock, I should think."

"Was the moon up?

"No, it had gone down about an hour before."

"What makes you think it was one o'clock?"

"Because it was ten when Mr. L—— went to bed. Then I sat up a long time,—I should think more than two hours, reading and praying, and thinking about my danger of being lost; and I had been in bed some time,—I cannot tell exactly how long—half an hour perhaps."

"Had you been asleep?"

"No, I *think* not."

"Were you asleep when you saw it?"

"Oh no; I was as much awake as I am now."

"Did you see the light and the bird with your natural *eyes*, the same as you see me now?"

"Yes."

"Where were they?"

"In my room."

"Did Mr. L—— see them?"

"No, he was asleep."

"If he had been awake, do you think *his eyes* would have seen them?"

"Certainly, I suppose so."

"Why didn't you wake him?—is no he fond of birds?"

"I don't know but he is fond of birds," said she,

with a very doubtful look, "but I never thought of waking him."

"Have you got a canary-bird?"

"No, sir," said she, as if doubtful of my meaning.

"Did you ever see a bird of Paradise?"

"No, sir, not alive. I have seen stuffed ones."

"Which are the prettiest,—the stuffed ones or the one you saw that night?"

She cast her eyes down, with a look of mingled sadness and confusion, evidently thinking by this time that I meant to ridicule her vision; but she replied, mildly and solemnly,—

"Nothing on earth can be compared with what I saw that night."

"Did the bird sing any?"

"No, sir."

"That is a pity. If he had only sung, then you would have had *a song* of Paradise. What became of the bird?"

"It went away."

"Why didn't you catch it and cage it? It would have brought a good price in Boston. Did it fly out of the window?"

"I said it went away; I mean by that, that the light and all I saw vanished away, and I saw them no more."

"How long did they stay before they vanished?"

"Only a few minutes."

"What did you do when they were gone?"

"I lay for a long time thinking about it, and feeling delighted and grateful to God."

"Grateful for the canary bird and the rainbow? Do you mean *that?*"

"No sir, not that so much; but grateful for God's great love to me, to pardon so unworthy a sinner."

"Did the bird tell you God had pardoned you?"

"No sir."

"What made you think he had?"

"What I saw, and my own happy feelings."

"What makes you happy?"

"Because I love God and trust in Christ."

"Would you have loved God, if you had not seen the bird?"

"I don't know; I hope so."

"When did you begin to feel so happy?"

"Thursday night."

"Just when you saw the bird, was it?"

"Yes sir."

"It is a great pity you did not catch that bird. If the sight of him is so effectual, we could carry him around here among impenitent sinners; and, as soon as they saw him, one after another, they would become happy, excellent Christians, and your bird would be worth more to convert sinners than forty ministers like me. Do you expect to see that bird again?"

"No, I have no such expectation."

"Now, Mrs. L——, do you feel sure all that was not *a dream?*"

"It was no dream," said she, seriously. "I was awake. Don't you think *I saw* that light, sir?" said she with an imploring look.

"No, madam; I don't believe you saw any such thing. I believe *you think* you saw it; but I believe it was all in your own imagination, and nowhere else."

She shook her head very emphatically, as if fixed in the opposite opinion.

"Mrs. L——," said I, "do you ever drink wine, or any stimulating drink?"

"No sir; not at all."

"Do you ever take opium or laudanum?"

"Not unless the doctor orders it when I am sick."

"Had you taken anything that night?"

"No; nothing but our tea."

"Do you drink *strong* tea?"

"No sir; I don't like it."

"Are you a nervous woman?"

"At times, I think I am."

"Were you nervous that night?"

"I was not sensible of being so. I was weary, and I felt very *sad.* I was quite excited at times before I went to bed, thinking of eternity to come."

"Mrs. L——, can you remember particularly what

you were thinking about that evening, just before you retired to rest? See if you can recollect, and tell me exactly what was in your thoughts just before you lay down."

After a considerable pause she replied,—

"I had been thinking and praying a long time, about my sins and my wicked, miserable heart; and I tried to give up all into the hands of Christ, as you had so often told me I must. I thought I did, and then I wondered that God did not give me peace. And afterwards I thought how happy I should be, if God would give me a new heart; and then I wondered how I should know it if He did."

"You thought," said I, "how *happy* you should be, if God would give you a new heart; and then you *wondered* how you should know it if He did. But you did not think of seeing a bird, or a rainbow?"

She opened her lips as if to answer, but cast her eyes downwards, and said nothing. A slight flush came over her cheek, but her look was that of sorrow, not of resentment.

Said I: "Mrs. L.——, I am sorry to trouble you with so many questions, and I do not wish to afflict you. Many things you say to me would almost convince me that you really had peace with God, if these things were not so mixed up with that vision which seems to have been the origin of your joy, and which *I know* was only a dream, or the work of your own imagination, while you were half asleep and half awake. If you rely, in the least, upon that vision, that miracle, as an evidence of your pardon; you rely on a mere fancy, a mere nothing. It is no evidence at all. It is just as much a proof that you will be lost, as that you will be saved. At best, your vision was nothing but a fancy, an imagination, coming from your nervousness, induced by the weariness of your brain when you lay down. I can account for your vision. You have just given me the clue. You had just been thinking 'how happy you should be,' if God accepted you; and you had been 'wondering how you should know it.' With these two ideas you went to bed,—one idea of great *happiness*, and the other of some wonderful thing, (you knew not what,) to lead you to that happiness. Then, in a state betwixt sleeping and waking, (when the imagination is most busy, and the reason and will lie most still,) your imagination just wrought out the *expected wonder*, to teach you something, (or convince you,) and the *expected happiness*, which you so eagerly longed for. This accounts for all you *thought* you beheld. Your eyes saw nothing. As soon as your astonishment and ecstasy had so fully waked you up, that the spell of your imagination was broken, and your eyes really began *to see;* your vision vanished. This is the truth of the whole matter, probably. God had no more to do with your light, your rainbow, and your new-fashioned canary-bird, than the devil had.

"Now, Mrs. L.——, I have only one thing more to ask you; but I am not certain that I can make myself understood. I will try. You know we speak of *remembering* things. We *remember*, because something made an impression on our mind sometime before—a thing capable of being remembered. We recollect the impression: that is remembering. Realities make an impression, and dreams make an impression also. And we remember *both*. But when we remember things that really took place, we have to recall the impression left on our mind *by facts*,—and when we remember dreams, we recall the impression left on our mind by *imaginations* only. Now, there is a difference betwixt the impression left on our mind by real occurrences, and the impression left on our mind by imaginations only, or by a dream; such a difference, that we are not very apt to mistake a dream for something that really took place. We can remember both, but they are not just alike. The impression of *a dream* is not exactly like the impression made by something when we were *awake*, though it may be very plain and deep. But there is a difference betwixt the impressions, and also betwixt the rememberings. Don't you think so?"

"Yes, I know there is."

"Very well. Now I want you to *remember* very carefully what you saw, Thursday night; and tell me whether the impression left on your mind then is *most like* the impression left by a dream, or most like the impression left by something when you were awake. And tell me whether your act of remembering most remembles the act of remembering a dream, or most resembles the act of remembering what took place when you were awake. Do you understand me?"

"Yes sir, perfectly."

"Very well. Now carefully consider the thing. Take time to think of it. Recollect what you saw Thursday night; and tell me whether your impression and recollection of it most resemble the impression and recollection of a dream, or something *not* a dream."

She sat in silence for two or three minutes, closed her eyes as if absorbed in thought, then rose and looked studiously out at the window, then sat down and closed her eyes for some two or three minutes more.

"Indeed, sir," said she, "I am at a loss. That *does seem* more like a dream than like a real thing. But I was awake. My eyes were open. I don't remember waking up."

Said I, "I don't wish you to *reason*, or *argue*, or *decide* anything about it, whether you were asleep or awake. I only wish you to tell me as you remember that night, whether your impression resembles most the impression of a dream, or an impression made when you were awake."

After a pause, she replied slowly and thoughtfully,—

"It is just like a dream; but I was awake, for my eyes were open."

"Very well, madam, I will not trouble you any more. If you want to know what *religion* is, ask your Bible, don't ask night birds, or night rainbows."

I saw this woman afterwards and conversed with her often. Had it not been for her vision, and the use she made of it, she would have appeared to me to be a humble child of God. But I had no confidence in her conversion.

Some few months after this, she proposed to unite with the church. I discouraged her. But after she had lived about a year as a pious woman, so far as I could discover, she was, with much hesitation, received as a communicant; and I knew her for some years afterwards, presenting satisfactory evidence of being a true Christian. In one of the last interviews I had with her, she told me she had become convinced that "the strange sights she saw on that Thursday night, existed only in her own fancy."

When I asked what had convinced her, she replied, "I have been sick since then two or three times; and when I was sick and very nervous, I had some other strange sights which I know were fancies, though they seemed as *real* as that one did."

"Perhaps they were *not* fancies."

"Yes, they were sir."

"How do you know?"

"Because, as soon as I went to examine into them they were gone. When I got up from the bed there was nothing there."

"Were you always in bed when you saw them?"

"Yes."

"What made you get up to examine?"

"Because I remembered what you said about the bird of Paradise, as I called it, and I was determined to know what these things were."

"But you could not catch them."

"No; as soon as I stirred and got out of bed the charm was broken."

"What were these things you call a charm?"

"Various things, such as splendid colors, beautiful animals, ladies dressed with great taste and in very rich, gay dresses, and moving like angels."

"Are you asleep when these things appear to you?"

"No, not at all; I am awake and thinking."

"What do you think they are?"

"I think they are nothing. But when I have been agitated, and become nervous and tired, after I get a little calmed down, and feel quiet and happy, these beautiful things seem to be before my eyes."

"Do you see them when your eyes are open?"

"Yes, sometimes, when the room is dark."

"Very well, madam, you have got right now."

"I wish," said she, "you would not say anything about that bird of Paradise, and the blue globe I told you about at first. I was deceived. I know they had nothing to do with religion, and I do not rely upon them at all as any witness that God has given me a new heart."

The religious treatment of persons of strong imagination and weak nerves, is one of the most delicate and difficult duties. The imagination has an extent of power over both the intellect and the body itself, of which few persons are suitably aware. The voices which are said to be heard by those religiously affected, the sights which are seen, the instances of falling down speechless and without power to move, the sudden cures of infirmity, said to be effected by the prayer of faith, the deaths which have occurred just as the persons themselves foretold, and for which they made all their temporal arrangements,—all such things are to be attributed to the power of the imagination and excited nerves.

Religion has nothing to do with them. Superstition and fanaticism transform them into miracles; but there is no miracle about them. Much less is there any religion in them. Religion is taught in the Bible. Ignorance and nerves should not attempt to add to it. The east wind is not a good gospel minister. Many of its *doctrines* are very incorrect.

In the case of this woman, the proper influences of divine truth were mingled up with the workings of an excited imagination and weak nerves, and her superstitious notions did not discriminate betwixt the two. She at first supposed, with solemn and grateful sincerity, that God had sent this vision to her as an assurance that she was forgiven. And it is not likely that all I said to her would entirely have corrected her erroneous idea, had not her subsequent experience lent its aid. But when she came to have other visions which resembled it, and on examination found them to be fancies only, her common sense led her to the conclusion that nothing but fancy created that beautiful light, that rainbow, that globe of blue, and bird of Paradise. There can be no security against the worst and wildest of errors, but by a close and exclusive adherence to the Word of God, to teach us what religion is.

Superstition.

I WAS sent for by a woman who was in great distress, in respect to her preparation for death. She was fully convinced that she should not live long. though now able to ride out daily, and seldom confined to her bed by her infirmity. She was a member of a neighboring church; but she said,—"I have no peace of mind, and no witness that God has given me a new heart."

I had not been acquainted with her before. She appeared to be an unimaginative, amiable woman, who loved her husband and her children, but she had not a very discriminating mind. Her wealthy, moral, but irreligious parents had done little for her, except to indulge her and train her in the love of money, and the enjoyments it can furnish.

I strove to instruct her in the way of life. I visited her almost every week for a long time. She gained little or nothing in hope. There was something strange about her, which I could not understand. Her mind would be drawn off from the very things which I was most anxious to fasten upon it. One day she mentioned to me what a "bright witness," as she called it, one of her acquaintances had. She told me what it was. "It was a great light that appeared to her, and filled all the room where she was." The silly girl who told her this silly story some years before, had sometimes induced her to attend religious meetings with her, among a class of people more apt to see such visions, and more fond of them than I am; and now, the poor woman's mind was constantly on the look-out for some such "great light." She said, "I want some witness to myself." With this expectation her mind was occupied; it was called off from the truth, and bewildered and confused by this superstition. Again and again I explained to her the unscriptural nature of all such notions, and taught her that such "great lights" existed only in the imaginations of people, very nervous or very silly, or both. I thought I had succeeded in dissipating her superstitious notions, and for some months (during the lapse of which I often saw her), I had hoped that she was led to put faith before fancy, and look to Christ and not to visions, for comfort and salvation. But after all this, being in trouble she sent for me. I went. She brought up the same story of a "great light," and asked me,—

"Why *don't I* see some such witness?"

"For three reasons," said I; "*first*, you are not

nervous enough; *second*, you are not *imaginative* enough; *third*, you are not *quite fool* enough."

Then I went over all the explanations of Bible religion again, and all the arguments to demonstrate the superstition of such notions as she had about some external witness, and expel it from her mind. She appeared to be convinced, *said* she was, and for some weeks seemed to enjoy a rational hope in Christ. I had a hope for her.

A few days before her death she sent for me again. She was in deep distress,—in despair. She asked me if I thought she should "not have some such bright witness before she died." She died without it.

Superstition is mischievous. It hinders the exercises of faith, where faith exists; it prevents faith where it does not exist. Superstitious people are silly. The sights they see, the strange sounds they hear, the voices whispering some words or some texts of Scripture in their ears, are nothing but fancies, not facts; and if they were facts, they would be no evidence at all that these persons had become the children of God. Bible evidences of religion are entirely different.

The Whistling Thinker.

"THERE are some instances of religious experience which can never be reconciled to a theological system." The expression of the old gentlemen startled me. I was closeted with the Rev. Dr. P——, a man turned of seventy—a divine of a good deal of celebrity in that part of the country. Forty years at least his junior, I had sought opportunity to consult him in respect to some difficulties and peculiarities, which troubled the hearts of two or three of my acquaintances. I wished to *learn*; and I thought from his years, and his high reputation, that he could instruct me.

I had just stated to him the case of an individual, and he made the remark which surprised me. As he did not add any explanation, and as I thought from his silence that he intended to leave me to digest the remark as best I could, while he whistled and looked out carelessly upon the sky; I repeated his words after him, "there are some instances of religious experience which can never be reconciled to a theological system," and then I added,—

"It appears to me, sir, if that declaration is *true*, then the religious experience of which you speak must be *false*, spurious; or else the theological *system* must be false."

"*Why?*" said he, gruffly.

"Because, sir, if the experience and the system are both *true*, surely they will not quarrel. Lies quarrel sometimes; truths never do. Things that agree with truth agree with each other. If a religious experience agrees with truth, (as certainly it *must*, as far as it *is* religious,) and a theological system agrees with truth, then they are alike; they need no reconciling. 'Things equal to the same are equal to one another.'"

"EUCLID!" said the queer old man; and then he began to whistle again, and look out at the window. In a few minutes he turned to me,—

"All you say is true," said he, in a careless manner; "but if you live to preach many years, and become much acquainted with people, you will find some Christians whose experience will not square with your theology."

"Then," said I, "my theology must be *false*."

The old man whistled again. I waited some time for him to finish his tune, doubtful whether he was thinking of me at all, or whether he whistled as a *means* of thinking. At last he ceased from his music; and, turning his clear, keen eyes upon me, he sat for some time in silence, as if he would read my very soul. I thought he was taking the dimensions of my understanding; and concluded, therefore, to wait in silence until he should get his measure fixed. After awhile, he spoke,—

"My son, don't you think I can defend the proposition I laid down, and convince you of its truth?"

"No, sir, not if I understand the proposition rightly."

("Whew,—) why can't I? (Whew, whew.")

"Because the proposition is not true."

"Perhaps it is not," said he; "but suppose you should meet with a person presenting every possible evidence of true religion in his views, and feelings, and conduct, year after year, and yet that same person had never been awakened, never had any change in his views and feelings respecting religion, as converts have, and was not in the least sensible of having been brought out of darkness into light at any time; how would you reconcile that experience with your theology about human depravity, and about regeneration? What would you say of such a person, after a sermon on original sin, or on conversion? How could you say he was 'born unholy and unclean,' as the Psalm Book has it, but had turned to God?"

"I would say, sir, that God had led him in a way that I knew not of, perhaps in a way that *he* knew not of, perhaps had renewed his heart in his infancy, perhaps had sanctified him *before* he was born, as he sanctified John and Jeremiah. But I would not admit, that his experience in religion could not be reconciled with my theological system."

After whistling awhile, the old gentleman looked up,—

"Who taught *you* to interpret Scripture? I don't believe Jeremiah, and John, and Paul, were sanctified before they were born. God certainly could have sanctified them then, and I believe He *does* sanctify and save infants,—some that never *are* born; but the Scriptures do not prove that Jeremiah and John were sanctified before they came into the world. What God says to the prophet, 'Before thou camest forth out of the womb, I sanctified thee, and ordained thee a prophet,' no more proves that Jeremiah was *regenerated* before he was born, than it proves that he was 'ordained a prophet,' and preached before he was born. The expression has reference only to God's predetermination, or election. The same is the case in respect to John. As to the rest which you said, I agree with all *that.* One may be truly born again, even in infancy."

"Well, then," said I, "how can your first declaration be true, that some Christian experiences cannot be reconciled with a system of theology?"

Again he whistled for a long time; then suddenly turning to me, as if he had whistled himself up into a thought,—

"It is *not* true. I supposed that you was a Seminary man, who had got a system of theology, with one leg and one crutch, not able to jump over a stump, and that, therefore, you could not reconcile *your* system with the facts you met; and I only wished you to understand that divine realities go beyond human systematizing, and if men will confine themselves to their narrow systems, the Holy Spirit will go beyond them. The church has been greatly injured by such men at times. At one period, nothing but *doctrines* will do; and so doctrines are preached, and prayed, and sung, till metaphysics have frozen piety to death. At another time, nothing but *practice* will do; and then religion soon degenerates into a lifeless form, an outward show, with no great doctrines to put life into the soul. At one period, nothing but Revivals will do, and Revival religion; and then, in the midst of that spirit of fanaticism, diffused by some noisy men all over the churches, a humble, faithful Christian will be looked upon with contempt, because he was not converted in a Revival; and a minister will lose caste, if he does not preach "*Revival, Revival,*" all the time. I have seen this again and again. The church that needs a minister will cry out, "we want a *Revival* man,—nothing but a *Revival* man will do for *us;*" and so they choose for a minister some proud boaster, who can talk of "Revival" more than of Christ. And another result of this proud spirit is, that when it prevails in our churches, our people by-and-bye come to undervalue the common means of grace, and they become *periodical* Christians; and then they undervalue the faithful Christian education of their children; they forget that the God of Abraham is still *alive*, and on the throne, a covenant-keeping God; they do not *expect* religious education in the family to be an effectual means of conversion, —they rely upon Revivals. And it soon comes to pass that the Revivals are scenes of mere excitement, delusion, and spiritual pride,—'stand aside, I am holier than thou.' At another period, the opposite error prevails. Revivals are looked upon with suspicion. They are not desired and prayed for. All excitement is feared. And then religion will run down into formality, and people will join the church when they get old enough, or when they get to have a family. There are many truly pious people who have become such under the influence of example and instruction in the family, and under the ordinary Sabbath-preaching, who never could give you any *special* account,—certainly not a *Revival* account of their conversion. These would not suit a Revival Christian. And Revival converts would not suit *them.* But all such things are wrong. They are the results of narrow systems."

Then he whistled again. But before I could collect my thoughts for any reply, he broke off from his tune in the middle of a bar,—

"*A theological system*, sir, *every minister of sense will have.* He cannot get along without it. A man can no more do without *a system*, than he can do without *a head.* But what I was after, is *this:* there are men of narrow views, linked to their system, and thinking their system contains all that religion contains; and they would not let anybody cast out *devils* any more than the disciples would, unless he would do it by *their* rule. These men love their system, and preach their system, and live in it, like a worm in a nut, and never get out of it, till, like such a worm, they get wings to fly beyond it. When death gives them wings to fly to heaven, they are out of their jail, and not before. In my opinion, Dr. Woods is such a man as Dr. Porter was before him. Dr. Taylor is such a man, (almost as much fettered as the rest of them.) Dr. Alexander, (one of the ripest saints,) is such a man. Dr. Dwight was such a man. And if you want an instance of such a man, whose fetters everybody can see, (and hear them jingle, too, at every step he takes,) look at Dr. Emmons, (poor fellow!) These are system men. Examine Dwight's Hymn Book.

How narrow its range is! How lean! It is worse than one of Pharaoh's lean heifers! It has just a few subjects; and passes over more than half the region of song, without a single note. I never could be confined to it. I would as soon consent to be confined to four tunes. Mear, Old Hundred, St. Martin's, and Durham, would do as well for all our music, as Dwight's Hymn Book for all our poetry.

"Now, my son, never get into a strait-jacket. You will find it pinch. It will make your bones ache. Many a minister becomes more familiar with his theological system than he is with his Bible; and not only so, but his system stands *first*, and when he gets hold of a text, he interprets it to square with his system, instead of paring and whittling off his system to make it agree with the text; and among his pastoral duties, he sticks to his Calvanism more than he sticks to Christ; and he would *pray* his system too, if the Holy Spirit didn't make his prayers for him. And in this way he systems his Bible into a corner, and his own soul into a nutshell. Never do *that*, in the pulpit or among the people. 'Preach the Word'—the *Word*, my son,—THE WORD! Are you a Calvinist?" said he, gently, after speaking in a voice of thunder.

"Yes, sir," said I.

"Then don't be afraid of an Arminian text: don't dodge, when you come across one. *Out with it;* it is *God's* text, and he don't want you to mince it. Are you a Seminary boy?"

"No, sir."

"*Down on your knees*, and thank God for it."

"I *have* thanked Him, sir, a hundred times."

"You'll thank Him ten thousand, if you live to my age."

"Are you opposed to what is called Calvinism?" I asked.

"*By no means*. I am a Calvinist. But I let the Bible make my Calvinism, instead of bringing my Calvinism to make Bible; and I claim the liberty of going along with my Bible, into a thousand corners beyond the limits of the system."

"You mentioned Dr. Taylor, with a sort of doubtful compliment about his being fettered; some ministers in my neighborhood have talked to me a great deal about Dr. Taylor. Let me ask whether you regard him as heretical?"

"No! *I* don't. But Dr. Taylor has committed *the Connecticut sin!* He is guilty of *thinking*, sir, of *thinking;* and for that reason, some people over in Jersey and Pennsylvania, and some in York State, count him a half heretic. But he only *thinks*, sir, that's all: and *thinking* is his original sin, and actual transgression too. Now, don't join in and cry '*mad dog*' about Dr. Taylor. *Wait*, till you are *sure you see the froth*. His *boys* don't understand him. Dr. *Taylor* isn't a *Taylorite.* Far from it, sir. His *boys* are Taylorites, but *he* isn't. I have had long talks with a whole score of ministers educated under him, and I KNOW that *not one Taylorite among them understands* Dr. Taylor's scheme."

"What *is* his scheme, sir?"

"His scheme of *doctrine* is John Calvin's, or John Howe's, or Edwards', substantially: his scheme of *philosophy* is his *own*, and no honor to him. Why, sir, he believes in original sin, and in the special influences of the Holy Spirit, (whether his boys do or not,) as much as you or I do. He wouldn't use my *lingo*, or, as he would express it, 'TER-MO-NOL-O-GY,' because he must have a word as long as *Yale College*, to suit 'the appropriate circumstances of his being;' but he preaches the same doctrines that I do. He is sound at the core. (I don't like his *philosophy.*) But you get into a *fight*, and Dr. Taylor will be one of the best *backers* you could have. He *thinks.*"

"You mentioned several men, sir," said I, "whose praise is in all the churches; but I do not exactly understand in what rank you mean to place them. Do you mean to speak of Dwight, and Taylor, and Alexander, and Emmons, as men of little mind?"

"Not *little*, my son; not *little;* but *limited, narrow.* Every one of them is more or less entangled with a system. Dr. Taylor came nearer to be a *free* man than any of the rest of them, when he was young. He flung off the system fetters nobly; but, like a *goose*, he went to work and hammered out a pair of his own, and they have galled him worse than the old ones would. The old ones had been used and got smooth—the *rust* worn off. These men are *great* men, *very* great men. They are *good* men; men of truth and faith and devoted godliness. They are *safe* men, *to teach* you on all the fundamental points. I should count you a heretic, and would not ask you to preach for me, if you did not agree with them on all the *fundamentals;* not because you disagreed with *them*, but because, disagreeing with them, I should know you disagreed with the Bible. My complaint about them is two-fold; *first*, they let their system limit their scope and range; and *second*, they put their system *foremost* in all religion."

"Well, sir, do you object to theological systems, catechisms, and confessions of Faith?"

"*No, no!*" said he, impatiently. "I *thought* you could *understand* me! I am no opponent of confessions of faith. If a man tells you he will have no creed or confession to stick to, ('nothing but the Bible,') set him down for a heretic or an idiot, or both. He *has* a creed if he is a Christian at all. And he will stick to it, if he walks in the Spirit, whether he is in the pulpit or in society. Yes sir;

he has a creed, if he is not a *downright fool!* Indeed, my young friend, our greatest danger at the present moment, throughout the whole of New England, lies just *here*; we have too much shortened our creeds, and forgotten our confessions, and ceased to preach the *great doctrines.* The doctrines are the great things after all. One of our prominent men, now preaching in the capital of our State, courts popularity by an occasional sneer at 'old, dead orthodoxy,' as he calls it. He is doing injury to the cause of truth. The seeds of error which he is sowing will spring up by-and-bye. If he does not become a heretic himself, his admirers and followers will. He does not believe the Westminster Confession of Faith, in my opinion; and, if that was a standard now among our churches and ministers, as it was once, when the Catechism was taught in all our schools, we should not have so many *creedless* ministers among us, ignorantly working to undermine the great principles of the Reformation, by sneering at 'old, dead orthodoxy,' like the Rev. Dr. ——. They hate the *doctrines*, sir. So you see I am not against systems and creeds; but I want a minister to have a *creed*, and a *heart* too. I want him to have a system; and then I want him to know that his system does not contain *everything*, and that he himself does not *know* everything. The Bible has a depth, and a richness, and an extent too, in its meaning, which no human system can express, Preach your *text* my boy, your TEXT, *right out*, and not your system."

The old man had waxed quite warm. He forgot to whistle, or look out at the window. I liked to hear him talk, and I was not disposed to have him think me quite such a novice as his manner towards me (though he was kind), seemed to indicate that he did. So I replied,—

"Perhaps I do understand you, sir, more fully than you give me credit for. But when you say, 'if I live to preach many years, and become much acquainted with people, I shall find some Christians whose experience cannot be reconciled with a Theological system,' I must still beg leave to say I do not believe it."

"*I took that back*," said he instantly. "I said that on the supposition that you were a *Seminary* man, cut to the length of the bedstead, and foolishly making your system everything."

"But, sir, you supposed a case of inexplicable conversion, and asked me how I could reconcile it with my Theological system."

"So I did; but I thought *then* you were a Revivalist, and I wanted to trip up your heels, so that you might pick yourself up and plant yourself on firm ground, and not think that all religion must work exactly according to your Revival mode. I *told* you that I agreed to all you said about that supposed case."

"Perhaps you did, sir; but you afterwards said 'the Holy Ghost will go beyond systems;' while I maintain that as certainly as my system is *true*, human experience in religion will neither contradict my system nor go beyond it."

"I meant to take that back, my son, I take it back now; if you are not a Seminary man or a Revivalist, or mounted on some other limping hobby. I only employed an expression to set you thinking. Mark me; I am not opposed to Theological Seminaries or to Revivals, I am only opposed to the injuries and abuses that grow out of them. If ministers and their people come to think that nothing but Revival will do, or nothing but a Seminary system will do; true religion will soon be eclipsed, either by fanaticism or bigotry,—and I want you to think about it. If Theological Seminaries would learn their place, and learn to keep it, they would do good. They may be good *servants* of the church, but they will be very bad *masters* of it. They want to be masters. Such is human nature. The church would do well to watch them. Cambridge is a beacon in *my* eye. The seeds of heresy and fanaticism are now sown thick, by those men who seek popularity by crying out '*Revival, Revival*, and Seminary, Seminary.' I am disgusted with their pride and their popularity-hunting."

The old man turned to the window again, and struck up another tune in a sort of low, whispering whistle. But before I had mustered my thoughts enough to know what to reply, he suddenly turned to me, solemnly,—

"Now we have come here to preach in a Revival. The Revival is God's work, and I rejoice in it. The converts *here* will appear very much alike; but let us not think that all other true converts must appear just so too, in their awakening, and repentance, and hope. There are many persons, (especially those who have had a careful Christian education, and have always been under the influences of Christian truth and example,) who come to be true Christians, and nobody can tell when they were converted, —they can't tell themselves. The Holy Spirit has led them gently and softly along. We can judge of them by their fruits, by their attachment to the great doctrines of truth, and their life of faith. We must not judge of them by the *way* in which they were converted. In all the substantial parts of religion, all true converts will be much alike. Their faith will be the same, their repentance the same, their reliance on Christ the same; and they will all hold substantially the same great doctrines,—(in their *hearts*, whether they do in their *heads* or not,) because it is by these doctrines, law to condemn, and grace to deliver, that the Holy Spirit moulds hearts. He moulds them alike. And for that reason I say that the *doctrines*, sir, the *doctrines* are our *tools* first, and our *tests* afterward. The Doctrines are the best Revival sermons,—mind, *the best.* Nettleton always preaches them. But we must not expect all our people who are converted, to feel them alike suddenly, or alike deeply :—

'God moves in a mysterious way,
His wonders to perform.'

But it *is* God who performs the wonders; and He performs them through His own *truth.* I am willing that He should use the truth suddenly or slowly, and convert a man as He converted Paul, or as He converted John."

"That is a part of my theological system, sir," said I.

"Then you and I agree," said he, with a smile. "You are not hood-winked or trammelled with a Seminary system or a Revival system. I perceive you *think;* and that makes me like you."

Turning again to the window, he struck up another tune, as his eye wandered over the valleys and the distant mountains of blue. Whistling seemed to be as natural to him as breathing. He appeared to whistle up his thoughts. And again, before I had time to contrive what to say, he turned to me,—

"Generations have their fashions, their foibles, as much as women about their dress. Seminaries and Revivals are the *fashion* of our age and country. These things have their advantages, but they have their disadvantages also. The two great dangers of the church in *our* day are these:—the church must have no ministers but Seminary ministers, and no religion but Revival religion. Both these exclusive preferences are *wrong*, foolish, and short-sighted. They do, indeed, partly balance each other; and so our Seminary ministers do not become altogether *book* ministers,—theorizing, speculative, and heartless as metaphysics; and our Revival ministers do not *all* become fanatics, with a bad heart, and *no* head. But the time will come, if God has good things in store for us, when the church will again welcome ministers who have never *seen* a public Seminary, and will welcome converts who do not tell a *stereotyped story* about their Revival conversion. These two hobbies of the age will get old and worn out by-and-bye; and then the church will be wiser than she is now. These hobbies *have* worked well; but the Seminary hobby is very stiff in the *joints*, and the Revival hobby has had his *wind* injured."

"To hear you talk," said I, "one would think you believed in a gradual regeneration."

"I believe," said he, "in *instantaneous* regeneration in *all* cases. But I do not, on that account, maintain that every regenerated sinner must be able to tell *when* he was regenerated. He may not *know* when, and *never* know till the day of judgment. But, in my opinion, he *will* know *who* regenerated him. I have very much ceased to *ask* persons whom I examine for reception into the church, *when* they became religious, or *how* their minds were affected. Principles are a far better test than mere emotions. They are more *reliable*, and more ascertainable too. My way *now* is, to inquire about their views of *doctrine*, of *truth*, and about some of their religious feelings *at the present time.* In my opinion, many a true child of God is afraid to come to God's table, and is kept away, simply because he cannot tell such an experience as he has heard of in others, and as he has been led to think universal with all true converts. He has had none of that *blazing* experience, (which I call *comet religion*, because nobody can tell where it comes from, or where it goes to, or what it is good for,) because he has been led gently to Christ, following the still, small voice, and does not know *when* or *how* he begun to trust Him,—*only*, that God has led him, as he never would have gone of himself. He has had principle, and conscience, and purpose, and faith, but not tumultuous and whirlwind emotion.

And, as I said before, in my opinion, there are many true Christians, who have been well taught from their youth, that never *can* tell *when* they turned to God; and if they attempt to fix on the day of the month, they will fix it *wrong*,—some, too soon, and many, too late."

"You spoke a little while since of mere excitements, fanaticism, and heresy, sir. I have a special reason for asking you, what is the fit mode of counteracting such evils?"

Instantly, he replied, with slow and measured words,—

"Preach *on the character of God.* Then, *on the depravity of man.* Then, *on the nature of holiness.* Then, *on secret prayer!* All fanatics have got a new God! My boy, I want you to take notice (put an N. B. to it, in your memory,) how the Bible in order to tear up error by the roots, brings up GOD HIMSELF, and tells what HE is. The old prophets do it, all through: 'Thus saith the LORD GOD: besides ME there is none else: *I* change not: holy, holy, holy, is the Lord.' The Apostles do it. Paul is full of it. He employed it on Mars' Hill, to convert the Athenian philosophers: he used it to knock over those who doubted about the resurrection; '*thou fool*,' says he, 'GOD giveth it a body!' Peter used it; 'one day with the Lord is as a thousand years!' All the Divine writers have it. It is their familiar thunder and lightning; and I advise you to borrow a little of it. It will purify the atmosphere all around you."*

In very much this strain, my aged counsellor went on for an hour,—relieved only by a whistling interlude; and sometimes, after a pause, roused again to utter some great truth, by some question which I ventured to ask him. He was full of thought. I have never listened to a man of more independent mind, or whose conversation was more rich in suggestions. He thought deeply and carefully, though perhaps many wise men would be slow to adopt all his opinions about men or about things.

My interview with him was of great use to me. He put me to *thinking*, which, he said, was "all that he aimed at."

Years afterwards, I was forcibly reminded of him, by a case which I am about to relate, and which I have here, in the following sketch, denominated *Unconscious Conversion.*

* When the Rev. Mr. Backus was ordained successor to Dr. Bellamy, in 1791, there was an aged, pious negro, belonging to the church. Soon after Mr. Backus' ordination, some one asked this negro how he liked Mr. Backus, whether he thought him equal to Dr. Bellamy. His reply was: "Like Master Backus very much—great man—good minister, but not equal to Master Bellamy. Master Backus make God big, but Master Bellamy make God bigger."

Unconscious Conversion.

In the discharge of pastoral duty I have never been more deeply interested or more perplexed, than I was in the case of a very affectionate and intelligent woman, whom I knew with great intimacy for several years. She was a married woman before I became acquainted with her. She was young in life, I suppose not more than twenty-five, and her husband was probably about thirty—not a religious man. I visited her as her pastor, soon after she had removed from another part of the country, and taken up her residence in the place where I lived. I was much pleased with her. She was a woman of refined manners, of excellent sense, of trained mind, of gentle and affectionate disposition, but withal of unusual firmness, having a mind and a heart of her own. Few women, as I believe, have ever adorned their station more than she adorned hers. As a wife, mother, friend; as a neighbor, as a daughter, (for I became acquainted with her parents and knew her demeanor towards them,) she was a pattern of propriety. A stranger to her might have deemed her manner somewhat reserved and cold, (as indeed it was to strangers,) for there was no forwardness about her. She was modest, unassuming, unobtrusive. But her reserve wore off by acquaintance; and though she never became imprudent, and never lost a just sense of a woman's dignity, she became peculiarly confiding and companionable. However, she was rather taciturn than talkative. Like a woman of sense, she took care whom she trusted, and what she said.

But there was a shade of melancholy which seemed to hang around her, quite noticeable to a keen observer, and yet not so distinct as to be visible, perhaps, to most of her acquaintance. Her half pensive look gave an additional interest to her intelligent countenance, (which had no small claims to be denominated beautiful,) and indeed there seemed to be a cast of sadness thrown over the very movements of her tall and graceful figure.

When I first became acquainted with her, I noticed this tender melancholy which hung around her like the shadow of a cloud; and I supposed that the twilight of some affliction still lingered around her heart, or that some secret grief was buried deep in her own bosom. After a more intimate acquaintance with her, I came to the conclusion that she had some trial of which she never spoke, but which preyed in secret upon her heart. I thought her appearance indicative of a concealed grief, which, like a worm in the bud, was preying upon her life.

On account of this opinion, I aimed to mention the subject of religion to her, in the most delicate and affectionate manner possible. I called upon her for that purpose. I found her alone. After a few moments of conversation I said to her,—

"I have several times mentioned the subject of religion to you, Mrs. C——, but you have been quite reserved; and I have called upon you to-day to converse with you upon that subject, if you will allow me such a favor."

"I am glad to see you, sir."

"Allow me to ask you whether you are a member of the church?"

"No sir, I am not."

"And do you think you are still living in unbelief, after all your opportunities?"

"I suppose, sir, I have no reason to think I am a Christian," said she, with a look of mingled solemnity and sorrow.

"Is it wise for you to neglect your salvation?"

"I know it is not wise, sir. My own heart condemns me," said she with much emotion.

"Then, madam, do not neglect it any longer. The favor of God is within your reach. He calls to you in His gracious kindness, and invites you to turn to Him for pardon and peace, freely offered to you through the great Redeemer of sinners. But how comes it about, Mrs. C——, that you have neglected salvation so long?"

"I do not know, indeed, sir. I suppose I have been too worldly, and too much led away by my own heart, though I have thought about religion a great deal all my life."

"I suppose so too. And I *know* you ought, instantly, to 'deny yourself, and take up your cross and follow Jesus Christ,' and not suffer your heart to be led away any longer."

She was much affected. I asked her some questions which she did not answer, because (as I then supposed), of a conflict in her own mind, betwixt a sense of duty and the love of the world. I therefore urged her as solemnly and affectionately as I could, to give her attention to religion without delay, and left her.

Again I called to see her. I inquired,—

"Have you been giving your attention to religion since I saw you?"

"I have thought of it very often, sir."

"And have you prayed about it very often?"

"I have *tried* to pray," said she sadly; "but I do not know as it was true prayer."

"Do you feel your *need* of God's blessing, as an undone sinner, condemned by the law of God, and having a wicked heart?"

"Sometimes I *think* I feel it; but I suppose I do not feel it as much as I ought to."

"Do you feel that you need Christ to save you?"

"I *know* it, sir; but I am afraid I do not feel it. My heart seems hard, very hard; I wonder at myself, my stupid self."

"It must be a very senseless or stupid heart, my dear friend, if it cannot feel the most solemn matter, save one, in all the universe. Nothing short of perdition itself, can be a more affecting and solemn thing, than to be an undone sinner without Christ to save you!"

"I am very sensible of my stupidity. I have often wondered at myself. I have tried to feel, but——"

She was overcome by this thought, and could not finish the sentence. She wept bitterly, though she evidently strove hard to control her emotions. "Pardon my infirmity, sir," said she. "I do not know why it is, but I cannot restrain my feelings. I hope you will not think me *quite* a child."

I assured her of my entire respect for her, and my attachment to her as a friend; that I was unwilling to say one word to make her unhappy, but that I wanted her attention to a happiness unequalled and everlasting.

"I know it, sir, I know it; and I thank you for all your kindness to me," said she with tears.

I besought her to "come freely, and affectionately, and fully to Christ, without any distrust and without any delay, because *salvation* is by *free grace.*

Afterwards I had several interviews with her, in all of which she was solemn and much affected, but ordinarily her *words* were few. I told her from time to time the same truths, which I was accustomed to urge upon the attention of other anxious inquirers. I referred her to the same texts, the same promises, the same cautions and directions. Months passed on in this way, and still she found no peace of mind, no hope. She did not come out of her darkness into the light of faith, as I had so long and so confidently expected; nor did she become any less solemn or less studious or less tender in feeling, as latterly I had so much feared. Indeed, at almost every interview I had with her, she would be melted into tears in spite of all her efforts; and then she would beg me to "pardon her weakness," as she called it, and apologizing for her emotions, she would say,—"I would not afflict you with these tears if I could help it. I know it must be painful to you to see me affected in this manner, after all you have done for me; and I feel that my state of mind is but a poor return for your kindness. But I assure you, my dear Pastor, I am not ungrateful to you, if I am unhappy."

I soothed and comforted her all in my power,

with the promises of God, and encouragements to trust in Him. I reasoned with her, and aimed to reach her conscience, and win her heart to the love of Christ. Again and again I taught her all God's truth, which I thought adapted to her state of mind. She heard it all attentively, kindly, and, as I sometimes thought, gladly. She never uttered an objection, complaint, or excuse. I confidently believed, as she continued to seek the Lord so assiduously, she would soon find peace, or be left to return to indifference. But it was not so with her. Through many months she continued, so far as *I* could see, in the same state,—solemn, tender, prayerful ordinarily, but uncomforted.

Her condition perplexed me, and very much grieved me. I had become greatly attached to her as a friend, and I believe she respected and loved me as her minister; and I could feel no reconciliation to the idea that she should continue in this unhappy condition. I blamed *myself* very much, for I supposed I must have failed to instruct her appropriately, even though she was desirous to be taught,—perhaps had not sufficiently explained the way of salvation, insisting upon those great doctrines of truth, through which the Holy Spirit leads sinners to repentance. Consequently I called upon her again, resolved to probe her heart, and, after some little conversation, inquired of her,—

"Have you yet found your heart at peace with God?"

"No sir, I am not at peace,—I am far from it."

"Do you still remain in the same state of mind that you have been in so long?"

"I am sorry to say, sir, that I can tell you nothing new about myself,—nothing different from what I have told you before."

"And certainly, madam, I can tell *you* nothing new,—can preach no new gospel, can tell you nothing different from what I have told *you* before. If you do not obey the gospel, nothing can save you. The gospel will not change. *You* must change. The gospel offers Christ to you, to enlighten you, to atone for you, to defend you from every danger. And since this offer is so free, and so kind, and so appropriate, and is made in the infinite sincerity of God, what hinders you that you do not accept it, and trust your Saviour humbly, penitently, gladly?"

"I wish, sir, I could tell what hinders," said she, sadly.

"My dear friend," said I, "have you ever really felt, and do you feel *now*, that you are an *undone sinner*, and have infinite need of Christ to save you?"

"Yes sir, I think I do. I never have had any doubt of that. I *know* I am undone, and I know I need Christ; but perhaps I do not feel it as I should."

"Do you *want* to feel it?"

"Yes, I know *I do*," said she, with some difficulty, and burst into tears. "I have prayed a great many times to be enabled to feel it more, if that is what I lack."

"Allow me to ask you if you have ever been fully convinced that you have by nature an evil heart, depraved, 'deceitful above all things, and desperately wicked?'"

"Yes sir; I know I have. I cannot conceive how anybody can doubt that, after examining himself at all. Perhaps I am worse than I suppose, or I should not continue in this sad state. I am fully sensible there is nothing in myself but sin."

"And do you think you can make your heart any better?"

"I am sure I can do nothing for myself. Certainly, I ought to be convinced of that by this time."

"Are you fully sensible that nothing but the Holy Spirit can meet the necessities of your poor heart, and bring you to Christ?"

"Yes, I have long felt it. I am sure I ought to know that, for I have tried often enough of myself to turn to God, and my heart is still the same."

"Why don't you give that heart to God, and

trust Him to renew it and control it, since you find all your own efforts vain?"

"I have often *tried* to do so, but it seems to be all useless."

"Do you constantly pray for Divine assistance?"

"I have always been accustomed to pray, in my poor way. At times I have neglected prayer for a little while, when I thought it did no good, and was afraid I should rely too much upon the mere act of praying, and when I have thought God would not accept such prayers as mine. But I do not often neglect daily prayer."

"Do you seek the Lord with all your heart?"

"I suppose not, sir; for if I did I should not remain in this miserable condition. I *try*, but it seems I fail."

"Do you rely upon any righteousness of your own to save you, or commend you to Christ?"

"I have no righteousness. I know very well there is nothing in me but sin and misery."

"Do you try to *make* a righteousness out of repentance, or humiliation, or faith, and thus expect your *religion* to commend you to the Saviour? Sinners sometimes seek *religion*, and think they must. But the Bible never tells them to seek *religion*—it tells them to 'seek *the Lord*.' And when they seek *religion*, in order to have their religion render them acceptable to God, all that is nothing but an operation of a self-righteous spirit. Do you think of being accepted in this way, instead of expecting God to receive you as you are, a sinner to be saved?"

"Perhaps it may be so, through the deceitfulness of my heart; but I am not conscious of it. I have thought of that point very often, since you explained to me the difference betwixt trusting to the righteousness of Christ, and aiming to establish a righteousness of our own."

"Don't you love the world too well?"

"Tho love of thc world *tempts* me, I am afraid, sometimes; but I feel that I am willing to forsake all for Christ."

"Are you willing *now* to give up yourself into the hands of Christ to save you, denying yourself in order to serve Him?"

"It seems to me that I am; but I suppose it cannot be so, for if I was I should not feel as I do."

"Christ offers to receive you *freely*, *now*, *just as you are.* He invites you to trust Him. Why do you refuse?"

"I *do* try; I have tried; I have tried for a long time, but I——" (her voice faltered, she could say no more.) I waited a little time for her to become composed, and then inquired,—

"Let me ask you, my dear friend, with all respect and affection, don't you indulge in some sin (sin of enmity, or envy, or discontent, or something else), some sin that keeps you from peace of conscience and peace with God?"

"No sir, I am not conscious of any such sin. I know I sin all the time. I struggle against it, but I do not *indulge* myself in any sin that I know of. If there is any such thing that keeps me from my Saviour, I should be glad to know what it is."

I recited to her some of the divine promises and directions as I had often done before, prayed with her, and left her.

Such conversations with her were repeated. She continued still the same. It was evident, as I thought, that I had not been able to profit her at all. In order to have a more perfect knowledge of her, if possible, I sometimes called upon her without saying a word upon the subject of religion. Her manner was cordial, and her conversation cheerful; but the old shade of pensiveness that hung around her, like a mysterious spirit, cast a sort of tender and touching melancholy over her whole appearance.

Several years had now passed away since my acquaintance with her commenced. She had been called to pass through some severe trials, in which I had sympathized with her and aimed to lead her to improve them rightly. She appeared to repose in me the most perfect confidence, told me her sorrows, consulted me in her difficulties, but continued without hope.

At one time I had great expectation that she would soon turn to her Lord in faith. She had a daughter, a young girl of sixteen perhaps, who became interested about religion and was led to hope in the mercy of God through Jesus Christ. For this lovely daughter she was most intensely anxious and prayerful. I strove to make use of this solicitude for her child, and of God's mercy to her, now in the bloom of her youth and beauty, as a means of leading the pensive-hearted mother to the same fountain of life. All *this* failed.

On one occasion when I called to see her, I asked,—

"Have you made any progress towards religion?" With trembling voice she answered,—

"I do not know as I can say anything to you, sir, on that subject, which I have not often said to you before. I am sorry to be obliged to tell you so. It must be very discouraging and unpleasant to you, after all your kindness and attempts to do me good. I do feel grateful to you for your attentions to me and to my child; but I make you a poor return when I am always compelled to tell you the same thing about myself, and meet you with these tears. I know it must be unpleasant to you. I wonder you have not been discouraged with me and left me long ago."

"My dear lady, don't think of *me*. It is *God*, whose kindness ought to affect you, and attract you instantly to his arms. I am sorry for you—my heart bleeds for you. I cannot give you up. I do believe God has mercy in store for you."

"I am sure my heart requites your kindness, my dear pastor; I am not ungrateful for it."

"And will you be grateful to *God*, to *Christ Jesus*, your suffering Lord, who bore the curse for you, who grappled with death and the devil *for you*, and opened your way into heaven?"

"I hope I am *not* ungrateful to Him," said she, sobbing aloud.

"Do you *trust* in Him, as a Friend to save you?"

"Oh! I am afraid not."

"You *may*—a thousand times, '*you may*.' 'Come, for all things are ready.'"

I could only exhort her, and pray for her.

I called on her again, and our interview was much the same as usual. I did not know but I was making her unhappy by my constant solicitations, and perhaps doing her harm; so I said to her,—

"My dear child, I will not press this subject upon your attention any more, if it is unpleasant to you to have me mention it. I have loved you, and aimed to do you good; but I have failed. I do not wish to make you unhappy. I will leave you hereafter entirely to yourself, if you desire it, and never say a word more to you on the subject of your religion."

Covering her face again with her handkerchief, she wept convulsively, as I went on to say,—

"I will do just as you desire; I will continue to offer you Christ and his salvation, or be silent on the whole subject, just as is most agreeable to ——"

"*Oh, sir,*" (interrupting me,) "I do *not* wish you to leave me. I wonder your patience has not been exhausted, and I am sensible it must pain you to see me always in this tearful condition. I am sorry to make you unhappy; but I hope you will never think me pained by your visits. I am *not*, I assure you. Almost my only hope is ——"

She could say no more, and I could utter no reply. I prayed with her, and promised to see her again. She *demanded* a promise.

On a future occasion, as I was conversing with her, I asked her,—

"Is it not strange that you do not *love* such a God?"

Greatly to my surprise, she answered,—

"I think I do love God, sir."

"How long do you think you have loved Him?"

"Ever since I was a little child. I cannot remember the time when I did *not* love Him. It has always seemed to me, as well as I know my own heart, that I did love God."

With amazement, I inquired,—

"Why did you never tell me this before?"

"I was afraid you would think me better than I am."

"And do you hate sin?"

"I have always hated it, (if I can judge of my own feelings,) ever since I can remember."

"*Why* do you hate sin?"

"Because it offends God, it is wrong, and because it makes me unhappy."

"Do you desire to be free from it?"

"Yes, I do, if I know anything at all of my own desires."

"Do you love to pray?"

"Yes, I love to pray,—it is my most precious comfort. Sometimes I feel it a task, I am afraid; when I fear that I am not sincere, and that my prayers are an offense."

"Is prayer a relief to you in trouble?"

"Sometimes it is. At other times a burden lies on my heart, which I cannot leave with God; indeed, commonly I have a burden left, because I am afraid I am not right with God."

"Do you *rely* on Christ to save you?"

"I have nothing else to rely upon; but I am afraid I do not rely upon Him as much as I ought."

"Do you *wish* to rely upon Him?"

"Yes, I do. It is my constant prayer that I may be able to do so. I know He is able and willing to save even me, unworthy as I am. I have never doubted that."

"Are you willing to *trust Him* to save you?"

"I certainly *wish* to trust Him."

"Do you receive Him as *your* Saviour?"

"I hope so; I *try* to do it."

"Do you feel grateful for what He has done for you?"

"Yes sir, I am sure I do."

"Are you *glad* to be in God's hands, and in His world, and let Him do with you as He will? You know He *will*, but are you *glad* of it?"

"Yes, I am. I would not desire to be anywhere else than in His hands. It is pleasant to me to think that He reigns over me and over all."

"Then are you not *reconciled* to God?"

"I don't know. If I was really reconciled to Him, I have always thought I should have more assurance of His favor. I am afraid to think I am reconciled."

"Do you love God's people?"

"Yes sir; their society has always been more pleasant to me than any other. I enjoy it."

"Don't you think that these feelings, which you have now expressed, are evidences of true religion?"

"I *should* think so, perhaps, if I had not always had them. But I have never been sensible of any particular change. I have *always* felt so since I was a little child, as long as I can remember."

I was utterly amazed! Here I had been for years

aiming to make conviction of sin more deep, instead of binding up the broken heart! I had been aiming to lead a sinner to Christ, instead of showing her that she was not a stranger, and an outcast! I I was ashamed of myself! I had often talked to this precious woman as if she were an alien from God, and an enemy; and now it appeared as if all the while she had been one of His most affectionate children, her very anguish consisting in this,—that she loved Him no more, and could not get assurance of *His* love towards her. It was true she had never told me these things before; but that did not satisfy me. I ought to have *learnt* them before. I went out and wept bitterly! I felt as if I had been pouring anguish into the crushed heart of the publican, as he cried, 'God be merciful to me a sinner!'

On my way home, I thought of what my old friend that whistled had said to me years before, and I was convinced that I had *practically* run into the error, against which his wisdom aimed to guard me. Over the recollection of the tears of anguish which I had so often caused this noble woman, in secret I poured out my own!

Afterwards I aimed repeatedly to show her what *were* and what were *not* evidences of saving faith; and she said to me more than once,—

"I should think myself a Christian if it were not for one thing; but I have had these feelings ever since I can remember: I have never been sensible of any such change as other people experience, and as the gospel mentions. I could not tell the time when I became a Christian, and am afraid to think I am a child of God."

So she felt; and she lived after this for months, downcast and burdened, with only an occasional gleam of sunshine to gladden her heart. I deem it not improbable that that secret grief which preyed upon her heart, and cast such a shade of melancholy over all her appearance, may have damped her religious joy and hope all along. I may not here record what it was. Gradually I discovered it, and it was cause enough, I am sure, to excuse all the melancholy which so long held possession of one of the noblest hearts that ever bled.

This woman had a *pious mother.* That mother taught her from her infancy, in a most faithful and affectionate manner; and it is probable that the gentle influences of the Holy Spirit renewed her heart in her early life, so that she "could not remember the time when she did *not* love God."

She finally came to a calm, but feeble and timorous hope that she was indeed a Christian. She hoped hesitatingly and humbly; as she said to me, "it is almost hope against hope." She removed to another part of the country, and *there* she and her daughter came, (on the same Sabbath, I believe,) for the first time to the communion table of their Lord. I have sometimes seen them since; they have sometimes done me the favor to write to me; they are still my precious friends; and I have reason to hope they are both on their way to heaven. When she arrives there, she may know what she will never know here,—*the time of her conversion.*

We are apt to have too limited views of God. We think we understand Him, but He constantly goes beyond us, and shames us. It is well for us to have wisdom enough to *be ashamed.* The man or minister, who thinks he can trace all the operations of God's Spirit upon the souls of men, or thinks that God's Spirit will be confined to the ways of his wisdom or modes of his imagining, knows very little of God. God sanctifies souls through the truth. *That* is about all that we know. If we think we have got beyond this in knowledge, and so understand the "different operations" of the Holy Spirit, that all true conversions will come within the scope of our favorite patterns, we have much yet to learn. That is a very common error with our Revivalists.

Many persons who have had a religious education, who have never thrown off the restraints of religious influence, and with whom the power of conscience and just principle has been felt, become truly the children of God, without any such sudden and sensible change in their feelings, as we often behold in others. I have learnt not to distrust the religion of such persons. They *wear* well. *Feeling* is not the only evidence of religion. Just principles, an effective conscience, and proper habits of life, are evidences of it also.

The Rev. Dr. A——, (now gone to his rest and reward,) once the distinguished and very useful pastor of a large church in the State of New York, said to me, more than twenty years since,—"After I was settled over my church, for about fifteen years we used to receive into the church on their profession of faith, from twelve to twenty persons every year. But we had no revival. Then, there was a great revival among us, and we received in six months more than all we had received before in three years. After that we had no more gradual admissions, or only a very few, for six or seven years. And so it has been ever since for a period of twenty years. Every few years we have a revival, and after it a dearth, and then another revival. And now, if anybody should ask me, which system I prefer, the revival system or the old one, I should have no hesitation in saying the old one. I know it is not for me to choose. God is a Sovereign, and sends his Spirit as he chooses; but I am sure our prosperity, on the whole, was greater, and our converts wore better, under the old system."

Ceasing to Pray.

At the earnest solicitation of a friend, very dear to me, who had herself just come to a happy tranquillity of mind, I sought an interview with her sister—an accomplished young woman, of about seventeen years of age. I found that the attention of my new acquaintance had been directed to religion some few months previous to this; but though her mind was still very tenderly affected, yet she had ceased to pray. She appeared very much discouraged and very miserable.

"I have given up trying to seek God," says she, "it does no good. I would give anything to be a Christian, but I never shall be!"

"You ought not to say *that*, my child," said I, "You do not *know* that. *I* know you may be a Christian, if you will; for God has never said, seek ye my face in vain."

"Well, sir, it seems to *me* that I can never be a Christian; I have that feeling; it comes over me every time I think about religion."

"And is that the reason why you have ceased to pray?"

"Yes, sir; my prayers will do me no good!"

"How do you know they will do you no good?"

"Because I don't pray with a right heart."

"And do you expect to get a right heart *without* prayer?"

"I don't expect to get a right heart at all, sir."

"Well, if you *could* get a right heart, would you get it without prayer?"

"I suppose not. But all my praying is only an abomination in the sight of God!"

"Does not God command you to pray, to seek Him by prayer; to seek His aid and favor?"

"Yes, sir; I know He does."

"Then is it not a greater abomination in His sight when you *neglect* prayer, than when you pray as well as you can?"

"Perhaps it may be," said she, sadly, "I don't know; but if I regard iniquity in my heart, the Lord will not hear me."

"Then you had better not regard iniquity in your heart. You ought to give God your heart; you ought to repent; you ought to 'cease to do evil,' and 'learn to do well.'

I then took up her Bible which was lying upon the table, and read to her, and explained the first five verses in the second chapter of Proverbs: the first ten verses in the fifty-fifth of Isaiah: and the twelfth and thirteenth verses in the twenty-ninth of Jeremiah. Then I appealed to her,—

"Is it not plain that God requires you to pray? and is it not just as plain that He connects encouragements and promises with that requirement?"

"Yes sir, I suppose it is."

"Then, will you obey Him?"

"I would, sir," said she, "if I had any heart to pray," and burst into tears.

"Do you *want* to have a heart to pray?"

"Oh, sir, I do wish I *had* one!"

"Then, cannot you ask God *to give* you such a heart? Cannot you go to Christ, and give up your heart to Him, and beg Him to accept you, since He loves to save sinners; and *trust* Him to put a right spirit within you, as He has promised to do?"

In this way I reasoned with her out of the Scriptures for a long time. It appeared to me that she was deeply sensible of her sins. She was evidently very miserable. She longed to be a Christian. But she was prevented from every attempt to seek the Lord, by the discouraging idea that her prayers would be useless, and were an offense to God. I had no expectation that she would gain any blessing without prayer, and therefore I requested her to listen to me, as calmly as she could, (for she had become much agitated,) while I should mention to her some things which I wanted her to remember. She tried to repress her emotions; and drying her tears, lifted her face from her handkerchief,—

"I will hear you, sir, very willingly; but you don't know what a wicked heart I have."

I proceeded,—

"The *First* thing I would have you remember is this: that your God *commands you to pray.* That is your duty. Nothing can excuse you from it. Wicked heart as you may have, God commands you to pray.

"The *Second* thing is, that *God connects His promises with these commands.* You have no right to separate them. The promise and the command stand together.

"The *Third* thing is, that when you do thus separate them (saying the promises are not for such wicked hearts as yours), and therefore refuse to pray, you *are not taking God's way*, but your own. You are teaching *Him*, instead of suffering Him to teach *you.* Your duty is to take *His* way. His thoughts are not your thoughts.

"The *Fourth* thing, therefore, is, you are *never to despair.* Despair never yet made a human being any better; it has made many a devil worse. Hope in God, by *believing* what He says. You need not have any hope in yourself; but you may have hope in God, and you may *pray* in hope. Never despair.

"The *Fifth* thing is, that your wicked heart, instead of being a reason why you should *not* pray, is the *very reason why you should* pray most earnestly. It is the strongest of all reasons. Pray just because you *have* a wicked heart. Such a heart needs God's help.

"The *Sixth* thing is, that a great many persons have thought, and felt, and talked about prayer just as you do; and afterwards *have found out that they were mistaken*, have prayed, and have become true and happy Christians. I could name to you, this moment, at least a dozen, whom I have known and have talked to, just as I do now to you. They have been persuaded to pray, and they are now happy in hope. If you will go with me, I will introduce you to some of them, and they will tell you their own story. Remember this: others just like you have found out their error. You may find out yours.

"The *Seventh* thing is, that your impression about prayer *is a temptation of the Devil*, it is a falsehood, a deception, a lie designed to keep you in sin and misery. Not that you think your *heart* worse than it is; but that you do *not* think God so gracious and merciful as He is, to hear the prayers of even such a heart. Resist the Devil and he will flee from you.

"The *Eighth* thing is, that this idea of yours (about not praying with such a heart), is just an *idea of self-righteousness.* You are 'going about to establish a righteousness of your own, and have not submitted yourself to the righteousness of God. Christ is the end of the Law for righteousness.' You wish to pray with such *a good heart*, that God will hear you on that account. This is pride, wicked, foolish pride, a spirit of self-righteousness, self-justification, and self-reliance. It is *this* which keeps you from prayer.

"Do you understand me?"

"Yes sir, I think I do."

"And are not all these things true?"

"I don't know but they are, sir."

"Then will you pray? Will you begin *now*, today?"

"Yes sir, *I will* try."

For a time she faithfully kept her promise. Several times after this I conversed with her, and though she did not appear to me to become more unhappy, yet she did appear to me to become more truly convicted. Her *conscience* seemed to be more awakened. Her mind seemed to be more influenced by the principles of truth, and I fondly expected that she would soon find 'peace in believing.' But she did not. She yielded to the old temptation. She neglected prayer; and, in a few weeks, divine truths ceased to affect her!

I strove to bring her back to her closet duty, but in vain! Years have passed, she is still without hope!

Continuing to Pray.

Having noticed from the pulpit, for several Sabbaths, the very fixed attention of a young friend to all that I uttered in my sermons; I called upon her at her residence. She had been a gay girl; and her social disposition, the pleasantness of her manners, her taste, and the almost unequalled kindness of her heart, while they made her a favorite everywhere, exposed her, as I thought, to be drawn into temptations to volatility and the vanities of the world. As I spoke to her of religion, her eyes filled with tears, and she frankly told me, that, for several weeks, she had been thinking very much upon that subject, and had been "very unhappy" in finding herself "so far from God,—just as you described in your sermon," said she "'*without God and without hope.*' That sermon told me my heart, and I have had no peace since. I am astonished at my sinfulness, and I am more astonished at my stupidity and hardness of heart." I conversed with her, and counselled her, as well as I knew how, and we kneeled together in prayer.

After this I saw her three or four times, within the space of a fortnight. She studied the way of salvation most assiduously, and, as I thought, with a most docile disposition; and she prayed for pardon, and for the aid of the Holy Spirit, with most intense earnestness. "I do want to love my heavenly Father," said she; "I do pray for the Holy Spirit to show my poor heart the way to the Saviour."

Calling upon her a few days after, I found that her appearance was very much altered. She was less frank than I had ever found her before; and though not less solemn perhaps, it was a different sort of solemnity. She appeared to be more downcast than ever, though not so much agitated, not affected to tears, but having now the appearance of fixed, pensive thought. The impression came over my mind, that she had been led to yield up the world, and that the peculiarity which I noticed in her manner and conversation, was the mute humility of a broken-hearted penitent, now musing over the world she had sacrificed, more than rejoicing over the Christ she had found. But after a little farther interrogation, I found it was not that: she was as far from peace as ever.

But I could not understand her. Her heart did not seem to me as formerly. She had no tears to shed now; her manner was cold, and unlike herself; her words were measured and few; her misery, which seemed deeper than before, had put on an aspect almost of sullenness.

It was somewhat difficult for me to ascertain her state of mind; but after a few minutes, yielding to my urgency to tell me her feelings as a friend, she said to me, with a fixed look of despair,—

"I am entirely discouraged! I never shall be a Christian! My heart is so wicked, that it is wrong for me to pray at all, and for the last three days I have not tried! I have given up all hope of ever being saved!" She thanked me for my kindness and good intentions; but gave me to understand, that she did not wish to have the subject of religion urged upon her attention any more.

I encouraged her to persevere in her attempts to gain salvation. Especially I enjoined upon her the duty of prayer, and said to her almost *precisely the same things* which I had said before to another friend, and which are recorded in the sketch preceding this, as eight things to be remembered.

As I was speaking to her in the way of encouragement, her look appeared to alter, her bosom heaved, she burst into tears, and sobbed aloud. Referring to this some weeks afterwards, she said to me, "When you encouraged me so kindly, that day, my whole heart melted; I would have done anything you told me; I thought, if God is so kind,

I *must* love Him, I *will* love Him." She promised to resume prayer again. She kept her promise. And about a week after that, light broke in upon her darkness; she was one of the most bright and joyous creatures, and, I am sure, one of the most lovely ones, that ever consecrated to God the dew of her youth. She has continued to be so. Her days are all sunshine. Her heart is all happiness, and humility, and love. "My dear pastor," said she to me, (when I asked what particular *truth or means* it was that led her to Christ,) "I never *should* have found my Saviour, if you had not encouraged me so kindly, and led me back to prayer. Prayer is *everything*, for God answers it."

These young persons, (mentioned in this, and in the preceding sketch,) were very much alike in conviction, in despondency, in temptation—they had the same means, the same ministry—the same truths were urged upon them in the same manner. Surely God is the hearer of prayer. If that other young woman could have been "led back to prayer," as this happy one expressed it; who can doubt that she would have been happy, too, in 'the kindness of her youth, and the love of her espousals.' If this page ever meets her eye, may it lead her back to prayer."

Human Ability.

A MEMBER of my church called upon me, with manifest solicitude, in respect to a friend of his, whom he desired me to visit: a young woman, who was a stranger to me. She was a member of the church, (but not of mine,) and though she was a resident in the place where I lived, she did not attend upon my ministry. I had reason to believe that she had tried it, but soon left the congregation because she disliked the preaching. She attended worship with another congregation, whose minister, as I suppose, preached many doctrines, not only *different* from those which I preached, but *contrary* to them. And I had little doubt that he would talk to inquiring sinners very differently from myself.

To visit this young woman under such circumstances was not pleasant to me. I should have to encounter her prejudices, and very likely should be obliged to contradict many things which had been taught to her; and, in such a case, it seemed to me almost beyond hope, that I should be the instrument of any good. However, she had consented to meet me, and it would be ungracious, if not unchristian, for me to refuse. I understood that a deep and painful anxiety, respecting her salvation, had troubled her for many months; and when her friend desired her to converse with me, she had consented *reluctantly*, I had no doubt. She told him she was "willing to converse with *anybody*," an expression indicative, as I thought, of no great confidence in myself, but yet it manifested an anxiety of mind.

I immediately called upon her. She was an intelligent young woman; her manners were refined, her education was excellent, and her well-trained mind was evidently accustomed to deep and extensive study. I am confident she has few equals in intellectual excellence.

She was in deep trouble. She had been a professor of religion for more than ten years, having united with the church in a distant part of the country, but for several years past she had been convinced that she was an unconverted sinner still.

Besides possessing a mind of great strength, she appeared to me to have much firmness of character, great power of discrimination, much pride of reason, and an independence which bordered hard upon obstinacy. But I thought she was of an amiable disposition. Her frankness pleased me, and I discovered in her such a tenderness and depth of sensibility as are not common. On the whole, I was much pleased with her—I esteemed her; but I feared that her firmness and her pride of reason would not easily yield to Christ, as prophet, priest and king. She had much philosophy and no faith.

"For years," (she said to me,) "I have been fully convinced that there is *something* in religion which I know nothing about, and know not where to find it." And as I endeavored to point out to her, as clearly and simply as I could, the way of salvation, explaining to her the great truths of Christianity; I soon found that her opinions came into conflict with the truths which I presented to her, and she seemed wedded to her opinions with an unequalled fondness, firmness and confidence.

She evidently disliked, and very *greatly* disliked, the whole system of truth which I urged upon her attention and her acceptance; but those truths to which she seemed most opposed, and which she was ready to call in question, combat, or explain away, were such as have respect to human depravity, the dependence of a sinner on the special influences of the Holy Spirit, and justification by faith in Jesus Christ, as making atonement for our sins, delivering us from the curse of the law, and securing to us the full favor of God. But she did not appear to be so *much* opposed to the atonement as to the Divine sovereignty and a sinner's dependence. She fully believed in "*human ability.*" She had not a doubt that a sinner possesses full power to come to Christ, to repent and turn to God. The idea that a sinner can do nothing of himself, which will have any saving efficacy, she could not endure. The doctrine of helpless dependence was unutterably odious to her. She said to me, as I was urging upon her heart some of the practical truths of God, "I believe as Mr. F—— believes." We had some little argumentation upon the points whereon we differed, but I soon perceived she was so much attached to her false system, had defended it so long, and had so much pride and false philosophy embarked for its support, that no direct demonstrations addressed to the intellect would probably avail to batter it down.

But *her system had not saved her*. That was her weak point. It had not led her to peace. It had not satisfied her heart,—a heart still wanting something, and roaming, like Noah's dove on weary wing, over a world of waters,—no rock to rest upon. So I waived all disputation, avoided theological points, (as much as I *could*, and still utter the truths appropriate to her,) and left her own wanting heart to convince her of the truth, by the pains of its own experience. I kindly assured her that there was salvation for her, a peace, and a repose, to which she was now a stranger; and encouraged her to seek the Lord with all her heart, under the direction of the Bible, and praying for the help of the Holy Spirit; for I was fully convinced that nothing but *the experience* of her own soul would correct the errors of her understanding, and lead her to believe the truths of God. If her "ability" was sufficient to repent without the aids of the Holy Spirit, I thought she had better try.

After several interviews with her, I was compelled to leave home, and I saw her no more for nearly a month. As I took my leave of her, I had little hope in her case. Evidently she was prejudiced against me, against my principles, and against all my preaching. Personally, therefore, it seemed impossible for me to have any influence over her. Her mind was filled with a system, in all its spirit, and all its influences upon personal experience in religion, entirely contrary to my religious views. She constantly heard preaching, which I thought, by her account of it, to be directly contrary to the truth which I was most desirous to impress upon her heart. I could not talk to her of seeking God, or explain to her the way of salvation, without coming into conflict with some of her darling opinions. And hence I could not expect that all I had said to her would be of much avail. Much as I esteemed her, I was half sorry that I had ever seen her at all.

On my return home about a month afterwards, I

called upon her, as she had politely requested. I found her in a very different state of mind. She was most solemn, but full of peace. Her mind was all light, her heart all joy. As she talked to me, every one of her thoughts was clear as a sunbeam. She related to me her religious exercises with so much precision, clearness, and graphic power of description, and in such sweet humility and loveliness of spirit, that I was utterly astonished: I thought I had never heard anything equal to it. On that account I asked of her the favor to write down the account she had given me,—her own religious history. She yielded to my solicitation, and a few days afterwards I received from her the following account, which I think one of the most instructive and graphic descriptions I have ever seen. I am sure the reader will join me in thanking her for allowing it to take a place in this volume.

"DR. SPENCER,

"Dear Sir—In compliance with your request, I transmit to you the following sketch of my religious history:

"Almost eleven years have elapsed since I made a profession of religion. I thought then that I was a Christian; but I made a mistake. I found out my mistake gradually. One thing was enough to teach it to me As weeks and months passed on, I found my path, instead of being like that of the just, 'shining more and more unto the perfect day,' only grew darker and darker; so that I finally feared its end must be in utter darkness.

"The time, when I first thought I had begun the Christian course, was during a Revival. The teaching I then continually heard, was, 'Give yourselves to God, and go right about serving Him,' as if doing *that* would of itself make one a Christian. I finally concluded that must be all; the importunities of friends were pressing me, and I at last expressed my determination and readiness to begin then the service of God, believing, as I was told, that we must not wait for light, we should find it in the discharge of duty. And herein I see now how the mistake of my life was made; my religion was one of works and not of faith. I knew nothing about faith.

"As time passed on, I became fully convinced, that there was no Christian principle at work in my heart. What then could I do? I always had a great repugnance to saying anything about my personal feelings; and if I should say I was not a Christian, and ask advice, I should only be told what I already knew, and what I heard preached every Sabbath day. I believed I might make my professed religion a religion of the heart, and there was no need of any publicity about it: as I was already a professor, why, it would make no great change in me. And I have tried to do so again and again, and wondered as often, why it was, that religion was a thing so utterly unattainable for *me.* This always made me miserable, except when I forgot it. And though I have sometimes almost forgotten it for weeks and months, still it has ever been a shadow in my heart, a secret blight upon everything.

"A few years since I spent a season in the State of Michigan, where I was under the influence and preaching of the 'Oberlin Doctrines.' My prejudices were against them, supposing some mysterious evil, I scarcely knew what, was lurking among them. But when I began to understand those views on depravity, ability, imputation, the atonement, &c., they pleased me exceedingly. They addressed themselves to my *reason* as I thought, and commended themselves to my heart. I found something tangible to work upon; and ever since, religion, as a speculative matter, has been to me the most interesting of all things. I adopted the views of Mr. F——, with my whole heart and soul; have ever since been openly committed to that faith, and everywhere its avowed and ready advocate.

"For some two years past I have taken very special interest in Theological discussions. I resided in W———, Pennsylvania, where every one belonged to the genuine 'Old School.' The Superintendent of the Seminary, in which I was engaged as a

Teacher, was a Clergyman of the Associate Reformed Church, and a large portion of the community were of that demonination. I was alone in my opinions, but openly committed to them. Last summer the Pastor of the Presbyterian church which I attended, formed a class among his young people to study the 'Confession of Faith.' I despised the book with my whole heart: but I joined the class and entered upon the work, all ready for a contest. A great deal of interest was soon awakened, not only among the members of the class, but it extended to others also. To me, finding myself alone as I was, it was a matter of most intense interest and excitement. I possessed myself of all possible aids, studied carefully, and if I found a point that baffled me, I sent it to a Reverend friend of mine, who was a disciple of Mr. F——, and in whose logic I had the utmost confidence. He allowed me to ask him as many questions as I chose, replied very fully to them all, and was ready to procure me all the means of information I desired.

"In the midst of this I was called away, all unexpectedly, suddenly, wonderfully; and I regretted it, because it put an end to my discussions, which were in prospect for the winter. I came here into a new world to me, and with work enough to occupy all my thoughts and all my time. Then I thought to myself, 'how shall I ever become a Christian now?' It seemed as if the most hopeful time had just passed, and now it was entirely out of the question; and I felt sad, as I thought 'perhaps God has given me to the world to take all my portion.' And during the first part of the winter I had little disposition as well as little time for serious thought.

"I had great difficulty in deciding what place of worship to attend. There were several things which might have induced me to attend upon your preaching, but then I thought, 'Dr. Spencer, with his blue Calvinistic notions, I shall quarrel with him every Sabbath.' No, I would not go there. I finally found preaching elsewhere much more congenial to my taste, and took a seat in that congregation.

"Some weeks since, I heard a sermon one Sabbath morning on human responsibility, which the clergyman brought out by dwelling very much on the god-like faculties with which we are endowed, and the obligations we are under to develop them. It pleased me exceedingly, for that had always been one of my favorite topics, and it tended to make me feel self-reliant and strong. In the afternoon, it so happened that I attended your church, where I heard a sermon on humility. Such a *contrast of sermons* really startled me! They actually came in conflict. If the thing could have been possible, I should readily have believed that the sermon of the afternoon was *meant* for a reply to that of the morning. I rebelled against it with all my heart. Yet I could not help thinking that humility, after all, was most truly Christian-like, and the most eminent Christians had always expressed just such humiliating views of themselves. It would be easy to be a Christian if I only felt so; but I could *not* feel so, for I did not *believe* we were such 'weak miserable worms,' and altogether between the impressions of the two sermons I was exceedingly troubled.

"About that time the things of religion were continually presenting themselves to my thoughts, with an unusual power. I realized as never before how utterly unsatisfying everything earthly proved. In all the past there had been nothing substantial or enduring; the future could promise nothing, but to repeat the emptiness of the past; and the present brought only the consciousness that I was sowing the wind and feeding on ashes! That higher and worthier life I almost despaired of ever attaining, for what more could I do than I had done? any other attempt would be but a repetition of struggles, that had been just as determined as they were unavailing. Yet there remained those fearful certainties—an eternity before me, and a soul in constant peril!

"Every Sabbath day these thoughts would possess me with such a fearful power that I would be led to form resolutions and purposes, immediately and with my whole heart to make one more trial to find peace with God. Yet, in the daily duties of the week, such thoughts would in a measure be dissipated, and such purposes forgotten. On one of those solemn Sabbaths, a few weeks since, notice was given by the clergyman, that during the week evening services would be held in the church, and that Mr. F—— would preach. That seemed like a message to *me*. It brought me to a point where I felt compelled to consider if this was not the time for the final decision. I found no interest or pleasure in the present, that need allure away my thoughts; I knew no better time could come in the future. More than all this, all unexpectedly my old prophet had appeared! I certainly should have no disposition to quarrel with *him:* all my combativeness would be laid at rest. I could receive whatever *he* would say. Not an excuse was left me. God had certainly met me half way. I dared not defer the work. I felt it must be done now or never.

"I resolved to attend these meetings. I went simply to learn what I should do. Though not very much prepossessed with his manner, yet in his matter I recognized the same Mr. F——, with whom I was already so well acquainted through his writings. His sermons were very much like those revival sermons of his, which were published some years ago. His philosophy came out occasionally in an incidental way, awakening most pleasing responses in my heart. I heard him with the greatest pleasure and satisfaction. Because I dared not then neglect any means that seemed to lie in my way, I went into the inquiry meetings. It cost my pride a struggle, yet I dared not excuse myself. At the close of a conversation I had there one night with Mr. F——, he said to me, in his peculiar manner, just as he was leaving me,—'Give your heart to God to-night. Won't you? Give your heart to God, before you go to bed: promise me.'

"'I have no faith in my promises,' said I.

"'*What?*'

"I repeated the answer, 'I have no faith in my promises.'

"'Well, make a promise,' said he, 'and stick to it.'

"But I did not then think how unwittingly I was confessing, in my answer, an inability I would have denied. God was then beginning to teach me the hardest lesson I had to learn.

"I came home from that meeting in a perfect sea of troubles. I was utterly amazed to find how much my pride had suffered, in putting myself in such a new attitude. I felt mortified, humbled, broken, in the desperate conflict. And I thought within myself, 'If I am so proud as this, perhaps it is only the beginning of what I must come to.'

"Then, not knowing what else to do, I resolved to see a friend of mine, who was a professor of religion, confess to him I was no Christian, and find what he would tell me. This resolve was just reversing my previous determination, and cost me another severe struggle. But after I had seen him, and all the thoughts of my soul had found utterance, it relieved me. Yet still my heart almost fainted, as I found how the committal had forced me on, shutting up all retreat against me.

"That night was with me a serious counting of the cost. I had begun somewhat to realize how my pride and will must suffer; and I brought into full consideration what more I might have to do. The idea of telling my friends about my personal religious feelings, was most repugnant to me: I had always felt it an insurmountable difficulty. I *never could* do it; and I had often feared this would prove a fatal hindrance. Every thought of this kind came up before me; and then I balanced all with my eternal interests. The question was settled decisively, finally.

"My friend had expressed a very earnest wish, that I should see you, sir. Well, I was in such deep waters, I told him 'I would talk with *anybody*.' The next day you came to see me; and after hearing my account of myself, you told me I had been 'going about to establish a righteousness of my own,' and therefore I had failed to find what I needed. You told me that my reliance always had been, and still was, upon my own powers and will to work out my salvation, without God to work in me. You said, I 'could not do it; I could do no thing of myself.' That was the hardest of all things for me to receive. I could not understand it. I did not believe it. I told you I *knew* I had got something to do. And afterwards, when I saw you, that was the point you continually endeavored to impress upon me,* that I could do nothing of myself. It seemed to me the darkest mystery in the universe. Anything on earth I would *do;* but here my understanding was hopelessly baffled. Yet when, two or three days after, you sailed for Savannah, I felt exceedingly disappointed. I heard it with the greatest regret, for your kindness to me,

* This representation is true, but defective. I did not fail to impress upon her attention, her *obligation* to repent, her *duty* to be a Christian, and the truth, that she had *much to do,* which she must do freely, voluntarily. But I insisted upon it, that her *help* was in God, that she was an undone and dependent sinner, to be saved, if saved at all, by grace through Jesus Christ. I did "continually endeavor to impress upon her, that she could do nothing of herself." It was needful to do so. That was a truth which she neither felt nor believed. I taught her, that she had "lost all ability of will to any spiritual good accompanying salvation," and that she needed the Holy Spirit to "enable her freely to will and to do that which is spiritually good." She speaks of her "favorite doctrine of ability." It was a favorite falsehood with her: and I "continually endeavored" to undeceive her.

and interest for me, had won my most sincere gratitude and affection.

"I had endeavored to avoid touching upon theological points. I did not wish to think of them. I felt that now it was another question with me. My theology was safe, and safely put away. I had not a suspicion that it was to be interfered with. I knew well enough the wide difference of opinion betwixt you and myself, and to enter upon any discussion would be most unprofitable and vain. Besides, you seemed no more inclined to treat upon theological points than I did. So I did not happen to think until afterwards, the bow you had drawn at a venture had sent its shaft with a tremendous thrust right upon my favorite doctrine of ability. It struck the doctrine as much as it struck me. Indeed it could not hit me without hitting the doctrine, for the doctrine was directly betwixt me and the arrow of truth. But you were gone, and I was left to think of it.

"Nothing yet seemed bringing me nearer to the light. I became almost discouraged. Human helps failed me, and I found that I failed myself. *It was so.* My utmost efforts of *will* were wholly ineffectual. I *did thoroughly prove them.* Anything on earth I was willing to do. As I had told you, 'I would die ten thousand deaths.' And my own multiplied endeavors,—my own experiences, did finally convince me that it *was not of myself to turn to God.* And then, with some sense that I was lost forever unless He did help me, I tried to look to Him for help.

"But then came my difficulty,—*I could not find Him!* The heavens were dark, my heart was dark, and the only God I could think of was a cold abstraction of my own forming! For a long time I struggled with that difficulty,—I *could* not find Him. Finally, the thought flashed upon me, 'there *is* a God.' (And then I recognized a familiar principle, when knowing the solution of a question *does exist*, we are patient to follow through all dark ways to find it.) 'It is *true*, though I have not yet found Him, there *is* a God,—God is.' It was like finding one spot on which I could rest. Wherever He was, *He* was the God I wanted. The idea of His *power* then possessed me. That was my first *realization* of any attribute of God. And it seems to me to show the wisdom of divine teaching, that when I had been full of miserable self-reliances, and vainly seeking in myself the strength to turn to God, the first attribute of His that I realized was *His power.* It came upon me with such force and vividness, that it seemed as if I had never before really believed there *was* a God. And then I remembered that He is '*mighty* to save.' That idea came so upon me, that it seemed to fill my whole being. Such a great and glorious Saviour then He was, that human pride might well be set aside for most humble thankfulness. *Such* an one I could worship forever. So different He seemed from what had been my own miserable conceptions of a Saviour, that I would find myself questioning if there *could* be *such* a Saviour. But yet it was most true,—I *felt* it to be true, and wanted to tell it to everybody in the house; besides, the whole Bible told of One just so 'mighty to save.'

"And then came new views,—clearer views of the atonement. I saw and felt how God himself had paid the ransom for a whole race ruined; He had himself borne the penalty; on Him was laid the iniquity of us all; it was all *done*, so that now there was nothing to *be* done, only to trust in Him to save us. It seemed such an *infinite* atonement,—so full, and it was so free; so that *every one* that thirsteth, may come,—whosoever will, may take freely. It was infinite *love* that, when extended to those so lost and guilty, became infinite mercy. There every sin might be covered and lost.

"That night I read 'my goodness, my fortress,' &c., and the thought struck me, is it so, then, that even a Christian has not his own goodness?—is his goodness Christ? Yes, it was so. In Him was all fulness, and *such* a fulness, then, there must be; whatever the sinner needed, whatever the sinner had not, was all found in Him. And it was such a new idea that the principle of holiness was not, after all, to be found in our own heart, but it was all in Christ,—Christ was the 'end of the law for righteousness.' He was our goodness, our righteousness, our sanctification, our redemption,—He alone our salvation. And when that idea fully broke upon me, I was lost in it. The *forms*, in which I had always brought God to my mind, had dropped away, and a new God,—a Saviour, seemed to have appeared out of heaven, and filled every place around me. It was an *uncreated* glory and purity all about me, and *such* a purity, and *such* a glory,—my only expression for it was, '*such a glorious Saviour*.' The intensity and vividness of that feeling and conception, which was the most glorious of anything that ever entered my soul, passed away after a time, but I was still happy in thinking there was just such a Saviour, until I attempted to express something of my idea to my friend who first directed me to you, and then it seemed to amount to nothing more than what I had known before,—what everybody knew, that there was a God and a Saviour.

"But it was a day or two after that before I happened to think, that here was another of my favorite doctrines torn up, root and branch,—that against imputation. But so it was; I felt it was gone. I knew in my very heart that Christ's righteousness was the only ground of acceptance. That expression, 'making mention of his righteousness,' struck me with peculiar force. And it came to me again and again, so full of meaning! But I did not feel a regret that my own former speculations were swept away, for the plan, as I now saw it, seemed so infinitely more glorious, that I could only rejoice in it. Not only had He paid our debt, but He clothed us also in His own robe of righteousness, that we need not depend on ourselves, or look for righteousness in ourselves, but find all in Christ. That was truly a glorious redemption.

"The vividness of these conceptions gradually dimmed, but still the *truth* remained. I *believed* everything that I had now learned, for *it was my heart's experience.* And because I found these impressions lost their vividness, and I did not feel them moving me, but felt how great a work was to be done in my heart; I could not, dared not think my heart was really changed; and I was continually fearful of falling again upon a false hope.

"About that time, in a prayer-meeting, I heard the minister to whose congregation I belonged, make the remark, as he was giving some directions to inquirers—'now we are not going to pray God to *enable* you to consecrate yourselves to Him; there is not a soul here but is able to do that.' He said it was 'just as easy, as giving away a book,' he held in his hand, 'all an act of his will.' That startled me. I *had just learned better!* I had found in my own soul, that 'it is *not* of him that willeth, nor of him that runneth, but of God that showeth mercy.' I did believe he was 'the Author and Finisher of our faith,'—even the *Author.* This boasted power of the human will, I found to be the very rock on which I had split before; so that that minister's teaching would not do for me. He had invited any who wished to see him, to meet him the next evening, and I had purposed to go; but now I would not venture.

"In the preaching of Mr. F—— hitherto, his peculiar doctrines had only come out incidentally. But a few nights after this I heard a sermon from him, almost entirely devoted to his peculiar views. He went on to speak of the fall, and that 'when man had changed his heart one way, he could as well do it the other,'—to speak also of an 'imputed righteousness,' which he seemed to think was 'the same as an imputed heaven' would be,—to speak of the power of example being the strongest moral force that could be brought to bear upon the mind, and this we had in Christ. He said that motives presented would work out their effects. These were the same things that I continually dwelt upon last summer. They now swept over me like a torrent, not *unvincingly* however, for *my own heart disproved them*—but with a strange power. It was like reviving what I had just buried. Those old speculations (which my own experience had *proved* to be *false*), all woke up fresh, and my mind was filled with them. It was true that sermon touched a chord that was dear to me, and I was compelled to have all the struggle over again. Clouds and darkness shut down over me, and I could not see my way out! But I did not go to hear Mr. F—— any more.

"By this time I began to look at my Theology in earnest, to see if anything therein was keeping me back from the light. And I finally acknowledged, that whatever the Bible said, whatever God taught, however it might come into conflict with my prejudice, *I must receive it.* I must take it, and learn it, and believe it as a little child, my own prejudice and *reason* out of the question. If Adam's sin had anything to do with us, why I must submit. And more than all else, if God did even ordain to leave some to everlasting punishment, I had nothing to say,—it was his right. That ninth chapter of the Romans, which I had quarrelled with more than any other chapter in the Bible, and had been determined not to receive, unless it could all be explained away; why, if God had really said so, I must take it, I must take it just as it reads, for, 'who art thou that repliest against God?'

And I could see now, that if it were so, it did more fully manifest the riches of his glory on the 'vessels of mercy.' His plans and purposes were none of my business. God would reign; and all I had to do was to be willing to be saved in the only way He had provided.

"But even after all this, I found myself in trouble For some days I seemed to have come to a stopping place. I could not go back. I knew not how to go forward. All was dark, and God was far away. I knew not what hindered me, or why I was in darkness. I could think of nothing which I was not willing to give up,—nothing that I was not willing God should do with me; and yet it seemed as if something must be wanting. Unquestionably the fault was in me; my deceitful heart had hidden away a part of the price, and I could not find it.

"I was remarking this difficulty to my friend, when he suggested that I seemed to be looking to my past experiences, fearful of being again deceived, and added, that never before in my life had I had such a course of thought. That remark struck me, and when I was alone that evening it induced a long train of reflections. I had never had such a course of thought before. *That was most true.* Never, in my life, not at all before, when I expressed the hope that I was a Christian, had I experienced anything like this. Never before had eternal things come to me with such reality and power, concentrating my whole soul upon one intense, absorbing thought. And now I bethought myself of all the various processes through which my mind within a few days had past. My very power of thinking surprised me. I thought, that while ever before I had found it difficult to fix my mind for any length of time upon my own eternal interests, now my soul's salvation had been the one thing continually before me. Engaged in my usual occupations, there was a constant under-current of thought, and when at leisure, my mind was filled with one intense, absorbing interest. Here certainly was one thing unlike what I had ever known before. In this respect I found myself a new creature. I reflected, also, that I had always revolted from telling my friends that I was not a Christian, or from expressing to them any religious concern, but now it was very different with me. I had actually surprised myself several times in thinking, with a sort of pleasure, how I would *tell* all my friends what wonderful things God had done for me. And it occurred to me now, how *unlike me* that was—how totally different from what I had always felt before. I was astonished, and said to myself, 'what has wrought this change?'

" Again, I reflected that night, I had been fully grounded and settled in a system of theology; it had been a matter of exceeding interest to me. I had believed it as fully and firmly as *reason* fully persuaded *can* believe. Neither had it been a mere prejudice of education. The prejudices of education and the influences under which I have always been, (except at one time for a few months,) would all have led me far enough the other way; but it was a theological belief, brought about by the power of my own reason. I honestly believed, when I rested on that system, and I believe now, that no force of argument in the world could have changed me. If I had not succeeded in sustaining my system I should have felt that the *truth* of it remained untouched,—I had only failed in the way of showing it. I had repeatedly heard all the strongest arguments that could be adduced against me, and they never moved me. The first sermon I heard after I came to this place was a sermon from Dr. Skinner, on "Depravity." It was a master-piece. As an effort of intellect, and for its logic, I admired it with all my heart. But I said, 'a man equally logical could answer him on the other side, and do even better *there*.' Besides, my pride was concerned; for I had been so openly and everywhere committed to my faith, I had contended for it so often and with so many, that this *alone* might make it a hard matter for me to retract; almost impossible. And besides all this, when I began to think about being a Christian now, theology had been left out of my thoughts.

I felt it was another thing that interested me. I did not wish to bring it up, and it never entered into my mind that it would be meddled with, much less that I should renounce one point. The idea of doing so I knew would have astonished me. Indeed, my attention had not been at all called to my theology, until arrested by finding it breaking away under me. But now, *understandingly*, *willingly*, I found I had given it all to the winds. *Human* agency seemed to have had nothing to do about it. Even you, sir, had to be called away, so I could not say your persuasion or influence had done it; and on the other hand, Mr. F.—— was right here to prompt me; nevertheless it was all gone. I had been almost entirely shut in to myself and my Bible, and there had been no form of argument or reason; the change had come about almost unconsciously to myself, like the wind blowing where it listeth. And now, what had done this? No person else had done it; and I felt that it *was not at all* like *me* to do it; it was the most unlike me of anything on earth; and then I felt convinced it must be some higher power—some divine agency. *It must be so.* And you cannot imagine with what tremendous power that conviction forced itself upon me; how it startled my very being! unless you know that my old speculations had led me to the conclusion that there was no such thing as the *special* influence of the Holy Spirit. I never could understand that doctrine of *special* divine influence. I thought it was irreconcilable with free moral agency, and so I concluded it was a delusion, or a mere figure of speech. But now I found God himself had taught it to me. The conviction forced itself upon me, that here was a work of God's Holy Spirit.

"And as I tried to account for all that I had experienced in any other way, (aiming to guard against being deceived again into a false hope,) that passage came very strikingly to my mind, where the Jews, when they could not deny that devils were really gone out, said, 'He casteth out devils by Beelzebub,' and Christ answered, 'A house divided against itself cannot stand; if Satan cast out Satan, he is divided against himself.' That might be a crafty suggestion, I thought; but it was not like Satan to do for me what I had experienced, nor was it like my own wicked heart to do it. It must be *God*, who was leading me by His Spirit, 'in a way that I knew not.'

"Then, in that night of reflection, I thought also of other things, many lesser things, in which, as it seemed, in spite of myself, I had been completely turned around. It did seem like turning the rivers of water. They were flowing backward against their current.

"Well *then*, I thought, if God's Spirit has done

such wonderful things in me, (and I could not now doubt it,) if He has already done things which I never before believed *could* have been done, then *He can do all things* else; and He would, I did believe He would, I could trust Him that He would; He would work in me to will and to do what I could never do myself. He would continue the work that He had begun, and finish it in righteousness. There I could rest; there the promises seemed to meet me. God's word was pledged, sure as His everlasting throne; He was faithful; the Word witnessed with the Spirit; and what He had promised, He was also able to perform. This was my light, my hope, and joy.

"And as I thus looked back, and saw how I *had* been led, I felt assured I might account, that the long-suffering of God was salvation; that He had purposes of mercy for me; and now, if He had met me, it had truly been when I 'was a great way off;' and He had received me in such a wonderful way, that He would have all the glory. I thought too, it was because He was a covenant-keeping God; and as He kept His covenant with faithful Abraham, because 'he *believed* God, and it was accounted unto him for righteousness,' so now He does keep His covenant with believing parents. And such faith as my father and mother exercised when they gave me to God, would be remembered and accepted.

This seemed to me like another added to the multiplied assurances of His faithfulness, that He *is* a God keeping covenant and showing mercy; and therefore, He kept me from an utter destruction, and followed me with purposes of mercy, to make me 'willing in the day of His power.' I did feel in my soul, that *He* had done everything for me, that had been done; so I could truly say, '*He* sent from above, *He* took me, *He* drew me out of many waters.' Whatever I had learned, He had taught me; and I did believe, that same Spirit of truth would yet lead me into all truth. And I rejoiced, that our salvation did not depend any more upon our own will, or our own power of enduring unto the end; if it did, I felt it would be a yoke harder than that which the Jews were not able to bear. It was wonderful to think, how the whole work was of God. He paid the debt; He clothed us in his own righteousness; His Spirit made us willing, and then continues to work in us, keeping us by the *power of God* through faith unto salvation. Such contemplations and experiences as these assured my heart, I felt that God was with me. The darkness is past; the true light now shineth.

"It seems to me now, that one of my greatest errors has been, making my *reason* the test for everything,—bringing every principle to the court of *reason* for trial. Starting in that way, it is not wonderful that I fell into error. I see now that *faith* is infinitely higher,—just faith in God and His word. Reason gets blinded, dizzy, lost, where faith is clear, calm, steady, and in a region of light. Reason *cannot* understand the things of the Spirit of God; not that they are contrary to it, but beyond it,—seen only by faith. And this is one of the most wonderful things that I have learned,—the beauty and power of faith. I never could understand it before. It has perplexed me a great deal. If it meant anything more than a mere intellectual belief, I could not at all apprehend it. I believe I finally concluded it did not. But *now* I see it as everything. The Bible is full of it. And to think that is all,—just to *believe* God is able and willing to do it all, and let him do it,—it is wonderful *that* should be such a stone of stumbling. Yet as I think of it, it seems to me I cannot conceive of any such other sublime act of the mind as that *faith in things invisible*, which the Christian exercises; and to think, too, that any one,—the very lowest orders of intellect can and do exercise it strongly; it must be the work of the Spirit of God. Really to believe in God, in a Saviour, in the power of the Holy Spirit, and to feel that the things of the soul and eternity are *realities*, seems to me like a new and wonderful thing. Even the thought that *there is a God*, as it happens to flash across my mind, *thrills* through my very soul. All these things,—it seems to me as if I had just been taught them.

"If I had been a Christian when I took hold of those theological matters it might have been different with me; but as it was, they pleased my unregenerate heart as well as my reason, and it startles me to think to what conclusions I was arriving. *I know* those doctrines well-nigh made shipwreck with me.

"The doctrine of election seems to me *now*, naturally, and necessarily to grow out of God's sovereignty. I rebelled against it, because I rebelled against Him. And now nothing melts me like it. To hear Him say, 'ye have not chosen me, but I have chosen you,' and then to think there was not a shadow of merit or claim in me, but it was all His own sovereign, absolute will and pleasure,—I can only say, 'not unto us, not unto us, but unto thy name be all the glory.' That He should have *predestinated* us unto the adoption of children according to the good pleasure of His will, is certainly in keeping with everything else that I have learned,—that it is all of God. 'Esaias is very bold,' but I begin to see how he may still be *right*, when he says, 'I was found of them that sought me not, I was made manifest unto them that asked not after me.'

"I know and feel that there is yet a great deal

to be done in my heart; but I believe I do feel more and more as if I could follow on through darkness and shadowy light, trusting that God will at length lead me out into perfect day. I cannot but think that my old rebellion is gone. I do feel willing that He should reign, and I rejoice that He does. And if I have any desire in my soul it is for God, for the living God, the God that reigns, and reigns in grace by Jesus Christ. While heaven once seemed desirable only as a place of security from eternal death, or at most, of intellectual pleasure, now what makes my heart go out for it is, that there I 'shall be like Him, for I shall see Him as He is.'

"And now it is my heart's desire to live 'as seeing Him who is invisible.' And whatever it costs me, I would be a humble, decided, constant follower of Christ, feeling in my own soul the power of that faith, that 'works by love, and purifies the heart,'—living the life which I now live, 'by the faith of the Son of God, who loved me and gave Himself for me.'"

* * * *

Conversion to God is conversion to truth.

The Faults of Christians.

Among my parishioners, at one time, there was a very industrious and respectable man, a mechanic, for whom I entertained a high esteem. I thought him a man of talents, and of much good feeling. He was about thirty years of age, was married, and his wife had recently become a child of God, as she believed, and had made a public profession of her faith in Christ. I had now the more hope of being useful to him, on account of his wife's experience of grace, and the uniformly happy state of her mind. He had also some other relatives who were members of my church, and were exemplary Christians. He was himself a constant and attentive hearer of the gospel every Sabbath day, and whenever I met him, (which was very often;) he was free to speak of religion, and confess his obligation and his anxiety to be a Christian. I had no small hope in his case. I had noticed the increasing depth of his seriousness. Besides, I knew him to be a personal friend to myself, very much attached to me, and on that account I had the more expectation of being able to influence his mind upon the subject, which now occupied, as he said, "all his thoughts."

After his wife had become a pious woman and a member of the church, he appeared to become more deeply impressed than ever before. The day on which she was baptized, and came for the first time to the Lord's table, was a most solemn day to him. He afterwards said to me, "when I saw my wife go forward before all the congregation to be baptized, I could not hold up my head, I was forced into tears, and I solemnly resolved to put off my salvation no longer. And I mean to keep that resolution."

After this, I took some pains to see him several times, for the purpose of personal conversation. He was thoughtful, serious, prayerful; and, as I thought, was 'not far from the kingdom of heaven.' But as the weeks passed on, I was surprised and sorry to find, that his religious impressions appeared to have come to a stand. They did not vanish; I could not say they had diminished; but they evidently had not become more deep and influential. He used to say to me: "I am *trying*, and I hope I shall yet be a Christian." I cautioned him against delay, and against any reliance upon the mere fact, that he *continued* his attempts, while he did not flee to Christ.

In this manner several months passed on. He

uniformly appeared solemn, often avowed his conviction of his lost condition as a sinner, acknowledged his need of a Saviour, and lamented the wickedness and hardness of his heart. But finding him, as I thought, very much stationary, I feared that his perceptions of Divine truth were not correct and clear, or that his impressions were only superficial or occasional. And therefore I aimed to deal the more plainly with him, and tried, in every way I could contrive, to bring the Gospel truths more clearly before his mind, and impress them more deeply upon his conscience and his heart. With the Law of God on the one hand, and the Gospel on the other, his conscience to condemn him and Christ to invite him, I hoped his heart would be brought to surrender in faith.

It was in one of these conversations, which I was accustomed to have with him, that he surprised me by expressing a thought, which I had never heard from him before. I had just asked him,—

"What *hinders* you, my dear sir, from being a Christian indeed, since all the grace of the gospel is so free, and since you are so sensible that you need it?" His answer was,—

"I think a great many more of us would be Christians, if *professors of religion were different from what they are.*"

"That may be," said I; "but you know, each

one 'shall give account of *himself* unto God.' *You* are not accountable for professors of religion, and *they* are not accountable for your irreligion."

"I know that," said he. "But how can we believe in the reality of religion, when members of the church and the elders too are dishonest, will lie and cheat, and make hard bargains, a great deal worse than other people?"

"Have you any doubt of the reality of religion?"

"Oh, no, I believe in the reality of religion. I believe in a change of heart, as much as you do."

"Then," said I, "*you* can believe in the reality of religion, somehow or other. In that respect *you* have not been misled by our 'dishonest elders and church members,' who drive such 'hard bargains, a great deal worse than other people.' As to the accusation, that our elders and church-members are such dishonest and hard men; I deny it: the accusation is not true. There may be some bad men in the church. There was a Judas among Christ's disciples. One of the chosen twelve was *a thief.* But that was no good reason why other people should reject Christ. The *general* character of our church-members is not such as you have mentioned. You ought not to condemn Matthew and the other disciples, because Judas was a villain."

"Well," said he (with some hesitation), "I know some church-members who are no better than other people, not a bit better than a great many of us who make no profession."

"Perhaps you do. But what of that? Will their imperfections do *you* any good? Will their sins save *you*, or excuse you?"

"Why,"—(hesitatingly),—"they ought to set us a better example."

"No doubt of that. And allow me to say, you ought to set *them* a better example. You are under as much obligation to set *me* a good example, as I am to set you a good example. You and I are under the same law. God commands *you* to be holy as He commands *me*. It is quite likely, that those church-members of whom you complain, would be better men, if it was not for such persons as *you*, persons who set them no holy example."

"Well; I believe many members of the church are great stumbling-blocks; I know they are."

Said I, "I believe many, who are *not* members of the church, are great stumbling-blocks; I know they are. You are one of them. You are a stumbling-block and a hindrance to many impenitent sinners, to your partner in business, to your neighbors, to your sisters, and other acquaintances. I am sorry for it, but so it is. If you would become a truly pious man, these persons would feel your influence constraining them to seek the Lord, and your example would be a stumbling-block to them no longer."

"I make no *profession* of religion," said he.

"That is the very thing," I replied. "You stand aloof from religion entirely, as if you disbelieved in it; and your example just encourages others to neglect it as you do. You once told me yourself how greatly it affected you, when you saw your wife come out to be baptized in the presence of the great congregation. If you would set such an example, it would probably affect others."

"*My wife* is a good woman; she lives as a Christian ought to live."

"Then you have at least *one* good example."

"If all professors of religion were like her, I should not find fault with them."

"And if *you* were like her, other people would not find fault with *you*. Your example would commend religion."

"Well; the example of a great many professors does not commend it to *me*."

"Why do you look at the *bad* examples? Look nearer home. Look at your wife's example. You are very unwise to let your thoughts dwell upon the faults of Christians at all; and when you do so, you hunt up a few professors of religion, who are not by any means a fair specimen of our church-members, and you take *them* as samples of all the rest. That is unfair. I am sorry you have run into this way of thinking. It will only lead you into error, and call off your attention from the eternal interests of your own soul. The faults of others cannot save *you*. I beg of you to think less about other people's sins, and more about your own."

"Well, I will. I know I have had my mind turned away from religion many a time, by thinking of the conduct of professors."

A few days after this I met my friend in the street, and asked him if he thought he had gained the "one thing needful?" He replied,—

"No, I don't think I have. But I believe I am as good a man as a great many who took the sacrament yesterday in your church."

"I am sorry to hear you talk of others again," said I; "you promised me that you would think of your own sins, and let the sins of other people alone. And now the very first sentence you utter, is a reflection upon some who were at the Lord's table yesterday. I am surprised at this. Your hard thoughts about other people will lead you, I am afraid, farther and farther off from religion."

"Very likely," said he, "but *I* can't help it. The members of the church set such examples, that my mind is turned away from religion by them many a time."

"Yes," said I, "the old prophet knew how that was; 'they eat up the sin of my people, and set their heart upon iniquity; they have left off to take heed to the Lord.' You are one of that stamp. You seize upon 'the sin of God's people,' as if it were bread to you; and then you forget to pray—you have 'left off' to take heed to the Lord.' After you have eagerly fed yourself upon the 'sin of God's people' for awhile, then you have no inclination 'to take heed' to anything God says to you. I advise you to eat some other sort of food. 'The sin of God's people' is a bad breakfast. It is very indigestible. The wicked seize upon it as if it were bread to the hungry; and the worst of it all is, that after they have eaten such a breakfast they have no family prayer; they do not 'take heed to the Lord.' That is your case, precisely; you complain of Christians, instead of praying for yourself. You *never* pray, after finding fault with members of the church for half an hour."

"How do *you* know I don't pray?"

"I know by the text which I just quoted. You '*eat up the sin of God's people;*' and for that reason, I know that the other part of the text belongs to you. You '*have left off to take heed to the Lord.*' Is it not so? Have you not left off, ceased to pray, since you began to find fault with Christians?"

"*Yes*, I own it. I am not going to deny it."

Said I, "I am very sorry you take such a course. You yield to a temptation of the Devil. The best Christians are imperfect, very imperfect. They do not profess to be sinless. You may see their faults, but you cannot see their penitence, and tears, and agony of spirit, when in secret they mourn over their many imperfections, and beg forgiveness of God, and grace to be more faithful. If *you* felt so, if *you* had had done wrong in public through thoughtlessness or overcome by some temptation, and then in secret should mourn bitterly over your fault; would you think it generous, would you think your disposition well treated, or even had any kind of justice done to it, if your neighbor should be going around complaining of your faults, as if you were a bad man?"

"No, I should not think I deserved that."

"Very well. These imperfect Christians have such secret mournings. And if you will go to them, and kindly tell them their faults, you will hear things from them which will alter your feelings about them; you will have a better opinion of their hearts than you have now, and a more just opinion too. Did you ever mention to these people the things you complain of?"

"No, I never did."

"I think you ought to do it. Certainly you ought to do it, or cease to make complaints about them to others. Jesus Christ has taught us our duty in such a case. 'If thy brother trespass against thee, go to him, and tell him his fault betwixt him and thee alone.'"

"That applies to Christians."

"It applies to *you.* You ought to be a Christian. And your neglect of one duty cannot excuse your neglect of another. You must not plead one sin as an excuse for another. If one of your neighbors had a bad opinion of you, surely you would much rather he should come and tell you what he had against you, and hear your explanation, than that he should tell it to other people."

"Yes, I should. But I have called nobody's name."

"I know it; and I complain of that. Instead of pointing out the guilty individuals, you complain of Christians in general; and thus you make the innocent suffer with the guilty. You make *religion* suffer, (at least in your estimation,) by the faults of a few, who profess to be religious people. How would *you* like it, if I should speak of the men of your trade as you speak of Christians, and say, 'Blacksmiths are villains, dishonest men?'

"I should want you to name the men."

"And I want *you* to name the men. Come, tell me who they are, and what they have done; and I promise you I will have their conduct investigated. They shall be tried before the proper tribunal. You shall be a witness against them. And if they are found guilty, they shall be turned out of the church; and then they will be complained of by you no longer, and the good name of religion will no more be dishonored by them."

"Oh, *I* can't be *a witness* against anybody."

"Why not? Can't you tell the truth? Will you make religion suffer, rather than bring bad men to justice? Will you injure the good name of all of us, 'church-members and elders too,' as you say, instead of lending your assistance to purify the church from unworthy members? Will you let this thing go on, and let it hinder (as you say it does), a great many of you from being Christians?"

"It is not *my* business to bear witness against church-members."

"Why do you *do it*, then? You *have* been doing it, every time I have met you, for the last three months. And though I have tried to persuade you to cease, you still keep on, bearing witness against 'church-members and elders,' every time I meet you."

"Well, I don't mean to *injure* anybody."

"No, sir, I don't think you do. The only one you injure is *yourself*. The general imputations which you so often fling out against professors of religion, are *slanders*. They are *not true*. You may *think* them true, but they are *not* true. I affirm them to be utterly unfounded and false. There may be indeed a few persons in the church, who are as bad as you declare them to be; but your general accusations are falsehoods. But suppose all you say, or even suspect, were true; suppose half of our church-members to be bad men; in the name of all that is common sense, I ask you, what has that to do with your religion? If half the money that is in circulation is counterfeit, does that make the good money in your pocket valueless? or will it lead you to refuse to take *all* money?"

"I don't want to have *counterfeit* money?"

"And I don't want you to have a counterfeit religion. The very fact, that you complain of counterfeit money, is full proof, that you believe there is such a thing as good money somewhere: and your complaint of counterfeit religion is full proof, that you believe there is such a thing as good religion."

"Yes, I believe all that."

"And you believe that you have not attained it."

"I suppose I haven't."

"And are you striving to attain it, or are you as anxious and prayerful about it as you were a few weeks since?"

"No, I don't think I am."

"Will you answer me one more question? Has not your seriousness diminished, and your prayerfulness ceased, very much in proportion as you have had hard thoughts, and made hard speeches about the faults of Christians?"

"I can't say no to that question."

"Then I wish you very seriously to consider, whether your fault-finding has not provoked God to withdraw from you the influences of the Holy Spirit! You *do know*, that your regard for religion and your attempts after salvation, have never been promoted by your complaining about Christian people. Thinking of their sins, you forget your own, as I have told you before. You foster in your own heart a spirit of self-righteousness, by your miserable and foolish way. I have warned you against it before, and I will now warn you again, if you will permit me. If you will go on in this way, God will leave you to your deceptions and your impenitence; you will live without religion, and you will die without it! I beseech you, therefore, as a friend, as a neighbor, as a minister, dismiss your thoughts about the faults of a *few*, (for they are only a few,) professors of religion, and seek from God the forgiveness of your own sins, and the salvation you so much need."

I left him. But he never sought me again. Fifteen years have since passed away, and he is still as far from God as ever. Often when I have met him, I have endeavored to draw him into some conversation upon religion; but he avoids the subject, and commonly shuns me.

The Holy Spirit would lead us to think much

about our own sins. It is a dangerous thing for us to dwell upon the imperfections of others. There are many in our congregations, who 'quench the Spirit,' by complainings and hard speeches about communicants of the church. The natural effect of this is just to dispel conviction of sin. "I am as good as many who belong to the church." If that declaration is true, it is utterly deceptive to the man that makes it. It leads him to think his sin and danger less than they are; it blinds his conscience. I never heard of any mortal, on the bed of death, apologizing for his irreligion by mentioning the faults of Christians.

Trying to Find God in the Wrong.

THE young woman who wrote the following letter had been known to me for years. I had often conversed with her upon religion, and she very much made it a matter of speculation merely, as I believed. The state of her mind now when she writes, (very different from anything I had ever known of her before), may be judged of by the following extracts from her letter :—

"For years I have not been indifferent to my personal religion, but the incubus that formerly held me within its thrall, still distresses me. Dreadful thoughts, that I dare not utter, against the goodness and justice of God, interrupt my efforts to do right, and so mingle with my petitions, that I have sometimes arisen from prayer in a sort of desperation—afraid *not* to pray, but afraid *to* pray; and I indulge in such fearful imaginations against the God of heaven, even while in the act of asking his blessing!

"I have often tried, sometimes successfully, to

lay this matter entirely aside, to give it up, hoping that in time some event, in the Providence of God, would occur, which would satisfy my mind and heart, and bring me to an involuntary decision. But I find that time and waiting do me no good, and shed no light upon my path.

"I have endeavored prayerfully to study my heart and analyze my feelings; and I can see no reason to hope that I have experienced a change of heart. I realize that I am deeply sinful; but when I try to feel grateful to God, that He has provided for me an atonement, and to the Saviour that He *is* that atonement, my spirit returns no response of tenderness and love—"a mail defends my untouched heart," that seems impenetrable to any appeal. Still it is my desire to live hereafter entirely to the glory of God.

"Christ is to me 'as a root out of a dry ground.' I see no beauty in Him 'that I should desire Him.' I feel no mournful sorrow for my sins; and my mind and heart seem constantly rising in dreadful questioning of every attribute of the character of God.

"I do not ask, as formerly, *why* these things are so? *why* I was created sinful? *why* I inherit the body of this death? My appeal to you is no longer to answer to me what God has never revealed, but it is that you will pray for me, that I be not utterly rejected of God, that He will hear my prayer and give me repentance and *faith in Christ.* Oh that I could feel that God is my Father, that Jesus Christ is my Saviour. Oh that I could *love* God, that Christ were precious to me.

"For many months I have wished for counsel on this great subject, and I have endeavored to come to a decision through prayer and study of the Bible. I have wished to visit you, but have feared that I was not sufficiently in earnest thus to commit myself. But I can stay away no longer. And *may* I come to you? And may I ask that you will respond to my letter? * * * It is my sincere prayer that you may be instrumental in shedding some light upon the cold and callous heart that prompts these lines."

* * *

Such was her letter. The next day I sent her the following answer:—

"Your state of mind has nothing in it new or uncommon. The same perplexities, the same discouragements, despondencies and 'desperations,' the same fitfulness and vain hopes of some undefined and undefinable good, which have so long affected you, have as much affected others. If your heart refuses to love God and trust in Christ, and in the strength of its rebellion not only refuses to obey your will but also entertains feelings, and leads to thoughts about God, which you dare not utter;' the same thing has afflicted thousands before you, so that you have no grounds for religious 'desperation' on this account.

"But on this point I have two things to say to you:

"*First.* It is well, (perhaps,) that you see so much of your heart's sinfulness. It *may* be well now and forever, if you *obey* the knowledge which truth and the Holy Spirit have given you. This *sense* of not 'loving God,' of finding 'no beauty in Christ,' of perplexity and fitful 'desperation,' constitutes a part of conviction of sin, and it proves the presence of the Holy Spirit striving with your soul.

"*Second.* After all you have learnt of the depravity of your heart, you have yet seen but a very little of it. It is a far more corrupt and abominable heart in the sight of God, than in your darkest or lightest moments you have ever imagined. You have conviction, but evidently your conviction is but partial or superficial. You know only a small part of your depravity and danger.

"And this leads me to say, that your failure to see appropriateness and goodness in Christ, and to feel an unbounded gratitude to Him, and to the love of the Father which gave Him, arises just from your *lack* of feeling your undone condition, and your *lack* of a heart right with God. If you knew we'l your lost estate, you would at least 'receive the word with gladness,' that there *is* such a thing as redemption for sinners; you would rejoice that one gleam of hope remains, that there is provision and possibility of salvation. And then you would *see clearly* that the best thing you could do, and the *first* you *ought* to do, is just to flee to Christ, an undone sinner, and fall into his arms, 'Lord, save, or I perish.' But even after you *saw that clearly* and determined to *do* that sincerely, another and a worse affliction would meet you, because you would find your obstinate heart refuse. And thus the very *amount of conviction* which you sometimes aim after, would not do for you what you are wont to suppose. Conviction is not the Holy Spirit. You need the infinite aid of the Holy Ghost. If you ever know your own heart well, you will know that you need it and must have it, or die an alienated, unconverted sinner! And *then*, prayer will be a reality with you; the cry of want, the voice of despair in self, the voice of hope in God and in God only. And then, if your resistance of the Holy Ghost does not provoke Him to depart from you; your seeking the Lord will be with your *whole* heart, and not as it hitherto has been, with only half of it. I refer you to Jer. xxix. 12, 13, 14; to Prov. ii. 1,—5; to Isa. lv. 6,—end. Your grounds of hope to bring you to faith in Christ must be the Bible and the Holy Spirit.

"Your reference to the high and mysterious things of God brings up a matter, which I think may easily be disposed of:—

"1. Whoever believes in a God at all, believes in an *infinite mystery*, and if the *existence* of God is such an infinite mystery, we can very well expect and afford to have many of his *ways* mysterious to to us; yea, our reason demands it. Why? how? wherefore? often demand things which not only lie beyond man to explain, but beyond man to *comprehend*, even if they were revealed by the tongue of an angel, or the lips of Jehovah himself!

"2. There are no more mysteries in religion than there are in nature, no more dark and unexplainable things. Our life is a mystery, and so is every tree and every flower. The power of our will over our muscles is a mystery. The same line of demarkation which separates knowledge from ignorance in natural things, separates knowledge from ignorance in religious things. The case is this (in general); we know *facts*, the *modes* of them, the *why*, the *how*, we do *not* know. In natural things we have no hesitancy in acting on the facts, though ignorant of the reason of them: for example, we breathe, though ignorant of the reason *why* breathing keeps us alive. And if we would act upon the facts of religion in the same manner, we should be Christians indeed.

* * * "You say you do not love God. You *ought* to love Him. Be ashamed of your heart (what a heart!), if you do *not* love Him. You have been, (are,) ashamed of it. And yet, when you try to make it feel, it will not feel at your bidding, 'a mail defends your untouched heart.' Do you not then feel your helplessness? Have you not an *experience*, which ought to make you both glad and grateful, that God has said to you '*in me is thy help.*' Fly to Him, fly now, fly just *as you are*, poor, vile, guilty, *lost.* Do you not know that Jesus Christ 'came to seek and to *save* that which was lost.' Delay has done you no good. It never can do you any. You wait in vain for 'some event of Providence to bring you to an involuntary decision.' Such a decision is an absurdity, no decision at all. And were it not so, it would be unacceptable to God, as it is contrary to the Bible. 'Choose ye this day whom ye will serve.' The choice must be your own.

"What hinders, that you should be a child of God? Is not salvation free? Is not the invitation to it flung out to you on every page of the New Testament? Is not Christ offered to you in all his offices? and are you not welcome to all his benefits if you want them? Is not the Holy Spirit promised 'to them that ask Him?' 'What more could have been done to my vineyard?'

"You say you want to be a Christian. What hinders you then? God the Father wants you to be a Christian. God the Son wants you to be a Christian. God the Holy Ghost wants you to be a Christian. Nothing can hinder you from being a Christian, but your own worldly, selfish, proud, obstinate, unworthy, and self-righteous heart."

* * *

The following expressions are taken from her reply:

"And is it *my* fault, that I cannot feel? I thought that I had done all I could, and that God was withholding from me His Spirit.

"My heart aches and is very sad. Do not let me deceive you; it does not *feel*, but it aches because it cannot. The heavens and the earth seem very dark."

I wrote to her in a second letter,—

"It seems to me your note requires from me the following remarks:—

"1. Your hesitancy and backwardness to speak of your feelings, to send your letter, &c., are things not uncommon with awakened sinners. Such sinners are often ashamed of Christ. You see, my dear girl, that if you would be His disciple, you must 'deny yourself, take up your cross and follow' Him.

I respect the shrinking modesty of your feelings, but I suspect that the *shame of sin* has also an influence upon you. If you shrink from Christ you cannot be His.

"2. The complaint that you 'cannot feel,' is an almost universal one with sinners whom God's Spirit alarms. It is one of the strongest of all proofs that the Holy Spirit is striving with the soul. Tread softly, my dear girl. 'Quench not the Spirit.' 'Grieve not the Holy Spirit of God.' Remember, 'my Spirit shall not always strive with man.' 'To-day, if ye will hear his voice.'

"3. Evidently you *try* to make your heart *feel.* I do not wonder at you. I do not blame you. But it will not feel for you. You cannot make it feel. Only one hope remains for you; give it to God, and He will make it feel,—to God as it is, hard, senseless, stupid,—to God in Christ, promising to be your Father and your friend.

"When you aim to make your heart feel, you are making (ignorantly) an effort of self-righteousness. You wish it to feel, because you think there would be some worthiness in its emotions. It is too hard for you. Give it to God *as it is,*—you cannot make it any better.

"4. You 'thought you had done all you could.' I suppose you have 'done all' you could' to *save yourself.* And yet you have accomplished nothing.

You cannot. Fly, then, to Christ,—to Christ, just *as you are,* just as unfeeling, just as unworthy,—to Christ *now*, 'while it is called *to-day*.' Be assured you are welcome to all His benefits.

"Finally, you are 'sad.' You ought to be joyful. You *may* be, if you will trust your Saviour. 'Rejoice in the Lord' is Bible exhortation,—a *precept.* Obey it. *Why* are you sad? Because you look into your dark heart, instead of looking *to Christ*, who died to redeem you. Look *up*, if you would have your eye catch the sunbeam that shall gladden you."

* * *

Her reply contained the following expressions:—

"How *can* I dare to ask or expect that Christ will accept of such a cold, strange, unloving, unfeeling heart, and not only *love* me, but allow me to ask of Him such vast favors? Surely there is no analogy to such a case in nature or reason. It seems to me as if, (pardon me), you don't understand *me.* If God ever softens my heart, I suppose it will follow as a matter of course, that I shall love Christ, and then I can dare to venture to go to Him. * * * I spoke of my *heart*, but I used a wrong expression. It seems to me as if, in regard to God, Christ, repentance, I am but senseless matter; *heart* I have none, and even my brain seems stupefied upon this great subject. * * * Oh, that I could 'look up and see the bright sunbeam that should gladden me.' The thought brings tears to my eyes,—would that it could thaw my very heart."

So she wrote. I sent the following answer:—

"Your present hindrance appears to me to be very much this:—you aim to do for yourself what the Holy Spirit must do for you. 'In *me* is thy help,' says God, and He would have you believe it. All along you have been aiming to work yourself up into a state of affection, which should bring you relief. But, my dear child, it is *God* that must bring you relief. You are to trust *Him*, rely on *Him*, leave all with *Him*. You cannot help *yourself.* You can no more put your heart right than you can pardon your own sins. Your heart has been too mighty for all your efforts, and will remain so. But it is not too mighty for God. There is help for you in Him, and you will find it if you will fling down the weapons of your rebellion, and submit to Him *in Christ.* * * * * Would to God, that you knew your utterly helpless condition, and would fall into the arms of the Saviour, who loves you and invites you to His arms. Go to your God and Saviour, my child, just as the prodigal went to his father, (Luke, xv.) and you shall be accepted as he was. If you do *not* go, you must find your grave in some far-off land! Go now. Go just as you are."

* * *

She afterwards referred to this letter. Said she, —"until I received that letter, I *never had* the idea that some other power must do for me. That letter first gave me the idea that I must go somewhere else than to myself. Not till then had I understood at all your former letters, directing me to the Saviour."

After this I had frequent conversations with her. Evidently she was perfectly sincere, and deeply anxious. But she could not perceive that her failure to gain peace with God was owing to anything in herself, nor could she believe that she was powerless in herself, in respect to putting her heart right, aside from God's help. Often she said to me,—

"I am very miserable. I do desire to love God. Above all things I wish to be a Christian. What is the reason I do not get some light?" I constantly presented to her the same truths which I had written, assured her of the fulness and free grace of Christ, and that it was her self-reliance and self-seeking alone which hindered her salvation.

One evening she left me in a most anxious and downcast state of mind. The next day, she said to me, "I have called, you will think, very soon. But I have come to tell you, that I am as happy to-day, as I was miserable yesterday. I found I could *do nothing.* I was helpless. I had exhausted all my powers, and still was just the same. All I could do, was to pray, and depend on God. I am nothing. Never before have I had such a sense of my sinfulness, and it is now sweet to think I may rely upon God." I asked her,—

"What hindered you so long?"

"All my life," said she, "I have stopped at the same place. I have read the Bible, and prayed, but my mind would find some difficulty, and stop there. *All my days I have been trying to find God in the wrong.*"

"Wherein were *you* wrong, yourself?"

"I was not willing to trust God. I thought (or *tried* to think,) it was not *my* fault that I was not a Christian. Your letter astonished me. How could I have been so ignorant of God? I did not know till I got your letter, that a sinner *might* come to Christ just as he is. It seems to me that people do not understand that. I never understood it before. I want you to preach that, so that people may know it. It was all new to me! At first I did not believe it. How could you know how I should be affected all along; and that, after I *should* see the sinfulness of my heart, and be determined to obey God, a 'worse difficulty would meet' me; my heart 'would refuse to trust?' I see it now. Before, I did not think it was *my* fault that I was not a Christian. I tried all the time to *put God in the wrong*."

Because this young woman had asked me to preach the same things to others, which had so much surprised and profited her; I requested her to make for me a written statement of her religious experience. A short time afterwards, she gave me the following:—

"Ever since I had given up the study of religious truth, as a mere intellectual speculation; I had for years tried to pursue it with and for my heart. Distressed with doubts and darkness, but hoping, that God would some time or other take them from me; I studied the Bible with prayer, and endeavored to be governed by its teachings, and enjoyed and appreciated spiritual things to such a degree, that my state seemed often very strange to me; for I realized that I did not love God, and felt no interest in Christ, and knew that without this there was no true religion. Still I felt no alarm, thinking it evidence that I was not vitally in error, because I was so desirous to be right. I thought I was *all but entirely* religious, but as these were fundamental wants, and as I was sincerely desirous to come to a decision upon this subject, I determined to attain them. But in this I could not succeed. I tried very hard, laboriously, but could not make myself love God. My mind in its efforts, invariably, at a certain point, came to a stop. I perceived that there was an obstacle there that always overthrew me, but could not tell what it was. I felt no pain at this, because I thought I had done all I could, when God withheld from me His Spirit, and, (can I express the dreadful thought!) that the fault was God's and not mine! But, as others did succeed, it must be that I could; and, afraid to die as I was, I persisted in using every faculty to gain my object, but it was of no use.

"I became convinced that all my trying, and all my searching, were in vain; and, tired of wearying myself longer in fruitless efforts, I determined to make a statement of my feelings to you, not doubting that you could soon enlighten me, and thinking that, as soon as I discovered the point that was now hidden from me, I should love God; and that then a knowledge of and interest in the Saviour would follow as a matter of course.

"I can give you no idea of the FAR OFF distance with which I had always regarded Christ. It is with difficulty that I can suppress the comments, that my heart instinctively responded to every sentence of your letters, as I read them. But I will only say, that my mind, heart, and senses, were in a maze, when I perceived their contents so contrary to my expectations.

"That my '*heart* REFUSED *to love God and trust in Christ*,'—that '*the Holy Spirit was striving with me*,' —that '*I knew only a small part of my depravity and danger*,'—that 'my failure to feel an unbounded gratitude to the Saviour, and to the love of the Father who gave Him, arose from my *lack* of feeling my *undone condition*, and my *lack* of a heart right with God,'—that 'I had been seeking God with *only half my heart*,'—were positions totally inadmissible to my belief, so strong was the impression on my mind that I was *nearly, entirely* right: and I was between laughing and displeasure, at the denunciations you pronounced upon my heart throughout, and especially at the close of your first letter.

"At first, I concluded that you had not in the least understood or appreciated me; and next, that you were unnecessarily severe; but by degrees the conviction began to steal over me, with a feeling that I cannot describe. *Is it so? Am I all wrong?* Is it *my* fault that I do not love God? *Has the Holy Spirit been striving with my heart?* when I thought I had been breasting the tide alone so long, and God had looked so coldly on my struggles?

"But a greater surprise awaited me; your remedy for my difficulties, when you directed me to 'fly to Christ *just as I was*.' 'When you aim to make your heart feel, you are making (ignorantly) an effort of of self-righteousness.' * * * 'It is too hard for you. Give it to God *as it is*; you cannot make it better.' . . . . 'You thought you had done all you could. I suppose you have done all you could *to save yourself*, and yet you have accomplished nothing. You cannot. Fly then to *Christ*—to Christ, *just as you are*—just as unfeeling, just as unworthy; to Christ *now*.' So you wrote to me.

"Here my heart fails me to express my emotions. I require another medium than words to tell what I felt. *Fly to Christ? just as I am?* to Christ *now?* Give *Him* my heart, *just as it is?* I have never thought anything about Christ. He has always been *last* in my thoughts; and fly to Him *first?* fly to Him *now?* stop trying, and He do all? Impossible! You did not understand me! My powers seemed stunned. I tried not to think about it; and after some days of perturbation I went to see you, hoping you would say to me something different—something on which I could act; but your remarks were all the same. I was very much disappointed, and listened in respectful silence—though thinking while you were speaking that you had little idea of their subsequent use to me. I came home without the slightest idea of doing as you had said, certain that you were not aware of what you had told me to do. But that I was *all wrong*, that I had not a single right feeling; that I was so far, far from God, when I thought I was all right, but in one item, (which would necessarily come right after I loved God,) was very distressing to me. What could I do? It seemed to me that I had a mightier effort to make now than ever before, and I was afraid I should die before I should have time to accomplish it. Oh, the troubled sea that tossed within my poor heart, I cannot bear to think upon! But do something I must. I tried to pray; but it seemed as if the heavens and earth were brass, above and beneath me. I examined the Bible, and all the references to the texts to which you referred me, and found that it substantiated your every word, and I began to feel that all you had said was true. And then I wondered that *you had never told me so before! I was sure that I had never heard it in any of the years of your sermons, to which I had so interestedly listened; and I could not remember that you had ever told it to me, in any of the previous conversations* that you had had with me. I was not conscious that I had ever before seen it in the Bible. *If* I had, I had *never comprehended it with even an ordinary amount of common intelligence;* it was an *entirely new truth.*

"Oh how can I describe my ineffectual efforts to grope and *feel after Christ*, through the *thick darkness!* I could not find Him. I could only cry, Jesus, Master, have *mercy* upon me; and ask Him to *take* my heart, for I could not give it to Him."

* * *

Delay: or, the Accepted Time.

A YOUNG man called upon me one Sabbath evening, and as soon as we were seated, he said to me,—

"I have accepted the invitation that you have so often given from the pulpit, to any who are willing to converse with you upon the subject of religion."

"I am glad to see you," said I.

"I don't know," he replied, "as I have anything to say, such as I ought to have; but I am convinced that I have neglected religion long *enough*, and I am determined to put it off no longer."

"That is a good determination," said I, "'Behold now is the accepted time, behold now is the day of salvation.'"

"Well, I don't know as that text is for me, because——"

"Yes, it *is* for you," said I, interrupting him.

"I was going to say, sir, I don't suppose I have got so far as that yet, so that salvation is for me *now*."

"You *told* me that you was 'determined to put

off religion no longer;' and therefore I say, 'now is the accepted time, now is the day of salvation.'"

"But I don't wish to be in a hurry, sir."

"You *ought* to be in haste. David was. He says, 'I thought on my ways and turned my feet to thy testimonies. I made haste and delayed not to keep thy commandments.' God now commandeth all men, everywhere, to repent, and you are one of them. And if you are like David, you will 'make haste and delay not' to keep God's commandments."

"I don't suppose I am in such a state of mind, as to be prepared to become a Christian *now*."

"Will disobeying God put you in a *better* state of mind, do you think?"

"Why, I don't know; but I have not much deep conviction. I know that I am a sinner against God, and I wish to turn to Him, and live a different life."

"Then turn to Him. Now is the accepted time."

"But I find my heart is full of sin; I am all wrong; I feel an opposition to God such as I never felt before."

"Then repent and turn to God instantly, while it is called to-day."

"But I don't suppose I can be ready to come to religion so *quick*."

"You *said* you was determined to put it off no longer, and I told you 'now is the accepted time.'"

"But I never began to think seriously about my religion till last Sunday."

"And so you want to put it off a little longer."

"Why I want to get *ready*."

"And are you getting ready? You have tried it for a week."

"No sir," said he in a sad manner, "I don't think I am any nearer to it than I was at first."

"I don't think you are. And I suppose the reason is, that you don't believe 'now is the accepted time.'"

"Oh, yes, I do; for the Bible says so."

"Then don't wait for any other time. Repent *now*. Flee to Christ *now*, in 'the accepted time.'"

"I have not conviction enough yet."

"Then it cannot be the 'accepted time' yet."

"But I have not faith enough."

"Then it cannot be 'the accepted time.'"

"Well, sir, I,—I,—I am not ready *now*."

"Then it cannot be 'the accepted time' *now*."

"But it seems to me, it is too *quick*," said he earnestly.

"Then it cannot be 'the accepted time,' and the Bible has made a mistake."

"But, sir, my heart is not *prepared*."

"Then it is not 'the accepted time.'"

With much embarrassment in his manner, he replied,—

"What *shall* I do?"

"Repent and turn to God, with faith in Christ to save you as a lost, unworthy sinner, *now* in 'the accepted time.'"

He appeared to be in a great strait. He sat in silence with very manifest uneasiness for a few moments, and then asked,—

"Is it possible that *any one* should repent, and give up the world, and turn to God *so soon*, when I began to think about it only last Sunday?"

"'Now is the accepted time,'" said I.

Again he sat in thoughtful silence, and after a time he asked me,—

"Is *salvation* offered to sinners *now?*"

"Yes, *now*. 'Now is the day of salvation.'"

"But it seems to me I am not *prepared* now to give up the world."

"That very thing is your difficulty. *You* are not prepared; but 'now is the accepted time.' You wish to put off your repentance and conversion to Christ till some *other* time; but 'now is the accepted time.' You and your Bible disagree. And if nothing else kept you from salvation, this would be enough. I beseech you, my dear friend, delay no longer. Now is God's time. 'Deny yourself, and take up your cross, and follow Jesus Christ.' You told me you was determined to put off religion no longer. I suspected you did not know your own heart, and therefore said to you 'now is the accepted time.' And now it has become manifest, that you meant to put off religion till some other time, all the while."

"It seems hard to shut up a man just to the present time," said he, in an imploring accent.

"If you were a dying man, and had only an hour to live, you would not say so. You would be glad to have the Bible say to you, 'now is the accepted time,' instead of telling you, you needed a month or a week to flee to Christ. It is *mercy* in God to say to you, 'behold now is the day of salvation,' when you do not know as you will live till to-morrow morning."

"Will you pray with me?" said he.

I prayed with him, and we separated. The last words I uttered to him as he left the door, were, "now is the accepted time."

Just one week afterwards he called upon me, "to give an account of himself," as he said,—

"I have got out of my trouble," said he. "Now, I trust in Christ, and I am reconciled to God, or at least I think so. I thought you were very hard upon me last Sunday night, when you *hammered* me, and *hammered* me with that text,—'now is the accepted time.' But I couldn't get away from it. It followed me everywhere. I would think of one thing, and then that would come up, 'now is the accepted time.' Then I would begin to think of something else, and it would come up again, 'now is the accepted time.' So I went on for three days. I tried to *forget* that text, but I *could not.* I said to myself, there is something else in the Bible except that; but wherever I read, that *would* come to my mind. It annoyed me and *tormented* me. Finally, I began to question myself, *why it was* that this plagued me so much? And I found it was because I was *not willing to be saved by Christ.* I was trying to do something for myself, and I wanted more time. But it was not done. Everything failed me. And then I thought, if 'now *is* the accepted time,' I may go to Christ now, wicked as I am. So I just prayed for *mercy*, and gave up all to Him."

The idea of this young man was new to me It had never entered my mind, that when one wants more time, it is "*because he is not willing to be saved by Christ.*" I suppose that is true. A delaying sinner is a legalist. Self-righteousness delays. How little the procrastinating know about their own hearts!

Physical Influence.

A MEMBER of my church, the mother of a family, was sick, and I visited her. In conversation with her I discovered that her mind was shrouded in darkness and gloom. I prolonged the conversation, hoping to be able so to present divine truth to her mind, that she should see some light, and gain some comfort from the promises; or if I failed in that, hoping to discover the cause of her religious darkness. But it was all in vain. I left her as dark as ever, without discovering the cause of her gloom.

I soon visited her again. She was the same as before. "Dark! dark! *all* dark!" says she, in answer to my inquiry. "I have not long to live, and I am sure I am not fit to die." She wept in agony. I pointed her to Christ, and recited to her the promises. I explained justification by faith in Christ Jesus, the undone condition of sinners, salvation by free grace, the offer and operations of the Holy Spirit, and the readiness of Christ to accept *all* that come unto Him. She only wept and groaned.

With much the same result I conversed with her many times. I could but imperfectly discover what had been the character of her religious exercises while she was in health; but she despised them all, and counted them only as deception. When I treated her as a backslider, and referred her to what the sacred Scriptures address to such persons, inviting them to return unto their God; the very freeness and friendliness of the invitations appeared to distress her. When I treated her as a believer under a cloud, a child of God, from whom our heavenly Father takes away the light of His countenance, for some reason which we cannot explain, —perhaps to manifest His sovereignty, perhaps to teach us our spiritual dependence, perhaps to arouse our efforts to draw nearer to Him, perhaps to teach us deeper lessons about religion, and give us richer experiences as He leads us, for a time, "in a way we know not,"—all these ideas appeared to increase her distress. If I treated her as an impenitent sinner, it was the same thing. Gloom, distress, despair, had taken possession of her soul!

After I had known her to be in this condition for several months, I called upon her, and to my surprise found that her mind was calm; her despair and distress had given place to hope and gladness of spirit. She could trust in God, she could submit to His will, rejoicing to be in His hands, she could rest upon the sufficiency of her Saviour;—"Jesus Christ is mine," said she, "and I am glad to be His."

Three days after this, when I saw her again, her light had departed, and all her former darkness and despair had returned. A few days afterwards, I found she had become calm and hopeful again, and then again in a few days I found her as gloomy as ever. Thus for months she alternated from gloom to gladness, and from gladness to gloom. I could not understand it. I studied her case, and tried in every mode I could think of, to find out why she should thus be tossed about betwixt hope and fear. But I studied in vain.

After awhile, as I was conversing with her one morning, when she was in one of her happy frames, I recollected that she had always been so whenever I had seen her in the morning, and had always been in darkness whenever I had seen her in the afternoon. I mentioned this fact to her, and asked her to account for it. She acknowledged the fact, but made no attempt to explain it. I explained it to her, as the result of her physical condition. Every morning, she awoke free from pain, and then her views were clear, and her mind comfortable. She continued in this comfortable frame till nearly noon, when, as her pain in the head returned, all her peace of mind vanished. This experience was uniform with her, week after week; and when I now called her attention to it, and explained her religious gloom as the result of her physical state, she was satisfied that the explanation was just. But, a week afterwards, when I saw her in the afternoon, her mind was as dark as ever; and then she rejected the explanation; she could not be made to believe that her darkness was owing to her disease. So it was with her, week after week. She had a comfortable hope every morning; she was in despair every afternoon. In the morning she would *believe* that her afternoon despair was caused by her bodily infirmity; but in the afternoon, she would entirely *dis*believe it. Thus she continued.

A few weeks before her death, and when her bodily condition had become different; all her darkness was gone, her mind continued light through the whole twenty-four hours; and she finally died in peace, with the full hope of a blessed immortality through our Lord Jesus Christ.

Despondency does not always arise from the same cause. It is difficult to deal with it; but there is one great principle, which has been of much use to myself, and which has some illustration in the following sketch.

Treatment of the Desponding.

In making visits to the sick, I became acquainted with a woman belonging to my congregation, with whom I had very little acquaintance before. She was in a very distressful state of mind. "I am a sinner," says she, "I am the vilest of sinners! I must soon meet my God, and I have *no preparation* to meet Him! I see before me nothing but His wrath, His dreadful wrath forever! Indeed I feel it this moment within my soul! It drinks up my spirit! God curses me now; and oh! how can I bear His eternal curse, when He shall cast me off forever!"

"God is *merciful*, Madam," said I.

"I know He is merciful, sir, but I have despised His mercy; and now the thought of it torments my soul! If He had *no* mercy, I could meet Him: I could take the curse of the Law, and it would not be the half of the hell which now awaits me! But oh, I *cannot bear*,—I *cannot* bear the curse of the *Law* and the *Gospel* both! I must account to the Lord Jesus Christ for having slighted His offers!

I have turned a deaf ear to all His kind invitations! I have trampled under foot the blood of the covenant! and I am soon to appear before Him, my *feet* wet with His blood, instead of having it sprinkled on my heart!" (She wept and wailed, as if on the borders of the pit.)

"Madam, there is *no need* that you should appear *thus* before Him. The *same* offers of mercy are still made to you, which have been made to you before. The same throne of grace still stands in heaven; the same God is seated upon it; the same Christ reigns as Mediator; and the same Spirit is still promised 'to them that ask Him.' The invitation of God is as broad as the wants of sinners: 'Whosoever will, let him take the water of life freely.'"

"I know it, sir; I know all that. And this is the burden of my anguish—the offer is so free, and I have no heart to accept it! If the offer was accompanied by any difficult conditions, I might think myself partly excusable for not accepting it. But it is all so free, and, *fool* that I am, I have all my days shut up my heart against it; and even now, I am rebellious and unbelieving. Oh! my heart is senseless as a brute's! it cannot feel! it is harder than the nether millstone!"

"I am glad you are sensible of that; because it prepares you to understand the promise, '*I* will take away the stony heart out of your flesh, and *I* will give you a heart of flesh, and *I* will put my spirit within you.' *God* says this; and you perceive He makes His promise for just such hearts as yours."

"Oh, I wish I could believe it! My heart won't believe. It disbelieves God! It makes Him a liar, because it believes not the testimony which God gave of His Son!"

"Madam, think a moment; if you did *not* believe that testimony, you could not be distressed on account of your *unbelief.* If you were hungry, and you did not believe there was any food upon the earth, you could not be distressed because you did not *believe* there was food enough. You might be distressed because there was no food, but you could not be distressed because you did not *believe* there was any; you would not wish to believe in a falsehood, or in what you deem a falsehood."

"I have not any doubt of the *truth* of God's Word, sir; but my heart does not *trust* in it. It *will* not trust. I have no faith."

"You have sometimes thought you had faith?"

"Yes, I *did* think so; but I was deceived. I have made a false profession. I have profaned the Lord's table! When I was a young woman, in Scotland, I first came forward, and I have attended on the ordinance of the table ever since, whenever I could. But I see now that I have been only a mere professor—one of the foolish virgins. For forty years I have been a communicant; and now, when my days are nearly done, the Lord frowns upon me for my sin. I feel it; I feel it. His wrath lies heavy on my soul! He knows I am an empty hypocrite, and he frowns upon me in His awful displeasure!"

"How long since you found out that you had no true faith?"

"I have suspected it a great many times, but I was never fully convinced of it till since I have been confined to the house with this sickness."

"Before you was sick did you enjoy a comfortable hope in Christ?"

"I *thought* I did, almost always after I made my first sacrament. That was a very solemn day to me. It was before I was married. I was nearly twenty, and my parents and the minister had often enjoined my duty upon me; and after a long struggle with my wicked heart, and after much prayer, I thought I was prepared. But I deceived my own soul! I have been deceived ever since till now; and now God fills me with terror! I shall soon meet him, and he will cast me off!" She wept piteously.

"Have you lived a prayerful life since you came to the communion first?"

"Yes, I have prayed night and morning; but I see now that I never prayed acceptably."

"Are you penitent for your sins? Do you mourn over them?"

"Yes, I mourn; but I have 'only a fearful looking for of judgment and fiery indignation.' My soul is in torment! God will cast me off! I shall be lost for ever! *lost! lost!*"

"It is a faithful saying and worthy of ALL acceptation, that Jesus Christ came into the world to *save* sinners."

"I believe it, sir. He is a great and glorious Saviour."

"*Your* Saviour, Madam, if you want Him to be."

"*No sir; no*, not *mine;* not mine." (Again bursting into tears.)

"*Yes*, Madam,—*Yours*, if you want him;—yours in welcome;—yours now, on the spot;—*yours*, if you will 'receive and rest upon him, as he is offered in the Gospel;'—*yours*, if you have never received him before;—*yours* still, even if you have profaned his covenant, as you say, for forty years. You have only to believe in Him with penitence and humility. Christ is greater than your sin."

As I was uttering these words, she continued to repeat the word, "*No, no, no, no*," weeping most distressfully. Said I,—

"Madam, suffer me to beg of you to hear me calmly."

"I will try, sir."

"I utter to you *God's own truth*, madam. I tell you Jesus Christ *is* for you. He is *offered to* you by the God of heaven. He proposes to be your Prophet, Priest, and King, to do for you all you need as a sinner to be saved. He is an all-sufficient Saviour. And in the presence of his merits, *I defy your despair*. Salvation is of grace—of *God's* grace,—of grace operating in the infinite love of God, and by the infinite humiliation of his Son. Here is fulness, the fulness of God. 'Christ is the end of the law for righteousness.' Jesus Christ did not fail in his attempt, when he undertook to redeem sinners. He did His work well. His love brought Him from heaven, and took Him through all the path of His humiliation, from the cradle to the grave. *He* bore the curse, and sinners may go free. He reigns in heaven, the King of glory, and sinners may meet Him there."

"Indeed, sir, he is a wonderful Lord. He hath done all things well. I am glad He is on the throne. When I can catch a glimpse of His glory, my heart rejoices."

"And His glory lies in grace, Madam; *such* grace that He invites you to cast all your cares upon Him, for *He careth* for you."

"I praise Him for it; I will praise Him forever. I rejoice that Christ *is* Lord over all."

She appeared to have lost her trouble. She had

become calm; and she continued to speak of the love of God, and the adorable condescension of Jesus Christ, for some minutes. She asked me to pray with her, and praise God for His wondrous grace. After prayer I left her, supposing that her despondency had been but for a few minutes, and would not return.

The next week I saw her again, as she had requested me to do; and I found her in the same deep despondency as before. She continued to speak of herself; and all I said to her gave no alleviation to her anguish.

Several times I visited her. Uniformly I found her depressed, and sometimes left her rejoicing, and sometimes sad. I could not account for it.

At length it occurred to me, as I was thinking of the different conversations I had had with her, that her mind had uniformly become composed, if not happy, whenever I had led her thoughts *away* from herself, to fix on such subjects as God, Christ, Redeeming love, the covenant of grace, the sufferings of the Redeemer, the Divine attributes, or the glory of God. Afterwards I tried the experiment with her frequently, and the result was always so. I finally stated to her that fact.

"Oh, yes sir," said she, "*I know that very well.* It has always been so with me ever since about the time I made my first sacrament. If I can get my mind fixed on my covenant God and Saviour, then I can rest. But how can I rest when I have no faith?"

"But, Madam, can you not *remember*, in your dark hours, what it was that made you have light ones? and can you not then recur to the same things which made them light, and thus get light again?"

"Oh, sir, I *cannot see the sun through the thick clouds.* God hides himself, and I cannot find him; and then I mourn. I know it is Satan that would drive me to despair. He shoots out his 'fiery darts' at me, and my poor soul trembles in anguish. I cannot help trembling, even when I *know* it is Satan. I have such awful doubts, such horrible temptations darting through my mind, and such blasphemous thoughts, that I feel sure God will cast me off."

This woman never recovered from her sickness; but the last ten weeks of her life were all sunshine. She had not a doubt, not a fear; all was peace and joy. Alluding to this, she said,—

"God does not suffer the adversary to buffet me any more. Christ has vanquished him for me, and I find the blessed promises are the supports of my soul. I fly to them. I fly to Christ, and hide myself in Him. I expect soon He will 'come again and receive me to Himself,' that I may be with Him 'where He is.' I shall behold His glory, and Satan shall never torment me any more."

She died in perfect peace.

There is a difference betwixt the despondency of a believer, and the despondency of an unbeliever. A desponding believer still has faith. It only needs to be brought into lively exercise, and his despondency will melt away. He becomes desponding, because he has lost sight of the objects of faith, and has fixed his thoughts upon himself and his sins. Let the matters of faith be brought up before his mind, and they are *realities* to him,—unquestionable realities. He only needs to keep his eye upon them.

The despondency of an unbeliever is different. He does not despond, because he has lost sight of the objects of faith, for he never *had* any faith; and there is, therefore, no preparation in his heart to welcome the doctrines of grace, of free forgiveness, of redemption through the blood of Christ, of eternal life for sinners. These things are not *realities* to him. His faith never embraced them. When, therefore, in his despondency, whether he looks at his own wickedness or looks at God, he sees only darkness. Especially, the love and mercy of God, the death of Christ for sinners, *all* redemption, are things as dark to him as his own soul. He does not realize them as facts; much less does he embrace them for himself. In the self-righteousness of his spirit he desponds, because he thinks himself too guilty to be forgiven. He is a mere legalist; he sees only the *law*,—not Christ.

But there is only one way of relief for believer and unbeliever in their despondency. They must look to Christ, and to Christ *alone*, all-sufficient and free. A believer has a sort of preparation to do this; an unbeliever has an obstinate reluctance. He thinks only of himself and his sins. Nothing can magnify equal to melancholy, and nothing is so monotonous. A melancholy man left to himself, and the sway of his melancholy, will not have a new thought once in a month. His thoughts will move round and round in the same dark circle. This will do him no good. He ought to get out of it.

Despondency originates from physical causes more than from all other causes. Disordered nerves are the origin of much religious despair, when the individual does not suspect it; and then the body and mind have a reciprocal influence upon each other, and it is difficult to tell which influences the other most. The physician is often blamed, when the fault lies in the minister. Depression never benefits body or soul. "We are saved by hope."

Unknown Presence of the Spirit.

As I was passing along the street one morning, I saw a lady, a member of my church, just leaving her house, and I supposed she would probably be absent a half an hour or more,—long enough for me to accomplish what I had often desired. There was a young woman, a member of her family, who was very beautiful, and reputed to be quite gay, to whom I had sometimes spoken on the subject of religion, but I had never found any opportunity to speak to her *alone.* I had thought that she was embarrassed and somewhat confused by the presence of this lady, whenever I had mentioned the subject of religion to her, and, therefore, I was glad to seize this opportunity to see her alone,—such an opportunity as I thought the lady indisposed to furnish me.

I rang the bell, and the young woman soon met me in the parlor. I then felt some little embarrassment myself, for I had rushed into this enterprise through an unexpected occurrence, and without much premeditation of the manner in which it would be most wise for me to proceed. I expected a cold reception, if not a repulse. I deemed her a very careless, volatile girl. I thought she would be unwilling to have me urge the claims of religion upon her; and the idea that much depended upon the manner in which I should commence, embarrassed me for a moment. But I soon came to the conclusion that I owed it to honesty and truth, to my own reputation for frankness, and to my young friend herself, to tell her plainly what was my intention in then calling to see her. I did so, in the most direct manner possible.

"I am *very* glad to see you," said she. "I have wanted to see you for a good while; for I want to tell you my feelings. I thank you for thinking of me, and being so kind as to come and see me. I should have gone to your house many a time, when you have so often invited persons like me; but when the hour came, my courage always failed me, for I did not know what to say to you. I am in trouble and know not what to do; I am *very* glad of this opportunity." She opened to me her whole heart in the most frank and confiding manner. Among other things she said,—

"I know I have been a thoughtless girl," (while her voice trembled, and tears dimmed her eyes,) "I have been gay and have done many things you would condemn, I suppose; but, my dear minister,

I have been urged into gaiety, when my *heart* was *not there*. I do not believe I am such a girl as they think I am, may I say, as *you* think I am? I know I have a wicked heart, and have too much forgotten God; but I have often wondered *what there is about me*, that makes my religious friends think that I care for nothing but——" She sprang from her seat, clasped her hands upon her face, and hurried out of the room, sobbing aloud.

In a few moments she returned. "I know you will pardon me for this," said she, the tears still coursing down her cheeks, "I do not wish to make any excuse for my sins, nor do I wish to blame *any one* for supposing me thoughtless; but I am sure *I want* to be led in the right way, *I am ready* to do all you tell me. I hope I can be saved yet."

"*Certainly* you can be, my child."

"Then tell me, sir, what to do."

I did tell her, and left her, one of the most grateful and affectionate creatures that ever lived.

As I took my leave of her and found myself again in the street, I commenced my old business of street meditation. My first emotion was gladness, the second shame: for I was ashamed of myself, that I had just been thinking of that young girl so differently from what she deserved, and that I should have gone into her presence, and opened my lips to her with no more faith in God. The next reflection was, how much more common than we think, are the influences of the Holy Spirit. God does often what we never give Him credit for doing. The influences of the Holy Spirit are more common than our unbelief allows us to think.

The inquiry then came into my mind, may there not be others of my congregation who would welcome me also? I stopped in my tracks, and looked around me for another house to enter. I saw one; I rang the bell, and asked for the elder of two sisters, a girl of about nineteen I suppose, and reputed to be very fond of gaiety. She soon met me, and I immediately told her why I had come.

"And I *thank* you for coming," said she. "I am glad you have spoken to me about religion. Why did you not do it before? I *could not* go to your house. I know it is my duty to seek Christ, and I *do want* to be a Christian."

After some conversation with her, in the whole of which she was very frank, and in the course of which she became very solemn, I asked for her sister.

"Yes sir, I will call her. I was going to ask you to see her; but *don't tell her* anything about *me*."

"Her sister came; and as the elder one was about to leave the room, I begged the younger one's permission for her to remain, stating to her at the some time why I had asked to see her. She consented, and the elder sister remained, I thought, gladly.

I then stated to the younger my message, and having explained her condition to her as a sinner, and explained the mercy of God through Jesus Christ, I was urging her to accept the proffered salvation, when she became much affected; she turned pale, covered her face with her hands,—"I *will try* to seek God," said she sobbing aloud. The elder sister, who had delicately taken her seat behind her so as not to be seen by her, clasped her hands together, overcome with her emotions, and lifted her eyes to heaven, while the tears of gladness coursed down her beautiful cheeks, as she sat in silence and listened to us.

I prayed with them, and soon found myself again in the street.

I immediately entered another house, in like manner, and for the same reason as before; and another unconverted sinner met me with the same mingled gladness and anxiety, manifesting the same readiness to seek the Lord.

By this time I had given up all thought of finishing a sermon which was to have been completed that day; for if I could find, among my unconverted parishioners, such instances of readiness and desire to see me, I thought my duty called me to leave my study and my sermons to take care of them.

selves, and to trust in God for the preparation I should be able to make for the pulpit on the coming Lord's day. I therefore went to another house, and inquired for another acquaintance, who was not a member of the church. I did not find her. But in the next house after *that*, which I entered, I found another of my young friends, who told me she never *had* paid any particular attention to the demands and offers of the gospèl, but that she would "neglect it *no longer*;"—"*I will*, sir, attend to my salvation," said she, "as well as I know how."

Here, then, I had found five young persons, in the course of a few hours, all of whom were "almost persuaded to be Christians." They all afterwards became the hopeful subjects of grace; and within six months of that morning were received as members of the church. I knew them all intimately for years, prayerful, happy Christians.

The strivings of the Holy Spirit are more common than we think. If unconverted sinners would improve these secret calls, none of them would be lost. These persons had been awakened before. Probably at this time, as formerly, they would have gone back again to indifference, had not their seriousness been discovered and confirmed. It is important to 'watch for souls.'

A Revival is Coming.

An aged woman, a member of my church, whom I frequently met, always appeared to me to have a more than common interest in the prosperity of religion; and whenever I saw her she had something to say in respect to the success of the gospel. Her heart appeared to be bound up in the welfare of the church. She would often inquire, "are any of our young people coming to Christ?"

One day as I was passing her house she called me in. Says she, "I asked you to come in here because I wanted to tell you a Revival is coming."

"How do you know *that*?" said I.

"We shall have a Revival here," says she "before another year is past."

"How do you know that?" said I.

"Dear me," says she, "now don't think me one of that sort of folks, who think themselves particular favorites of the Lord, as if they were inspired; I'm none of that sort, by a great deal. But I have got faith, and I have got eyes and ears, and I believe in prayer. Perhaps you may think me too certain, but I tell you a Revival *is coming;* and I don't know it by any miracle either, or because I am any better than other people, or nearer to God. But, for this good while, every day when I have been out in my garden, I have heard that old deacon," (pointing to his house,) "at prayer up in his chamber, where he thinks nobody hears him. The window is open just a little way off from my garden, and I hear him praying there every day. He is not able to leave his house much you know, because he has got only one leg; but if he can't work he can pray; and his prayers will be answered. I am sure a Revival is coming, and I should not be surprised if some of his children should be converted. I am not so foolish as to think I am a prophet, or to think I know the secrets of the Lord. I am none of your fanatics. But remember, I tell you a Revival is coming. God answers prayer. You will see."

A Revival did come. Before a year from that time more than a hundred persons in that congregation were led to indulge the hope, that they had been "born of the Spirit." Among them were a son and a daughter of that old man of prayer, and a grandson of this woman who "believed in prayer."

There was no miracle or inspiration in this aged woman's confidence. She employed only faith, ana her own careful observation. "God answers prayer," says she; and she had noticed that earnest prayer was offered, such as had prevailed before.

She was not so singular as she supposed. Others expressed the same confidence, and about the same time, and for a similar reason. One of them said to me, "I notice *how they pray*, at the prayer-meeting in the school-house up Bridge street, every Tuesday night." God does answer prayer.

Much that is foolish, fanatical and wicked, has been preached and published about prayer for Revivals, within the last twenty-five years. Men have maintained that the prayer of faith will produce a Revival at any time, and in any place. And the prayers which have been offered on that principle have sometimes been shocking to contemplate; while the fanatical "Revivals," (so-called,) which have followed them, have done inconceivable mischiefs. A spurious spirit has crept into the church, and spurious conversions have deceived many. Said a minister of no small notoriety to his congregation, "they accuse me of trying to get up a Revival here, and I *am* going to get up a Revival here, so help me my Maker." Horrible! How unlike the gospel—how unlike the humble spirit of reliance and faith!

The Broken Resolution.

As I was one day in familiar conversation with a man, who was a member of my church, and, as we all thought, was one of the most faithful and happy Christians among us; he surprised me, by a half desponding expression about himself. On my inquiring what he meant, he frankly told me what had been his experience, in respect to his comforts of hope.

He said, that he entertained a hope in Christ, and united with the church, when he was a young man. He was now about fifty years of age, and still retained his hope. "I believe I am a Christian," said he, "but I am not the *happy* Christian that I once was." He then went on to tell me more particularly the history of his heart. He said, that for some time after he made a public profession of religion, his faith became more and more established, and his hope more fixed and clear; till he finally arrived at a full assurance of his gracious state, and lived for some years in perfect peace, and commonly in the sweetest joy and delight. As these happy years glided by, he never was troubled with a single doubt about his piety, he had no dark days, no discouragements, not an hour's interruption of his precious communion with God.

Several years had passed away in this happy manner, when a melancholy change came over him. He recollected well the time, and remembered it with deep distress. He said, that he and several other members of the church, after some conversation about the state and prospects of religion in the congregation, agreed to hold a meeting for conference and prayer, in a familiar way. They held it. "It was a precious meeting," said he, "or, at least, it was so to me. My faith was strengthened, my joy was great."

Just at this time, filled with gratitude and love on account of God's gracious goodness to him, he resolved most solemnly that he "would be more faithful." "But," said he, with the deepest solemnity and sadness, "*I did not keep that resolution.* And since that time, I have never been able to get back my former assurance and peace with God! I have a hope, a strong hope, but my former *peace* is gone! I have prayed, and repented, and labored, to get near to God; but I have never been able to rejoice in such happiness as I used to have!"

In answer to my question, he replied,—

"No, I am not conscious of any *indulgence* in sin,

though I sin every hour; nor do I know as I was unfaithful in any one thing in particular. I do not know why God frowns upon me so long; but I know I did not keep my resolution, and my *enjoyment* in religion is very much gone!"

"Perhaps," said I, "you have sought enjoyment too much."

"I thought of that years ago," said he, "and left off *seeking* for it, in any other way, than in serving God."

"Perhaps you think too much of your service," said I, "and too little of the free grace of Christ."

"I think not," he replied. "I never put *my* duties into the place of Christ, betwixt me and God."

"Do you *receive* Christ as your *own* Saviour?"

"I think so: if I did *not*, I should despair. I have *hope* in Christ; but I live on, with a saddened heart. And now, whenever I find Christians rejoicing, I always want to caution them not to be unfaithful, as I have been."

"Do you doubt the reality of your conversion to Christ?"

"No, I have not that trouble; but I have not such delights of peace and joy as I had once."

"Do you expect ever to attain your former happiness?"

"I trust,—I *hope* I shall not *die* without it. I could not die in any peace, as I am now!"

"Is not all this darkness your own fault? Do you believe it is God's will that you should go mourning all your days?"

"I know it is my *own fault*, the result of unfaithfulness and broken resolutions; but I do *not* know as I can now overcome the evil; I have tried for years, but *God* keeps me in this state."

I aimed to convince him that *God* did not "*keep* him" in it, but that he kept *himself* in it. Before I had finished what I intended to say to him, we were interrupted, and at that time as well as on several future occasions, he avoided saying anything to me about himself in the presence of other people. I afterwards asked him privately why he avoided the subject. He said he was afraid he should bring others into darkness, and injure the cause of religion, if he spoke of his trouble. I had several conversations and arguments with him, but they seemed to be useless; he would reply, "God keeps me in this darkness." I proved to him, both by Scripture and by argument, that God did *not* keep him in it,—that he kept himself in it. It might tire the reader, if I should record here the half of the conversations I held with him. Let the last one suffice. He replied to what I had just said to him,—

"I think I *have* faith; and why do you say *unbelief* keeps me in darkness?"

"I believe, too, that you have faith; but I believe you fail to exercise it on a particular point, on which you have special need to exercise it."

"What point do you mean?"

"Last Tuesday evening," I replied, "you attended the prayer-meeting in Bridge street. You offered the last prayer. I heard you. After I left another prayer-meeting, I came across that way, intending to make some brief remarks in your meeting, as I had just done in the other; but when I got to the door, I heard your voice in prayer, (for the door was open,) and I did not go in. Just at the close of your prayer, I walked silently away in the dark. I wished to avoid saying anything to *any one* who heard that prayer. I believed that anything I could say would do more harm than good. Do you recollect how you prayed?"

"No, not particularly."

"Well, I will tell you. You prayed that the Lord would convince unconverted sinners,—that He is infinitely kind and gracious, willing and waiting to save them; constantly calling to them, 'turn ye, turn ye, for why will ye die?' You prayed that they might be led to *believe* in God's willingness to accept them, to adopt them as His own children, and make them blessed in His love. You prayed that the Holy Ghost would lead them to a right understanding of the invitations and promises of

His word, so that they *might know* that 'a way and a highway' is opened to them into His full love and everlasting favor. You prayed that they might see and know, that if they were not happy in God's love, and in the hope of dwelling with Him forever in heaven, it was their own fault, because they would not *believe* in our blessed Lord and Saviour Jesus Christ, and turn to Him. You prayed that anxious sinners might hear Jesus Christ saying unto them, 'come unto me all ye that labor and are heavy laden, and I will give you rest.' In this manner you prayed, and I have repeated some of your expressions exactly as you made them."

"I recollect it now," said he.

"Very well. Now what *I* mean by your not exercising faith on an important point is precisely what *you* meant in that prayer. You meant, that what God was waiting to give, they were not willing to receive; that they did not *believe* in His mercy to sinners, through Christ, and did not come and accept it freely, and without hesitation or fear. *You* meant that they might be happy and safe, if they would flee to Christ and trust Him; and what *I* mean is, that you prayed exactly right, and that you yourself ought to exercise the same faith and same freedom in coming to Christ, which you prayed that *they* might exercise. Precisely the same peace and joy in God which your prayer implied as offered to them, is now positively offered to you, and in precisely the same way. You ought to *believe* this. You ought to *act* upon it. And I am surprised, that while you can see 'the way, and a highway open' for them, you cannot with the same eyes see it open for you."

"But," said he, "I am not like them. They have never sinned in the way I did. They have never known peace with God, and such enjoyments as I had once."

"That may be true," said I, "but you make a distinction which God has *not* made. Nowhere in His word has He said anything to imply an unwillingness to be reconciled to backsliders, and to restore unto them the joys of His salvation; or to imply that He is *less* willing and ready to fill them with peace, than He is to give peace to unconverted sinners who turn to Him."

"But it seems to me," he replied, "a greater sin to forsake Him, after having once experienced His gracious love."

"Let it seem so, then. I do not say it is not. But when you hesitate to believe in His readiness to forgive you, and smile on you as He used to do, I say that you 'limit the Holy One of Israel,' as He has not limited Himself."

"I know He freely invites unconverted sinners to come to Him.'

"And do you *not* know, He invites backsliders just *as* freely? How often He called upon the Israelites who had offended, and when they turned to Him restored to them His favor. Just so He treated David and Peter. Just so He has treated at times almost every Christian on earth. He performs what He has threatened and promised:—'if they break my statutes and keep not my commandments, then will I visit their transgression with the rod, and their iniquity with stripes; nevertheless, my loving kindness will I not utterly take from him, nor suffer my faithfulness to fail. My covenant will I not break, nor alter the thing that is gone out of my lips. Turn, Oh backsliding children, for I am married unto you.'"

"I know it is so in general," he answered, "but are there not some sins that are exceptions?"

"*No;* what business have *you to make* exceptions when God has made none? Suppose Sarah Parker had said to you, just after your prayer, 'Mr. H——, I know the way is open for sinners in general, but are there not some sins that are exceptions?' what would you have said to her?"

"I should have assured her that Christ gives a universal invitation to all sinners, without exception."

"Well, give the same assurance to *yourself.* Will you direct others in a way in which you yourself have no confidence to proceed?"

"Others are not like me."

"Are you better or worse?"

"It seems to me I am a great deal worse."

"What if Sarah Parker should say to you, 'it seems to me that I am a great deal worse?' Her 'seems to me' would be as much in place as your 'seems to me.' Neither of them proves anything. The question is not how 'it seems to you,' but how it seems to God—what *He* has said, and we are to believe; what provision is made for us in Christ."

"I wish I could see it as you do; but, somehow or other, I cannot get out of my darkness, and don't know as I ever shall."

"Perhaps not," said I; "but I assure you the spirit and efforts of self-righteousness will never help you out."

"Do you think it is *self-righteousness* that keeps me in the dark?"

"*Unquestionably*," said I.

"Then I should be glad if you would explain it to me, for I cannot see *how*."

"Precisely as the self-righteousness of a convicted sinner keeps *him* in the dark, when he is 'going about to establish a righteousness of his own, and has not submitted himself to the righteousness of Christ.' He does not 'receive Christ and rest upon Him alone for salvation, as he is offered in the Gospel.' He tries to save himself. He tries to be righteous enough to be saved; and if he cannot think himself to be so, he desponds and wanders in the dark, *because* he does not trust Jesus Christ. And though you trust Jesus Christ for eternal life, yet you limit your faith, so that you do not trust Him to make peace for you *now;* to be your light, and hope, and joy, in reference to your unfaithful ness and broken resolution. *That sin* you make an exception. You do it in the spirit of self-righteousness; and the evidence of this is found in the fact, that you think *God keeps* you in the dark, because your transgression was *so bad.* It is the darkness, then, of self-righteousness. On that one point, you have a self-righteous spirit, a spirit of *legalism,* to think of the *extent* of sin, and weigh it and measure it by *Law,* instead of exercising full faith in Christ, to be your peace with God."

"It may be so," said he; "but if it is, I am not sensible of it. It appears to me, that I am *not* looking for any righteousness in myself, to furnish ground for any confidence and peace with God."

"You think so. But at the same time you mention your offense as a very bad one, and your case as 'an exception,' which shows that you turn (on that point) from the *Gospel* to the *Law,* in the spirit of a self-righteous legalism. You do not, indeed, *exult* in self-righteousness, but you *despond* in self-righteousness. You do not *appropriate* Christ to yourself on that one point, and accept of peace through Him, and take confidence and comfort to your heart. But, on the contrary, just like an entire unbeliever, and in his spirit of legalism, (which is always self-righteousness,) you think of the magnitude of your offense, and thus fall into darkness and gloom. Instead of this, you ought to think of the magnitude of Christ, and accept *Him* alone as *all* and *enough*."

All I could say to him furnished him no relief. He continued in much the same state as long as I knew him, one of the most faithful of believers, and yet one of the most sad. A pensive gloom, a deep, and settled, and heavy sadness, hung almost constantly over his soul, which all his faith and all his hope could not dispel! His hope had lost its brightness, his faith its buoyancy; indeed, both faith and hope seemed to have retired in a great measure from his *heart*, and lingered only around his *mind*. Melancholy state! "God appears to me now," said he, "a great way off! I pray to Him from a distant land; but he does not allow me to come near! Still I am always happy at prayer-meeting."

I found it impossible to persuade him to feel that he might come near, if he would; just as any other sinner might. He would reply,—"My *mind* is convinced, but my *heart* has not any of its old feelings of freedom and nearness to God. But I mourn in silence. I don't wish others to know how I feel, lest it should injure the cause of religion!"

This good man may have been mistaken in reference to the primary cause of his loss of peace; but the probability is, that he thought rightly. And it is probable, too, that many Christians have the distressful feelings of outcast, and distant, and disinherited children, by reason of their unfaithfulness, after their God and Father had given them peace. It is dangerous for a child of God to let his heart wander from home. Bitter, bitter are the tears of unfaithfulness.

What can I do?

In a pleasant interview with a young woman of my congregation, who had recently been led to a hope in Christ, she particularly desired me to see her brother. She had had some little conversation with him, and thought he would be glad of an opportunity to speak with me, for he had some difficulties which she thought troubled him. I immediately requested the favor of seeing him, and in a few moments he came to me. Said I,—

"I asked to see you, sir, because I wished to speak with you on the subject of religion. Have you been considering that subject much?"

"Yes sir, a good deal, lately."

"And have you prayed about it much?"

"I have prayed sometimes."

"And have you renounced sin, and accepted the salvation which God offers you through Christ?"

"No, I don't think I have."

"Don't you think you *ought* to?"

"Yes, if it was not for one thing I would."

"What thing is that?"

"The doctrine of election."

"How does that doctrine hinder you?"

"Why, if that doctrine is true, I can do nothing."

"What can you do if it is *not* true?"

"Why, I don't know," said he, hesitatingly, "but what have *I* to do? *I* can do nothing. It is not my business to interfere with God's determinations; if he has foreordained whatsoever comes to pass, as the Catechism says he has."

"Well, do you think he *has?*"

"*Yes!*" said he, (with an accent of much impatience.)

I then tried very carefully to explain to him our duty, our freeedom of will, our accountability, God's gracious offers of both pardon and assistance; and that God's secret foreordination is no rule of duty to us, and can be no *hindrance* to our duty or salvation. As I thus went on in the mildest and most persuasive manner I could, his countenance changed, he appeared vexed and angry, and finally, in the most impudent and passionate manner, exclaimed,—

"I don't want to hear any such stuff as that! If God has foreordained whatsoever comes to pass, what have I to do?"

"Just what He tells you to do," said I.

"I can do *nothing*," he replied furiously.

"Did you eat your breakfast this morning, sir?"

"Yes, to be sure I did!"

"How could you do it, if God has foreordained whatsoever comes to pass? *you* can do nothing. Did you eat your dinner to-day?"

"Yes, to be sure; I don't go without my dinner."

"What did you eat your dinner for, if God has foreordained whatsoever comes to pass, as you say he has? What have you to do? You can do nothing. Do you mean to go to bed to-night?"

"Yes; I shall try."

"What will you '*try*' for? What have *you* to do? You can do nothing. If God foreordains whatsoever comes to pass, it is not your business to interfere with God's determinations. Will you answer me one question more?"

"Yes."

"Why do you say 'yes?' What have you to do? You can do nothing. God has foreordained whatsoever comes to pass, and you have no business to interfere with his determinations."

He appeared to be confused, if not convinced; and after a few more words, I asked him if he could tell me plainly what he himself meant, when he said he could do nothing.

"*No*," said he, "I don't know *what* I mean."

"Can you explain to me how, in your view, the foreordination of God makes you incapable of doing anything, or hinders you?"

He hesitated for some moments, and then answered,—

"No, *I* am not able to tell anything about it."

I then carefully explained to him his duty, his freedom of will, his accountability to God, and earnestly strove to persuade him to dismiss his cavillings and come to immediate repentance, as God requires, and as a rebel against God ought to do, while mercy solicits him to salvation. He seemed to be somewhat affected; and when I explained to him more fully that the foreordination of God did not take away his liberty, power, or accountability, he appeared to be convinced. I invited him to come to me, if he ever found any more trouble or hindrance, or difficulty of mind, and tell me what it was. But he never came. He frequently muttered some objection to his sister, on the ground of predestination; but he never afterwards introduced that subject in conversation with me. Yet I was not able to persuade him to be a Christian; and now, after fifteen years more of his life have passed away, he still remains in his sins; entirely neglecting all public worship, manifestly a hardened sinner.

It is not safe for a sinner to trifle with Divine truth. The falsehood, insincerely uttered as an excuse, comes to be believed as a truth. Sad state,—given over to believe a lie!

Religion and Rum.

A MAN about forty years of age, with whom I had previously but a slight acquaintance, called upon me one evening, in the greatest anxiety of mind. Seldom have I seen a man more agitated. He had become suddenly alarmed on account of his condition as a sinner. His feelings quite overcame him. He wept much. I answered his questions; and urged him to repent and flee to Christ, now in the 'accepted time.'

He was an intelligent, well-educated man, who had seen much of the world, and evidently had moved in good society. He conversed with much fluency and correctness, evidently possessing a quick and ready mind. His parents, as he told me, were communicants in a neighboring church, and until about three weeks before he came to my house, he had been accustomed to attend church with them. He had a good degree of intellectual knowledge on the subject of religion. He was evidently a man of sound understanding.

He continued to call upon me frequently for some

months; but he attained no peace of mind,—no hope in Christ. I was surprised at this. He appeared, from the first, so sincere, so earnest, attended all our religious services so punctually, and in all respects manifested so much determination, that I had confidently expected he would become a Christian indeed. And as he continued in much the same state of mind, I aimed to teach him the truth more carefully, and examine into his views, and feelings, and habits, in order to ascertain, if possible, and remove the obstacles, (whatever they might be,) which kept him from yielding to the Holy Spirit. But I could not even conjecture, why a man, who appeared to know the truths of the gospel so well, and feel them so deeply, should not make some progress in his religious attempts. I noticed nothing peculiar or remarkable in him, unless it was some degree of fitfulness, and the ease and frequency of his tears. He wept more than I had been accustomed to see men of his years weep.

I mentioned his case to one of the officers of the church, with whom I knew he was acquainted, and requested him to converse with him. He complied with this request. He had several conversations with him; but he was disappointed and perplexed, as much as I had been. "He weeps," said he, "and that is pretty much all that I can say about him."

A few weeks after this, and while his tearful

seriousness continued, I saw him one day in such company, that the thought was suggested to my mind, whether he did not indulge himself in the use of intoxicating drink. I made inquiry about this, and found it was so. The next time he called upon me, I told him, as plainly as words could possibly express it, that I had not a doubt, but his drinking was a device of the great adversary to keep him from salvation. He appeared to be surprised—did not deny drinking, but positively denied that he ever drank to any excess. I aimed to convince him, that any drinking at all of stimulating liquors was an excess *for him*. Again and again, I urged him to quit. He promised he would, but he did not. On one occasion he confessed to me, that he had resorted to brandy, in order "to sustain himself," as he expressed it, at times when his "mind was burdened and cast down with the thoughts of another world." I explained to him the folly, the danger, and wickedness of dealing with his serious impressions in that way. He promised to do it no more. But he kept on,—he lost all regard for religion,—he forsook the church,—and now he is ten years nearer death,—an irreligious man, and probably an intemperate man.

Mr. Nettleton once said to me, "if a hard-drinking man gets a hope, it will be likely to be a false hope."

The Word of a Companion.

On Monday, the day after the administration of the sacrament of the Lord's Supper, a young man of my congregation called upon me in great agitation of mind. He said he felt that he was "a great sinner," that he could "not bear to live in the condition he was in," that his "attention had been anxiously turned to the subject of salvation several times before, but he soon forgot it again," and he "was afraid it would be so now." Said he, "I have wanted to come and see you a good many times, but I never *could* make up my mind to do it till yesterday."

I was not surprised to see him. The exercises of the communion Sabbath had been more solemn and joyful for the people of God, than any such exercises that I have ever witnessed; and as similar occasions of communion had often before been times of awakening for those who were not communicants, I had *expected* that the same things would be experienced *now*. I told him this, and aimed to make him realize the solemnity of the fact, that the Holy

Spirit was striving with him. I noticed in him two things, which particularly characterized his state of mind,—the depth of his convictions, and his fixed determination to turn unto God.

As I was to leave home that day, and should not see him again for several weeks, I took the more care to teach him the gospel truths, and to impress them upon his mind. And because his attention had been arrested before, and he had gone back to indifference; I aimed to convince him that his danger lay on that very spot, and his only security was to be found in a full and instant determination to 'deny himself, and take up his cross and follow Jesus Christ.'

He left me, and such was my impression of his fixed *purpose*, that I had little doubt or fear about the result.

On my return home a few weeks afterwards, he immediately called upon me. He came to tell me of his happy "hope in God through Jesus Christ *my Saviour*," as he emphatically expressed it.

Some months afterwards he united with the church. But in making, at that time, a statement of the exercises of his mind at the period when he first came to see me; he mentioned one thing which astonished, instructed and humbled me. After mentioning his anxieties, his sense of sin, and his interview with myself, he added, "that day one of my *companions* spoke to me on the subject of religion. *That determined me.*"

This was the turning point therefore. *I* thought he was "determined" before: he thought so: he appeared to be. Indeed I had never witnessed the appearance of a more full and fixed determination in any anxious inquirer, save one; and it was the very thing which gave me such a confident expectation of his conversion. But I was greatly mistaken. His heart wavered and hesitated and hung round the world, till one of his "companions spoke to him." That young companion was the successful preacher after all. Suppose that "companion" had *not* spoken to him; what would this young man have done? We cannot tell; but there is a high degree of probability that he would have done just what he had so often done before,—would have quenched the Spirit and gone back to the world. Such companions are greatly needed.

Salvation ought to be urged upon the *will*, the *choice*, the "*determination*" of sinners, up to the very point of their "receiving Christ and resting upon him alone for salvation, as he is offered in the gospel." Such an urgency is never out of place. The *will* is wanting, the determination is wanting, in every unconverted sinner, whether he believes it or not. The Bible has it right,—'*choose* ye this day whom ye will serve.'

Fasting and Prayer.

THE sixteenth day of March, in the year 1831, was observed, by the church, in which I was pastor, as a day of fasting and prayer. This appointment was made with special reference to the out-pouring of the Holy Spirit,—to seek, by united prayer, the revival of God's work in the midst of the congregation. The meetings for prayer were held in the church, and a large portion of the members were present.

The next week, as I was returning home from a religious meeting late in the evening, and had turned into an unfrequented cross-road, in order to shorten the distance I had to walk; I was startled at the sudden sound of footsteps behind me, which seemed to be those of a man rapidly approaching me in the dark. I did not know but some evil-minded person might intend to do me harm in that obscure place, and under cover of the impenetrable darkness of one of the darkest nights that I ever saw. I did not choose *to run*, for, in that case, I should never know why I was so hotly pursued. I felt glad, that I had some corporeal strength; and though I cannot say, that my courage very specially forsook me, yet I had no particular liking for a hostile attack and a tussle in the dark. As the footsteps so rapidly approaching me appeared to be directly in my rear, like a lover of peace I crossed to the other side of the road; and not preferring an attack in the rear, I stopped and faced about. My pursuer espied me, and, without slackening his pace, ran directly towards me across the street, till, coming within ten feet of me, much out of breath, he called my name. "That is my name, sir," said I. He came close up to me, panting for breath, and stopped in silence. After a few heavy and rapid breathings, he spoke. He told me who he was, and why he had run after me. He was a young man of my congregation, to whom I had never before spoken. I did not know him personally. He had just come from the school-house where I had been preaching; and, not willing to be seen by his companions speaking to me, he had waited till they were out of the way, and then run after me, through the obscure street into which he had seen me turn. He wanted to see me, for he felt that he was "a sinner unreconciled to God, and in danger of hell." "What shall I *do?*" said he; "I can't live so another week. Is there any way that such a one as *I* am can be saved?"

I had a long conversation with him standing there in the dark, (for he did not choose to go home with me,) and I found, that his first impressions of any particular seriousness had commenced in the church, on the *Fast-day*, the week before. He was an apprentice in a mechanic's shop, where there were more than a dozen other irreligious young men. The master of the shop (not a professor of religion), told the whole of them, that if they wished to attend church on the Fast-day, they need not work. They accepted his proposal. And as he himself afterwards told me, *that* was the reason why *he* went to church that day himself. He said, he "did not expect the boys would take his offer, but would prefer to stay at home and work;" and if they had done so, he should have done so too; "but when they were all going to church," says he, "I was *ashamed* to stay at home."

That young man, his employer, and almost the entire number of those young men in the shop, became communicants in the church before the close of that year. Thirteen persons were received into the church, whose seriousness commenced *that day, in the church*, while the *people of God were praying* for that *very thing*. 'The Lord is with you while ye be with Him.' 'Before they call I will answer; and while they are yet speaking, I will hear.'

God Reigns: or, Despair

I DO not deem it a departure from the purpose or the title page of this publication, when I insert the following sketch of experience, which I copy from a paper which lies before me. The author of it, a clergyman, is still living, and still exercises the functions of his Pastoral office. He here writes a little sketch of his own sad experience, which I am permitted to copy from his own hand-writing, though it was not designed for publication, being in a letter to a friend. As he has here explained how it was, that he rose out of the dark and turbid waters of despair, the explanation may be of some service to others,—as I know it has been to his friend. Despair is opposed to faith, and every sinner on earth has the right to oppose faith to despair.

The following is a part of the letter:

"MY DEAR FRIEND,

"You say I am always happy, but you know little about me. I am not accustomed to obtrude my griefs upon others, for awakening a painful and useless sympathy; and I have sadly learnt, that there may be griefs utterly beyond the power of others to understand, and which, therefore, their sympathies cannot reach. But I have seasons (and they are not unfrequent), when my soul is cast down within me. I am sure *I* can sympathize with any and every trouble of your darkest hours. * * *

"It is not a year since I found myself involved in all the horrors of darkness. I had hoped that such a season would never again return upon me; but it did. I had formerly learnt, that ill health, or rather nervousness in any state of health, has a great influence in bringing on depressed feelings; and at the period to which I now allude, I was fully conscious of my nervous condition, and I recollected and reflected upon its influence. But this did not help me out of my trouble. Day by day the darkness settled down upon my soul, deeper and deeper. I could see *no* light! I was no Christian! The Bible was a sealed book to me; Christ was as a fiction, and salvation as a dream. Prayer was not so much of a mockery, as *a lie*, for I felt that I did not *believe* what my lips uttered, when they said they called upon God. I did not believe in God. I was a dark sceptic. I could realize *nothing*, but my own wretchedness; and in the depth of that wretchedness I cursed the day in which I was born! Many and many a time I wished I never *had* been born, or had died when I first saw the light. Many and many a time I wished myself a dog, a horse, a stone, *anything* but myself. I could realize nothing, rest on nothing, believe nothing.

"No pen can describe the horrors I endured. They were of every sort. I can only give you a few hints of them.

"Blasphemous thoughts, not lawful to utter even here; temptations which I may not name,—things that would freeze your blood,—yea, things which made me feel that hell itself could be no worse,—would be darted through the mind, without volition or control! My poor soul was their sport. She had no power over them, not an item. She was tossed about, like a leaf in the storm, helpless, hopeless. At times, things would flash over my mind, like the flashes of the pit, as I thought; for I could not account for them in any other way. It was as if Satan spoke to me, to jeer at me, and taunt me, and triumph over me in his malignity:—'where is your God *now?* what do you think of prayer *now?*' These ideas would come with such suddenness and vividness, so involuntary, so surprising to myself, that I could not believe them the production of my own mind; it must be that Satan was permitted to buffet me, and expend all his malice upon me, giving me a foretaste of hell.

"In my agony I used to roll upon the floor of

my study, hour after hour, in despair, thinking it a sin, a shame, an impossibility for me to make another sermon. I knew I was not fit to preach. I thought I should be only acting a part, only playing the hypocrite *knowingly*. I would have relinquished the ministry if I could. But what could I do? I *must* preach. And after I had put it off as long as I could, and had scarcely time enough left to prepare for the Sabbath, I used to get my texts, and enter upon the composition of my sermons, feeling that I was the most miserable and most unworthy being on this side of the pit, and that I should soon be in it. When I got engaged over my sermons, I used to forget *myself;* and then, as my thoughts were occupied with the truth of God, I would become interested in the study, and get along pretty well till Sunday was over. I would preach like an apostle, and go home in despair! I tried every device, but no relief came.

"I went to a distinguished clergyman, and told him my case. He was kind to me. He said some wise things to me. But he began to say to me, that God was disciplining me, to prepare me for some greater usefulness: 'Stop! sir,' said I. 'I cannot receive that!—I *can't!* I *can't!* It does not belong to me. I thought of that, but my conscience rejected it as a snare of the devil, to keep me at peace in my sins. I told him I *knew* better; I was afraid, and had good reason to be afraid, that I never had any religion;—I could not live so, and certainly I could not die so. I told him that I could comfort others, and lift them out of such troubles as *seemed* to resemble mine,—*had* done it,—was skilled in doing it,—if nothing else, I could *beguile* them out of their despair, without their knowing how I did it; but I could not comfort myself; my case was different, and I could not receive the same truths I preached to *them.* The ideas and promises which cheered them could not cheer me. I told him I had often thought myself like the man of gloom, who applied in his despair to some friend, perhaps minister, and his friend said to him, 'divert your thoughts,—take exercise, amusement,—go to hear Carlini play,' (a famous harlequin, attracting crowds at the time.) 'Alas! sir,' said he, in despair, '*I* am Carlini myself!' And so was I. I went home in despair, weeping along the street as I went.

"While I was in just this state, perplexed, agitated, tormented night and day, fearing and half expecting I should become a maniac, I had occasion to take a woman to the mad-house. (She would go with *me*,—her friends could not manage her.) As I rode along with her in the carriage, and conversed with her, I felt in my soul that *I* was more fit for the mad-house than she! I left her there. As I came out, I looked around upon the grounds, the trees, the sky, and knew nothing, and doubted everything, and thought of *myself*, my torment of soul became intolerable! It was with difficulty that I could restrain myself from screaming out in my agony! I got into the carriage to go home. The young man who was with me made some attempts at conversation, but I could not attend to him; and finding my answers incoherent, I suppose, or finding me mute, he looked at me with astonishment, and afterwards left me to myself.

"We rode on. I could realize nothing—believe nothing. I did not believe there was a God! I felt that I was sinking down into the madness of despair! a forlorn, hopeless, eternal wreck! a wretch too wicked to live, and not fit to die!

"By-and-bye my mind began to question and reason. *I am*—that is certain. These are *trees*—that is a *river*—yonder is the *sun*. All these things are certain. But where did they come from? They did not make *themselves*. *I* did not make myself. There is *dependence* here. They do not *govern* themselves. There is *order* here. The sun keeps his place, and is now hiding himself in his west in due time. '*There is a God!* Yes, there *is* a God!' That was the first gleam of light. I held on to that idea; '*there is a God, there is a God, there is a God!*' I kept affirming it in my mind. I felt I had got hold of *one certainty*, and I would not let it go. I could believe *one* thing.

"In a moment, (for these ideas flashed through my mind like flashes of lightning,) I got hold of another idea, another *certainty*, and then linked the two certainties together. It was *order*, dominion. God *has* dominion. Yes, *He* rules. '*God reigns!*' said I. It was an ocean of light to me! It flooded the universe! '*God reigns! God reigns! God reigns!*' I kept repeating these two words mentally, '*God reigns! God reigns!*' It was triumph to me. It was glory. I almost leaped from the carriage. I groaned aloud under the burden of my joy. (The young man started up and gazed at me. I did not notice him.) I held on to the idea. '*God reigns!*' said I. I dared not let it go; '*God reigns!*' I dared not let any other idea enter my mind; '*God reigns! God reigns! God reigns!*' said my exulting soul.

"Then came a contest within me,—a conflict like the clash between thousands of opposing sabres! I felt the full power of my idea, if I could but hold it; but the assaults that were made upon it came like the shock of battle! One thought after another seemed to heave over my soul, like the waves, to dash me from my rock! You are a lost sinner; vile—a wretch! '*God reigns!*' said my soul. You are a hypocrite! '*God reigns!*' said my soul. You are a fool! '*God reigns!*' You are a madman! '*God reigns!*' You *are* mad, for no sane mind ever acted in this way! '*God reigns!*' I am certain of *that*—'*God reigns!*' Wo to you if He does! '*God reigns!*' What do you know about God? '*God reigns!*' You are a sceptic, an infidel! '*God reigns!*' God has abandoned *you!* '*God reigns!*' You are moved this moment by the power of the Devil! '*God reigns!*' said my exulting soul.

"Thus one temptation after another dashed upon me, and all I could do was to hold on to my rock. '*God reigns!*' At one moment I trembled, as an onset was made upon me; the next moment I triumphed, as the onset was hurled back by the power of the *one certainty* I wielded. I was sinking, amid the dark surges that dashed over me. In an instant I was above them all—governed them all—and could have governed a thousand such oceans, because '*God reigns!*' I opposed that shield to every wave of midnight—to every shock of scepticism—to every 'fiery dart,' that Satan hurled at me. I held it up, and defied despair and the Devil. I turned it in every direction, upon every foe, every fear, every doubt; 'GOD REIGNS!' and I wished to *know* nothing else.

"I came home holding these two words over my poor soul, now settled, soothed down to perfect peace—calm, happy. I did not want to think anything, know anything, care for anything: '*God reigns!*' and that is enough.

"Gradually I got hold of other truths, and employed them, I hope, in faith; but for many days I needed nothing to fill my soul with delight, but that glorious idea, '*God reigns!*' '*God reigns!*' It saved me from being a maniac.

"This is but a very imperfect glance at one of my dark seasons. It can give you only a partial idea of them. No pen can ever describe them, and no imagination conceive of their horrors, unless the positive experiences of despair have been such as to make imagination ashamed of its feebleness.

"I do not wish the return of such seasons. They may, indeed, have been of some use to me, as my wiser friend suggested; but I do not like such discipline; I do not wish to learn the power of faith, by being scorched by the blaze of hell.

"Never can I even recollect those dark trials, without being overcome with emotion. I wish I could forget them. But they are burnt upon my memory, and I have not been able to write this without many tears. God grant you may not be able to understand me now, or at any time hereafter. But if you ever should come into such depths, I know of but one way to get out:—FAITH, FAITH, FAITH. You must not *try* to get out. You must let *God take* you out. You can do nothing for yourself. You might as well breast the dash of the ocean, or brave the thunder of heaven. You must let God 'hide you in the cleft of the rock, and cover you with His hand!' You must just exercise *a passive faith*,—much more difficult than an active one. At least *I* have found no other way. *Reason* with such feelings?—reason with a whirlwind as soon,—with a tempest,—with the maddened ocean! You *cannot* reason with them. They will take you up, and dash you about like the veriest mite in the universe. Look;—do nothing but look. God reigns. Jesus Christ is King. Leave ALL to HIM:—it is Faith."

It was a bright doctrine, to which this minister clung in the time of his trouble. It is a great truth, "God reigns," and, therefore, 'grace reigns through righteousness unto eternal life, by Jesus Christ our Lord;' and, therefore, no sinner on earth need ever despair.

The Last Hour.

ONE of the most distressing instances of religious darkness and despondency, that I have ever been called to witness, was that of a poor girl, whom I first knew when I was called upon to visit her in her last sickness. She was not twenty years old, her health had departed, she seemed to be doomed to an early grave. A seated pulmonary affection deprived her of all hope of recovery, and she had no hope in God. From her earliest childhood she had had excellent religious instruction. Her parents were pious people, and though they were poor, they had carefully educated her. She had been a scholar in the Sabbath school from her childhood, under the weekly instructions of a teacher who loved her, and who had taught her with assiduity, kindness, and skill. But though she had been long the subject of religious impressions, and had carefully studied her Bible, and earnestly prayed to be directed into the path of life, she had never found peace with God.

When I first knew her, none but herself had any special fears that her life was near its end. She was then able to be about the house, and sometimes, in pleasant weather, to walk out into the fields. But she had given up all expectation that she should recover, and she now addressed herself to the work of preparation for death, to which she looked forward with an indescribable anguish. She regarded it as the commencement of eternal woe.

At first I felt no peculiar discouragement, on account of her religious depression. I regarded her fearful distress of mind, as only the natural accompaniment of a just conviction of sin, and confidently expected that she would soon be led to hope and peace in believing. But it was far otherwise with her. She attained no peace. As week passed after week, she continued in the same despondency, receiving no light, no hope, no comfort. She read, she examined, she wept, she prayed in vain. And as her health declined more and more, her mind became wrought up to an intensity of anguish most distressful to witness. It was enough to melt any one's heart, to hear her cries for mercy. Never did a sinner plead more earnestly to be delivered from going down to perdition. She cried for mercy, as if standing in the very sight of hell! She had not a single gleam of light. Her soul was dark as a double midnight, and seemed plunged into an ocean of horrors. No one, I am sure, could have listened to her dreadful wailings, without feeling a sympathy with her, which would have wrung the heart with anguish.

I visited her often, conversed with her many times, taught her most carefully all the truths of the Bible, which I supposed could possibly have any tendency to awaken her faith in Christ, and prepare her to meet Him ; but I never had any evidence to the last, that anything I ever said to her was the means of any benefit.

I wondered at her continued despair. It seemed to be the more remarkable, on account of the clear views which she appeared to have, of the character of God, of His holy law, of her condemnation by it, of her wicked heart, of redemption by Christ, and of the faithfulness of God to fulfil all his promises. I often examined her thoughts and feelings on all such points as well as I could, in order to detect any error into which she might have fallen, and which might be a hindrance to her faith and peace, and in order to persuade her to trust all her eternal interests to the grace of the great Redeemer. She had not a doubt about any of these truths. She knew and bewailed her guiltiness and depravity, she fully believed in the love of God towards sinners, and the willingness of Christ to save her, unworthy as she was ; she said she hated sin with all her heart ; she longed to be holy ; she did not believe that she hated God, though she would not say that she loved

Him; she admired "the kindness and love of God our Saviour" towards sinners; and wanted, above all things, to have an interest in His redemption, and be *sure* that He had accepted her.

Months before her death I believed that she was a child of God. I thought I could discover every evidence of it, except hope, and peace, and the spirit of adoption. She had now come to believe that she had some love to God; "but," says she, "I am afraid God does not love *me*, and will cast me off forever, as I deserve."

I strove, in every possible manner, and time after time, to lead her to the peace of faith. By holding directly before her mind the character of God, the redeeming kindness and work of Christ, and especially God's free invitations and firm promises; I strove to lead her to an appropriating faith, which should beguile her into a half-forgetfulness of herself, by causing her to delight in God. By teaching her according to the Scriptures what are the evidences of a new heart, and then by taking her own declarations to demonstrate to her that her own exercises of mind and heart were precisely these evidences; I labored hard to induce her mind to rest upon the "witness within,"—a witness really there (as I believed), if she would only hear and heed its voice. I explained to her what I honestly supposed to be the cause of her darkness, that is, her bodily condition, which prevented her seeing things as they were, by throwing a deceptive and dismal cloud over everything that pertained to herself. At times, when she appeared to me to be coming out of her gloom, and to be standing on the very borders of a light which she could not but see; a single recurring idea about herself would fling her back into all her darkness, and she would weep and wail in despair.

I had been describing heaven to her, and referring to its song of redemption, 'who loved us, and washed us from our sins in his own blood,'—

"Others will be in heaven," said she, "but *I* shall be cast out! From the distant region of my doom, I shall behold my companions by the river of life, happy, happy spirits, perhaps I shall hear their song; but no such home *for me!*"

"How came they there?" said I. "They were not saved by their goodness. They were no better than you. Jesus Christ saved them by his blood, and he offers to save you."

"He passes *me* by, sir. He called them, and they obeyed the call in due time; but he does not call *me!*"

"*He does,* my child, He *does.* He calls you *now,* 'Come unto ME.'"

"If He does, sir, I have no heart to hear Him! My day is past! my day is past! I shall be cast off as I deserve! Oh, I wish I had never been born!"

"Your day is *not* past. 'Now is the day of salvation.' "

Her only answer was tears and groans.

Such was her melancholy condition, as she declined more and more. Her strength was now almost gone. She evidently had but few weeks to live, if indeed a few days even remained to be measured by the falling sands of her life.

One day, (some weeks before her death,) after I had been stating to her the evidences of a regenerated state, and she had clearly described to me her own views and feelings, which seemed to me to accord with these evidences in one particular after another almost throughout the entire chapter; I said to her, with some earnestness,—

"Mary Ann, what do you want more, to convince you that you are a child of God? What do you expect? If these things do not convince you, what could? What evidence more do you *want?* Do you want an angel to come down from heaven here to your bedside, to tell you that you are a Christian, and shall go to heaven as soon as you die?"

"Oh, yes," said she, in a transport of emotion, clasping her death-pale hands, "*that is just what I want—just what I want.*"

"That is just what you cannot have," said I; "God is not going to give you any such *kind* of evidence."

I then explained to her, how she must rest upon spiritual evidences, as all Christians do, and not on any evidence of the senses, or supernatural occurrence outside of her own heart.

As she approached fast her end, and evidently could not survive much longer; I was greatly disappointed and saddened, that her mind continued in the same unbroken gloom. I had not expected it. I had looked for a different experience. But it now seemed that her sun must go down in clouds!

One Sabbath morning, just before the time of public service, I was sent for to "see her die." She could still speak, in a very clear and intelligible manner, better than for weeks before. Her reason was continued to her, all her faculties appeared as unimpaired and bright as ever. All that I could discover of any alteration in her mind, appeared to me to consist simply in this,—she now thought of *herself* less, and of her God and Saviour more. I told her, as I was requested to do, that she was now very soon to die. The bell was tolling for me to go to the pulpit, and, having prayed with her, commending her to her God, I gave her my hand to bid her farewell. "Will you come to see me at noon?" says she.

"My dear child, you cannot live till noon. The Doctor says you cannot live half an hour. I will come here as soon as I leave the church."

I went to the church and preached; and as soon as the service closed, I went immediately to her house. She was still alive. One of her friends met me at the door, and hastily told me, that soon after I left the house, an hour and a half before, she avowed her perfect trust in Christ, and her firm confidence that He would "take her home to heaven." "I am full of peace," said she, "I can trust my God. This is enough. I am happy, happy. I die happy." A little while after, she said she wanted to see me "once more." She was told I was in church, and that she could not live till the sermon was closed. "*I shall live*," said she firmly. She seemed to refuse to die. She inquired what time the service would close, and being told, she often afterwards inquired what time it was. She watched the hands of the clock, frequently turning her eyes upon them, in the intervals between her prayers and praises and rapturous thanksgivings. As I entered the room she turned her eyes upon me; "Oh," says she, "I am glad you have come; I have been waiting for you. I wanted to see you once more, and tell you how happy I am. I have found out that a poor sinner has *nothing* to do only to believe. I am not afraid of death now. I am willing to die. God has forgiven me, and I die happy,—I am very happy. I wanted to tell you this. I thought I should live long enough to tell you. I thought God would not let me die till I had seen you, and told you of my joy, so as not to have you discouraged when you meet with other persons who have such dark minds as mine was. Tell them to *seek* the Saviour. Light will come some time, if it *is* at the last hour. I prayed God to let me see you once more. He has granted my last prayer; and now—now I am ready."

Her voice faltered; she could say no more. I prayed some two or three minutes by her bedside; we rose from our knees, and in less than five minutes more she was dead. 'Blessed are the dead that die in the Lord.'

It was pleasant to hear this dying girl affirm her faith, and to witness her joy at the moment of death. But I do not know that this joy amounted to any more real evidence of her effectual calling to Christ by the Holy Spirit than she had presented before. Faith is one thing, and feeling is another. It is the faith that saves. It is the feeling that comforts. But the faith may exist where the feeling is wanting. The principle may exist where its action is wanting.

If this poor girl had died in all her darkness and fears, I should not have despaired of her. Amid all her glooms of guilt, I thought she exhibited proofs of faith. It seemed to me that it was faith, which made her attend to the truths of the Bible, with such careful scrutiny and enduring perseverance, at the very moment when she saw no light in it for *her* ;—that it was faith, which made her pray so fervently and without faltering, month after month, at the very time when she did not suppose she received any answer ;—that it was faith, which kept her, in her most gloomy times, perfectly free from any besetting doubt that there *is* salvation for sinners in Jesus Christ, freely offered to them in the love of God ;—that it was faith, which made her so perfectly assured that peace with God is attainable, and made her long for it as the only thing she cared for ;—yea, that it was faith, which gave to her very glooms their most terrible aspect, creating such a confident and continued conviction that if Christ was not found, everything was lost. Her grief was not that of an alien and an enemy, but that of an affectionate, but disinherited child. The very point of her anguish consisted in this,—namely, that she believed Christ to be a full and free Saviour, and yet could find no evidence in her heart that she trusted in Him. The promises were precious things in her heart's estimation, but they seemed to her to be precious things which she did not embrace. She distrusted herself, but not God. She was afraid to believe that she was a believer. She was so tremblingly afraid of getting wrong, that she dared not think she could possibly be right. On this ground,

I was led to believe that Mary Ann was a child of God, long before that memorable light shone on her soul in the hour of death. She was in darkness, not because she had no faith, but because she did not believe she had any. She had a title to heaven, without having eyes to read it.

Her mother, father, and physician, (who was a pious man), all her friends, as I suppose, regarded this bright close of her earthly experience very differently from myself. They appeared to look upon it as the commencement of her faith, thinking that God had first appeared for her in that time of her first triumph and joy. Such an idea in similar cases, I suppose, to be common, and I suppose it to be an error, and a very misleading one, especially to many unconverted sinners. Such unconverted sinners hear of instances like this, and, therefore, *hope* that it may be just so with themselves, when they shall be called to die. On the ground of this hope, they speak a deceitful peace to their own hearts, without any definite, determined, and prayerful efforts to prepare for death,—just leaving it to that coming hour itself to bring along with it the preparation they need. Their secret thought is,—such a one, who always *lived* without religion, died in peace at last, and why should not I? Delusive thought, and often fatal! These persons never stop to inquire what had been the previous heart-history, the struggles, and prayers of those, whose peaceful death they mention. They themselves are not *living such a life* as their now departed acquaintance did, who died in peace; and, therefore, they have no good reason to think they shall *die such a death.* Too hastily they say of such a one, "he lived all his life without religion." They say what they do *not* know, and what probably is *false.* If any one would hope to *die* like Mary Ann, let him *live* like Mary Ann. Her supreme aim, and her agonizing prayer for months, sought the favor of God. To gain this, she omitted nothing which she deemed a duty,—she deferred nothing to a future hour. To gain this was all her desire, and no discouragement could make her falter, or turn her aside. 'Go thou and do likewise,' if thou wouldst *die* like Mary Ann.

The Dawn of Heaven.

SIXTEEN years after the death of Mary Ann (mentioned in the preceding sketch), I was summoned to the sick-bed of her sister. She was a younger sister, whom I had never seen since she was a mere child, and of whose religious character I had no knowledge. She had married; and after many trying changes, she was now in the city of New York. A kind lady, one of my own friends who resided in that city, and who had formerly known something of her family in another State, had accidentally heard of her illness, had called upon her, and now did me the favor to bring me the sick woman's request, that I "would go and see her." She told me I should find her in a very destitute condition, very much unbefriended and alone, though she had herself done something for her, to make her a little more comfortable. I received this message in the evening, and early the next morning I made my way to the house, to which she had directed me.

I found the sick woman in a boarding-house, among strangers, where nobody knew her except her husband, and manifestly nobody cared for her. She was in the garret, in a little room close under the roof of the house. The scanty furniture and the whole appearance of the room, showed me, at a glance, how unenviable was her condition. There was but one chair in the room, and this was used for a table (the only one she had), on which were placed some vials of medicine, a tea-cup and a saucer, which constituted all the furniture of the room, except her humble bed. But all was neat and clean. If there was scantiness, there was decency.

As I entered the room, I perceived at once her hopeless condition. She was emaciated, pale, tormented with a hollow cough, unable to speak but in a whisper, and her cheek was flushed with that round spot of peculiar red, with which I had become too familiar to mistake it for anything else than the fatal signal. I approached the bed on which she was lying, told her who I was, and offered her my hand.

"I am *very* happy—to see you," said she (speaking with effort and only in a whisper, and compelled to pause at almost every word). "I did not suppose—you would remember me—at all,—and for a long time—I could not have courage—to send—for you,—or—let you know—that I was here. But I remembered—you visited—my sister,—Mary Ann,

—when *she* died,—and I had—a great desire to—see you."

"I am very glad," said I, "to be able to see you; but I am sorry to find you so ill. I wish I had known that you were here, sooner."

"You are—very kind, sir;—but I was—afraid to trouble you. I have—not seen you—before,—since I was—a little child;—and I supposed—you had—forgotten, that—there was such a person. I am very thankful to you—for being so kind—as to come—to see me."

"Have you been sick long?"

"Yes sir,—a good many—months. I have lately—been growing—much worse,—and I want now—to get home—to my mother,—this week,—if I can. I think—I should be better there—for a little while,—though I cannot tell."

"Do you think you are well enough to go home?"

"I hope—I could go—in the boat—and live to get there. The hottest—of the summer—is coming on soon—and our place here—is very uncomfortable; but—most of all—I want to see—my *mother*,—*once* more—before I die." And the big tears rolled fast over her fevered cheeks.

"I hope," said I, "you may be able to see her; but you do not seem to have much strength just now."

"Indeed, sir,—my strength—is—all gone. I cannot—stand on my feet—any longer. Before I became—so weak—I used to work with my needle—and help my husband—earn something;—and then, we had—a more comfortable place. But I can do nothing—now—and so we came—to this—garret—to save rent."

"Have you much pain?"

"Yes sir—I am in—great pain now,—the most—of the time."

"Do you expect ever to get well?"

"Oh, no sir,—I shall—never get well. I know I am—to die—before long;—the consumption—is—a hopeless disease. This painful cough—will soon end—my days."

"Are you afraid to die?"

"Oh, no sir," said she with a smile, "Jesus—is my hope. He—*will* save me."

"Trust Him," said I, "you trust eternal rock. He has promised,"—

Interrupting me, she replied,—

"What *can*—anybody want—more than the *promises?* It seems to me—the promises—are enough—for everybody;—*so sweet*—they are so *full.* Why, God—has promised—to make—an everlasting covenant—with us—poor sinners!" And tears of joy coursed down her smiling face.

I conversed with her as long as I thought it best

for her. All her conversation was in the same happy strain. She appeared very much exhausted, and I had little hope that her desire to "see her *mother once* more," would ever be gratified. Indeed I did not think she would live till sun-set. I prayed with her, and promising to call again in the afternoon, I left her.

Some little arrangements were made for her comfort, and in the afternoon I called there again. She was evidently worse, but her joy was full. Said she,—

"I bless my God—for all my pain—for the disappointments—of my past life,—and the strange—strange way—in which—he has—led me on. I have had trials—many trials. My husband—did not prosper—as—he hoped—to do,—and sometimes—we have been—in distress. But—my trials have—done me good. Now we have few wants.—You know I cannot—eat anything now,—and I hope—his wages—will keep him—from suffering. I came—to this—little room—when I—could not work—any longer,—on purpose to relieve him. The rent—is cheaper—here—in this—little garret,—and I want to be—as little burdensome—to him—as possible. I used to think—when I first made a profession—of religion—trials would—overcome me;—but God makes me happy—in them. I find—if one—is not worldly—trials are easy—to bear;—and if—we look towards God—and heaven—they are—nothing at all—but mercies."

"And does your husband feel as you do? Is he a pious man?"

She turned her languid head upon her pillow, glancing around the room, to see if the nurse who had been procured for her, had left the room, and perceiving she was not there, said she,—

"I suppose—I may speak—freely—to you—about my husband,—since—we are alone. He is not—religious,—and that is the trouble—of my heart."

She could say no more: she wept and sobbed aloud. After a little time, becoming more composed, evidently struggling to suppress her emotions, she continued,—

"I must leave that—I can't—speak—of *him*. Oh, it seems to me—as if the careless, who neglect—salvation,—have never—read—God's promises. If they had—and knew—what they meant—they could not—help trusting—them. I am happier now—than ever—I was before. It is sweet to—suffer—this pain,—when Christ—puts such delights—into my soul."

She was now stronger than I had expected to find her. I prayed with her, and promising to see her again the next day, I left her.

I was prevented from calling to see her the next morning, as I had intended; and when I called in the afternoon, I perceived her end was very fast approaching. Her countenance was changed, her pulse more feeble and fluttering, her voice was now perfectly restored, and she could speak with strong, clear articulation. She mentioned her recovered voice as an instance of God's goodness to her, and both she and her husband took it as an evidence that she might live to reach her home. To me it was only an evidence to the contrary. She did not appear to be at all aware how near she was to death, and still entertained the hope of starting the next day, "to go home to her mother." I felt very reluctant to crush that hope; but I thought she ought to be made acquainted with the prospect before her. She was still very weak and in some pain, and when I mentioned her sufferings to her, and expressed my sorrow that she had so much to endure; her face lighted up with a glad smile: said she,—

"Oh, it is *pleasant* to suffer, when we know it is *our God* that brings us to it. He does not afflict me too much. My poor body is weak and almost gone; but my God fills me with the delights of his love. My heart is full of joy. I am perfectly happy. I shall soon be where Christ is, and love Him forever."

"I suppose," said I, "you are aware that you cannot now last but a little while; and are prepared to go, at any moment when God bids."

"I have no desire, sir, to get well. Why should

I have? There is nothing in this world for me. You see we have nothing. I have parted with all my little furniture and my clothes, to get bread and pay our debts; and I don't want the world; it is nothing to me now, and I leave it willingly. I am happy. God makes me happy. Christ is enough for me. I love to trust God's promises. I trust Him for all I want, and He makes me very happy. Death seems like nothing to me. It is my friend. I welcome it. Dying is only a step, and then I shall be at home, at home;" and tears of joy coursed down her smiling face. The last word—*home*, which she had uttered, seemed to remind her of her earthly home, and she added,—

"To-morrow, I hope to go home to my *mother*, and see her and all my other friends once more; *perhaps* I may."

"I am afraid not, my dear friend. You are very low, and I wish you to be ready to die at any moment."

Turning her death-glazed eyes upon me, she asked,—

"Shall I die *to-night?* If you think so, *tell* me *plainly*. Don't weep so for me. I thank you for all your kind sympathy; but I am perfectly happy. God fulfils to me all His promises. I leave all in His hands—gladly, joyfully. But I think I can live to get home. *You* think I shall die to-night. I thank you for letting me know it; and I am *ready* if God calls. But if I am alive, may I see you in the morning? God will reward you, I know, for all your kindness to me."

"Yes, my child; you may expect me here in the morning; but if you have anything you wish to say to me, you had better say it now."

"I have no more to say, but to thank you again. Your kind words have done me great good; and it has been sweet to me, *very* sweet, to join with you in prayer. Help me to praise God for the delights that fill my soul. Don't weep so for me."

I prayed with her, and praised God as she desired, and then bade her *farewell*. "Do not think I weep because I am sorry," said she, "I weep because I am overcome with joy. Delights fill my happy soul. This is the dawn of heaven. My heaven is begun. Dying is sweet to me. I go to my blessed Lord. I thank you for coming to me. Farewell, farewell."

Early the next morning I returned to that privileged garret. It was empty! Even her corpse was not there! She had died about four hours after I left her; her body had been placed in its coffin, conveyed on board the vessel, and on the very day in which she expected to see her "*mother once* more," her mother received the lifeless corpse of her child.

It now lies buried in the grave-yard of her native valley. She and Mary Ann sleep side by side.

And they shall rise together from the dead, in that coming day when our Lord Jesus Christ shall be revealed from heaven, 'to be glorified in his saints, and to be admired in all them that believe.'

If grace is there, how instructive, how glorious is

THE DEATH BED OF THE POOR.

"Tread softly—bow the head—
In reverent silence bow;
No passing bell doth toll—
Yet an immortal soul
Is passing now.

"Stranger! however great,
With lowly reverence bow;
There's one in that poor shed—
One on that paltry bed—
Greater than thou.

"Beneath that beggar's roof,
Lo! Death doth keep his state
Enter—no crowd attend:
Enter—no guards defend
This palace gate.

"That pavement, damp and cold,
No smiling courtiers tread;

One silent woman stands—
Lifting with meagre hands
A dying head.

"No mingling voices sound—
An infant wail alone;
A sob suppressed—again
That short, deep gasp, and then
The parting groan.

"Oh! change—Oh wondrous change—
Burst are the prison bars;
This moment *there*, so low,
So agonized, and now
Beyond the stars.

"Oh! change—stupendous change!
There lies the soulless clod;
The sun eternal breaks—
The new immortal wakes—
Wakes with his God."

THE END.

The following is the Table of Contents of the former series of "A Pastor's Sketches:"

www.ingramcontent.com/pod-product-compliance
Lightning Source LLC
LaVergne TN
LVHW021140110826
845150LV00005B/1080